Researching Young Children's Perspectives

What ethical dilemmas face researchers who work with young children?

Researching Young Children's Perspectives critically examines the challenges and complexities of rights-based, participatory research with children. Rather than approaching these dilemmas as problematic issues, this book positions them as important topics for discussion and reflection.

Drawing from their own rich experiences as research collaborators with young children in internationally diverse settings, the authors consider the ethical, methodological and theoretical frameworks that guide best practice in research with young children. Each chapter poses points for consideration that will inform and challenge both the novice and experienced researcher, such-as:

- How 'participatory' can research be with infants under eighteen months?
- When should listening through observation stand alone?
- What is the distinction between methodologies and methods?
- How can *all* young children be assured of a voice in research?

The authors also present seven separate case studies which demonstrate exemplary research with young children. Each study is accompanied by insightful commentary from the authors, who highlight the issues or difficulties faced and propose potential solutions.

If you are a student at undergraduate level or above, this book will give you all the confidence you need to conduct your own high quality research with children.

Deborah Harcourt is Professor of Early Childhood at the Australian Catholic University, based in Brisbane, Australia.

Bob Perry is Professor of Education in the Murray School of Education at Charles Sturt University, Albury-Wodonga, Australia.

Tim Waller is Reader in Early Years Education and Coordinator of the Childhood Research Cluster at the University of Wolverhampton, UK.

Researching Young Children's Perspectives

Debating the ethics and
dilemmas of educational
research with children

Edited by
Deborah Harcourt,
Bob Perry and Tim Waller

 Routledge
Taylor & Francis Group

LONDON AND NEW YORK

First published 2011
by Routledge
2 Park Square, Milton Park, Abingdon, Oxon, OX14 4RN

Simultaneously published in the USA and Canada
by Routledge
711 Third Avenue, New York, NY 10017

Routledge is an imprint of the Taylor & Francis Group, an informa business

Typeset in Galliard by Keystroke, Station Road, Codsall, Wolverhampton

British Library Cataloguing in Publication Data
A catalogue record for this book is available from the British Library

Library of Congress Cataloging-in-Publication Data
Researching young children's perspectives : debating the ethics and
dilemmas of educational research with children / edited by Deborah
Harcourt, Bob Perry and Tim Waller. — 1st ed.
    p. cm.
1. Education–Research–Methodology. 2. Qualitative research.
3. Quantitative research. 4. Inclusive education–Research. 5. Early
childhood education. I. Harcourt, Deborah. II. Perry, Bob, 1945–
III. Waller, Tim.
LB1028.R388 2011
370.72–dc22
2010034975

ISBN13: 978–0–415–60490–1 (hbk)
ISBN13: 978–0–415–60494–9 (pbk)
ISBN13: 978–0–203–83043–7 (ebk)

Contents

PART II
Case studies of high quality research with young children 83

Illustrations

Figures

Tables

Notes on contributors

Angeliki Bitou is currently a PhD student in the School of Education at the University of Wolverhampton, UK. In 2006, she took an MScEcon in Early Childhood, at the University of Swansea, UK. She is also a preschool teacher in Early Years Setting (Βρεφονηπιακός Σταθμός) in Greece. Angeliki's recent research interest is with children under three years old and their experience in early years education and care; young children's right to participate in planning the curriculum in early years settings in Greece and England; and practitioners' perspectives in England, Greece and Sweden on children under three years old.

Ben Bradley is Professor of Psychology and Presiding Officer of the Academic Senate at Charles Sturt University, Bathurst, Australia. Ben's current research projects include: (1) the historical origins of psychological discourse about 'the mind', with particular reference to the effects of Darwin's writings on the primacy of groups in human psychology; (2) the developmental origins of group mind, through the observation of babies in all-infant groups; and (3) through the curriculum renewal project embodied in the CSU Degree Initiative, Ben is promoting experience-based teaching in higher education (including psychology), as argued for in his recent book *Psychology and Experience* (2005, Cambridge University Press).

Clare Britt is currently completing her PhD at the School of Teacher Education, Charles Sturt University, Australia. Clare's current research interests include re-imagining possibilities in the early years of primary school; arts-informed research; researching with children; discourses of hope; and theorising place and space in education. Clare is inspired by her professional and personal communities of friends, family and colleagues, who challenge her thinking and encourage her creativity. Most importantly, she is inspired by the children with whom she researches and works, who motivate her to keep working towards transformation of the ways schooling can be imagined and enacted in Australia.

Heather Conroy is Senior Director of Pedagogy, EtonHouse Preschools, and Academic Head, EtonHouse Education Centre (an early childhood teacher training and professional development institution) in Singapore. Heather's work involves mentoring students and teachers to support understanding of themselves as action researchers. Her collaborative work with teachers, influenced by the work of colleagues in Reggio Emilia, aims to amplify children's rights to parents and the wider community, and to provide a platform for children's perspectives of their preschool experience to be made visible. Research interests also include mentoring and teacher development. Based in Singapore, Heather is an Australian educator who has lived, worked and travelled within Asia in the past few years.

Sue Dockett is Professor of Early Childhood Education in the Murray School of Education at Charles Sturt University, Albury-Wodonga, Australia. Sue's current research encompasses investigations of educational transitions, educational issues confronting children and families in marginalised contexts, children's play, and the engagement of children and young people in research that matters to them. Much of Sue's work is undertaken in collaboration with her partner, Bob Perry.

Liz Dunphy is Senior Lecturer in Early Childhood Education at St Patrick's College (Dublin City University), Dublin, Ireland. Liz teaches and coordinates a range of pre-service and in-service childhood education courses. Her research interests include young children's mathematics, early childhood pedagogy and the assessment of early learning. Liz was involved at management level in the development of *Siolta: The National Quality Framework for Early Childhood Education* (Centre for Early Childhood Development and Education, 2005). More recently, she has contributed to aspects of the development of *Aistear: The Framework for Early Learning* (National Council for Curriculum and Assessment, 2009). Liz loves to visit the west of Ireland with her family and friends.

Jóhanna Einarsdóttir is Professor of Early Childhood Education at the School of Education, University of Iceland. She is currently the director of the Centre for Research in Early Childhood Education at the University of Iceland. The aims of the centre are to increase and promote research in the field of early childhood education and serve as a forum for development in the field. Her professional interests include continuity and transition in children's learning, children's well-being and learning in preschool, and research with children. Jóhanna recently became a proud grandmother of two baby girls.

Thérèse Farrell is a practising primary school teacher. She has been teaching young children in a suburban school in Dublin, Ireland, for a number of years. Her postgraduate studies have primarily focused on the skills and dispositions that young children acquire as a result of their participation in play. She has a particular interest in eliciting children's voice and incorporating children's ideas into her classroom provision. Thérèse currently lectures part-time in Early Childhood Education in Saint Patrick's College, Dublin.

Alma Fleet is Associate Professor at the Institute of Early Childhood, Macquarie University, Sydney, Australia. Having taught in schools in California and Scotland, advised in Australian children's services, and with continuing involvement in early childhood teacher education, she is passionate about educational change. Her current major research projects include systemic change in the first years of school through practitioner enquiry, and supporting the professional pathways of Aboriginal and Torres Strait Islander early childhood teachers. She writes with colleagues about the potential of pedagogical documentation for socially just practices in education. Alma wishes she had more time researching with children.

Joy Goodfellow is Adjunct Senior Lecturer at Charles Sturt University, Bathurst, Australia. Joy is particularly interested in lived experience as a phenomenon. Her career in early childhood education has culminated in research activity around professional experience, practitioner inquiry and, more recently, the role of grandparents as regular child care providers. In her retirement, she is working with a team of university researchers investigating the lives of infants in formal child care arrangements. Joy has six grandchildren and is challenged by those who are much more technologically savvy than she is.

Colette Gray is Head of Research Development at Stranmillis University College, the Queen's University of Belfast. She is a Visiting Professor (Child Development and Education) to Plymouth University and a chartered developmental psychologist. Her research interests include the impact of special needs on all aspects of the young child's learning – particularly children with a visual impairment and autism; the ethical challenges of participatory research; gender and underachievement. Married for over 35 years, in the future, Colette looks forward to a time when she can engage her grandchild in fun-filled participatory research studies.

Deborah Harcourt is Professor of Early Childhood at the Australian Catholic University, based in Brisbane, Australia, but working across five campuses which also include Sydney, Canberra, Melbourne and Ballarat. Deborah's current research interests include children's standpoints on quality (in Singapore, Italy, Australia, Israel and Romania); children's decision-making roles in medical intervention and medical procedures; ethical protocols when researching with children; informed consent processes when inviting young children to participate in research; and providing culturally safe contexts for Indigenous early childhood teacher education students. Deborah shares her life with JB (aka Mr Mom), her 'surfer boy' of 25 years, and their four children, Sam, Hunter, Hugh and their gift from Cambodia, the beautiful Maya, who all tolerate mum's long and frequent absences from home.

Linda Harrison is Associate Professor of Early Childhood Education at Charles Sturt University, Bathurst, Australia. Linda's research and professional work focus on the quality of young children's experiences, interactions and relationships in non-parental child care. Her areas of expertise include observational and self-report methodologies for assessing infant–parent attachment, child–adult and child–peer interaction, and early childhood environments, including home-based care, child care centres and school. She is a principal researcher involved in several longitudinal investigations of infant, toddler and preschoolers' experiences of non-parental child care and early education, including the *Longitudinal Study of Australian Children*.

Hartmut Kupfer works as a trainer with childcare centres' staff in LebensWelt GmbH, an organisation providing services for immigrant families in Berlin, Germany. Hartmut is especially interested in children's and teachers' participation in kindergarten cultures and in the different ways languages are involved in these processes. Collecting examples from his practice, he studies the dialogical interplay of teachers' and children's voices in 'everyday concerts'. At home, he and his partner Johanna Mierendorff also get lessons about children's perspectives. His teachers here are Karl (8) and Konrad (12).

Sharynne McLeod is Professor in Speech and Language Acquisition at Charles Sturt University, Australia. She is the editor of the *International Journal of Speech-Language Pathology* and is an elected Fellow of the American Speech-Language-Hearing Association and of Speech Pathology Australia. Sharynne provided expertise in the development of the World Health Organization's children and youth version of the *International Classification of Functioning, Disability and Health*. Her research focuses on children's speech and foregrounds the right of everyone (particularly children) to participate fully in society. Listening to children is an important part of both her work and her life.

Bob Perry is Professor of Education in the Murray School of Education at Charles Sturt University, Albury-Wodonga, Australia. Bob's current research interests include powerful mathematics ideas in preschool and the first years of school; ethical tensions in researching with children; student decision-making on staying on at high school; starting school within families with complex support needs; preschool education in remote Indigenous communities; transition to school for Indigenous families; and building community capacity. Bob shares his life with his partner, Sue Dockett, and their son, Will, both of whom ensure that he keeps his feet firmly on the ground.

Niklas Pramling is Associate Professor in Education at the Linnaeus Centre for Research on Learning, Interaction and Mediated Communication in Contemporary Society (LinCS), University of Gothenburg, Sweden. Niklas' main interests are children's learning in the arts and the role of metaphor in learning and knowledge formation.

Ingrid Pramling Samuelsson is Professor of Early Childhood Education at the Department of Education, Communication and Learning at the University of Gothenburg, Sweden. Ingrid's main research interest is focused on curriculum questions, how young children learn as well as how teachers can provide opportunities for this learning. Two of the current issues are children's perspectives, and 'preschool didactics' from a perspective of young children's sense making in different areas, such as emergent mathematics, literacy, natural science, aesthetics, etc. Ingrid holds a UNESCO Chair in Early Childhood Education and Sustainable Development and is the World President of OMEP (Organisation Mondiale pour l'Éducation Prescolaire: www.omep.org.gu.se).

Frances Press is Senior Lecturer in Education at Charles Sturt University, Bathurst, Australia. Fran is interested in the way in which relevant government policy supports or works against the creation of a strong, robust and child-responsive early childhood sector. Her particular research interests are the impact of corporate child care provision; early childhood programs for infants and toddlers; the construction and enactment of quality in early childhood education and care settings; and the creation of sustainable integrated services for children and families.

Sue Robson is Principal Lecturer and Subject Leader for Early Childhood Studies at Roehampton University, London, UK. Sue's current research interests include the development of young children's self-regulation and metacognition; parent–professional relationships; young children's creative thinking; children's voices in research and practice; and the impact of physical and social environments on young children's activity. Sue is also interested in research in higher education contexts, particularly student self- and peer-assessment, and student conceptions of collaboration. Sue lives with her husband, Ken, and two daughters, Charlotte and Isabella, who have both always given her lots of practice in listening to children's perspectives!

Anne B. Smith is Emeritus Professor at the University of Otago, Dunedin, New Zealand, formerly Director of the Children's Issues Centre. Her research interests are in Childhood Studies and Children's Rights theory. She is the author of *Understanding Children's Development* (1998), and co-author of *Advocating for Children* (2000), *Children's Voices* (2000), *Children as Citizens* (2009) and *Learning in the Making* (2009). She has a particular interest in young children's learning; quality early childhood environments; family discipline, early childhood centre and school influences on children. Anne has been a passionate advocate for children for 40 years and now has five young grandchildren.

Jennifer Sumsion is Professor of Early Childhood Education in the School of Teacher Education at Charles Sturt University, Bathurst, Australia, and Co-Director of the National Centre for Research into Early Childhood Education and

Care. Jennifer's research interests lie in the use of innovative theoretical, methodological, pedagogical and collaborative approaches to address enduring challenges within early childhood education research, policy and practice. Recently, she was co-leader, with her colleague Linda Harrison, of the national consortium that developed 'Belonging, Being and Becoming: The Early Years Learning Framework for Australia'. Jennifer and Linda now lead the national Early Years Learning Framework research network.

Sarah Te One is Lecturer in the Faculty of Education at Victoria University of Wellington, New Zealand. Sarah is currently teaching childhood sociology, children's rights and researching parent support and development in early childhood services. She has been involved in several research projects including New Zealand's early childhood Centres of Innovation. Sarah's interests are in young children's rights in early childhood education which include their rights in research. Sarah lives with her husband Mark. They have three almost adult children, Mohi, Annie and Miriama, three cats and a dog. The Te One whānau (family) live in a small seaside village and are actively involved in community life.

Tim Waller is Reader in Early Years Education and Coordinator of the Childhood Research Cluster at the University of Wolverhampton, UK. Tim is also a Convener of the Outdoor Learning SIG in the European Early Childhood Education Research Association (EECERA) and an active member of the Early Years SIG in the British Educational Research Association (BERA). He was formerly Director of Postgraduate Studies in the Department of Childhood Studies at Swansea University. Previously he taught in nursery, infant and primary schools in London and has also worked in the USA. His research interests include outdoor learning, pedagogy and social justice in early childhood. Tim is Director of the *Longitudinal Evaluation of the Role and Impact of Early Years Professionals (in England)* – a three-year project commissioned by the Children's Workforce Development Council. Since September 2003, he has been coordinating an ongoing research project designed to investigate children's perspectives of their outdoor play. This project has involved developing and using a range of 'participatory' methods for research with young children. He has also helped to establish the Men in Childcare Network in Wales. Recently, he has edited the second edition of *An Introduction to Early Childhood: A Multi-Disciplinary Approach* (2009, SAGE).

Cecilia Wallerstedt is a PhD student in Arts Education at the Academy of Music and Drama, University of Gothenburg, Sweden. Cecilia has a background as a teacher in music and mathematics in an upper-secondary school. In her PhD thesis she is investigating teachers in preschool and primary school who are trying to develop in children the ability to discern time in music. Her research interests are content-related questions for music education, listening as a foundational musical ability and teaching and learning from the learner's perspective.

Eileen Winter is a chartered educational psychologist and Director of Academic Programmes at the Institute of Child Education and Psychology in the Republic of Ireland. Her specialist research interests cover all aspects of special needs including autism, dyslexia and the impact of profound and multiple disabilities on children's health and well-being.

Foreword

This book marks an important pause in the development of participatory early childhood research. The debate has moved from reiterating the case for listening to young children's perspectives in research and demonstrating how this can be achieved, to identifying the ethical parameters which need to be in place. The interest among policy-makers, practitioners and researchers in these developments makes it more important that these ethical 'way markers' and boundaries are debated and made explicit rather than merely assumed. A way marker may provide a reminder of territory covered and a chance to reconsider intended directions.

The contributors draw on detailed examples from research conducted with young children across a range of countries, including Australia, Singapore, Iceland, Sweden, England, Germany, Greece, Northern Ireland, Ireland and New Zealand, and represent some cross-national academic research partnerships. This diversity of research practice emphasises the similarities and differences in the sociocultural contexts in which these theoretical and methodological reflections have taken place.

Research with pre-verbal children and children with disabilities, just two of the subjects approached in this book, present particular questions where ethical way markers should be placed. How 'participatory', for example, can research be with infants under 18 months and when instead should listening through observation stand alone?

Other way markers refer to time: children's time and adults' time. Making methodological strides has opened up further queries about the research questions with which it is appropriate to 'bother' children. This becomes more important the further the research agenda is from the everyday lives of young children. Sudden policy interest in evaluating service provision can lead to the desire for quick consultations to policy-driven timescales. An alternative may be for researchers and practitioners to help policy makers draw on the wealth of new understandings being gathered about young children's perspectives on matters about which young children have 'first hand' knowledge. 'Experiences of starting school' is one such topic which has been greatly enriched by reflecting on children's visual and verbal narratives. Such accounts as illustrated in this volume draw on 'slow listening' which requires adults, whether practitioners or researchers, to slow down and step back in order to see and hear in new ways. 'Slow listening' may run counter to our fast-moving culture but offers rewards in building up a new body of knowledge from children (including those under five) about their lives.

This book also presents a pause in the development of participatory early childhood research by encouraging researchers to reconsider *methodological* frameworks alongside *methods*. The challenge here is to look beyond the tools on offer to articulate the values and principles which inform their use. This is of particular importance where the tools have wide appeal, as can be the case with digital technology. It is easy to hand over a camera to a young child. It is harder to articulate the values and principles which will underpin such a tool's use in a research context. This topic of visual research methods with young children is explored in detail in several chapters here.

Shining a theoretical and methodological light on these questions can bring into sharper focus broader ethical questions about involving children, young people and adults of different abilities in the research process. Researching young children's views and experiences concentrates methodological and ethical thinking in ways which may have wider implications beyond early childhood. Researchers, within and beyond Early Childhood Studies, are well placed to bring new questions into the open and to join in emerging discussions about people-centred research.

Alison Clark
Senior Lecturer in Childhood Studies
The Open University, Milton Keynes, UK

Acknowledgement of reviewers

Many people have assisted the editors in reviewing various versions of the chapters in this book. Initially, leaders of author teams read through and commented on the chapter drafts. After revision, chapters were sent to external reviewers who are experts in the field of researching with children but who did not have any connection with writing the chapters. The editors and authors are very grateful for the independent critique provided and acknowledge the assistance of the following:

Aline-Wendy Dunlop, University of Strathclyde, Scotland
Ann Farrell, Queensland University of Technology, Australia
Anne Graham, Southern Cross University, Australia
Anna Klerfelt, University of Gothenburg, Sweden
Valentina Mazzoni, University of Verona, Italy
Jane Murray, University of Northampton, UK
Sally Peters, University of Waikato, New Zealand
Jonathan Sargeant, Australian Catholic University, Australia
Nigel Thomas, University of Central Lancashire, UK
Tuija Turunen, Charles Sturt University, Australia and University of Lapland, Finland
Susan Whitaker, EtonHouse Education Centre, Singapore.

Commencing the conversation

Deborah Harcourt, Bob Perry and Tim Waller

Background to the book

This book is the product of a collaborative effort by the members of the European Early Childhood Education Research Association (EECERA) Special Interest Group (SIG) *Young Children's Perspectives*. EECERA is a self-governing not-for-profit association that celebrated its twentieth anniversary in 2010. It provides a relevant academic forum in Europe for the promotion, development and dissemination of high quality research into early childhood education. One of the ways in which EECERA raises the visibility and status of early childhood research is through the establishment of networks of researchers and the facilitation of collaboration and communication between them. To this end, SIGs are formed on particular early childhood research themes and are the responsibility of two co-conveners, of different nationalities, to support cross-national collaborations within and across the groups.

The SIG *Young Children's Perspectives* was formed by Deborah Harcourt (Australia) and Alison Clark (United Kingdom) at the EECERA Annual Conference held in Malta in 2004. At that time, the group comprised a membership of about ten academics/researchers from Europe and Australasia who were investigating children's voices in research. As a relatively new discipline in early childhood research, the group sought to do the following:

* generate critical reflection on children's perspectives and children's rights;
* support and encourage cross-national perspectives on seeking children's perspectives;
* support SIG members' research in a collaborative and cooperative manner;
* share innovative and reflexive research on children's perspectives and children's rights.

As a result of the papers presented at the 2004 conference, a special edition of *Early Child Development and Care* was published in 2005 with SIG member Wendy Schiller (Australia) as guest editor. The group continued to meet at successive conferences (Dublin 2005, Reykjavik 2006), and as a result of the high quality papers presented by members at the 2007 Prague conference, a second special edition of *Early Child Development and Care* was commissioned, and subsequently published in 2009, with SIG members Wendy Schiller (Australia) and Jóhanna Einarsdóttir (Iceland) as guest editors. At the 2007 meeting, the SIG said farewell to Alison Clark as one of the co-conveners and welcomed Jóhanna Einarsdóttir as the new co-convener. Membership now stood at about 30 researchers from around the world.

The next SIG meeting, held at the EECERA conference in Stavanger (2008), saw the 'birth' of this book. The papers presented by members of the SIG reflected not only the growing interest in researching with children, but the growing ethical and practical tensions that were challenging researchers. These included issues around children's rights, informed consent, methodologies, data collection methods, researching with children with special educational rights and access to marginalized children. In response to the challenges, and also to highlight the thoughtful research being undertaken by members, a call for expressions of interest was sent to members of the SIG with the view to producing an edited book with authors from as many nationalities and perspectives as possible. The book would be divided into two parts so that the ethical and practical dilemmas could be examined in detail in the first section, while the second section would give practical examples of research with children that would provide pivotal points of discussion.

In February 2009, the editors agreed upon 11 of the expressions of interest whose authors were then invited to write a (first) draft chapter for further consideration. In order to ensure that the manuscript would undergo a rigorous academic review process, the editors first provided initial comments to the authors in order to support the development of a suite of chapters that would be complementary. In May, each author was invited to participate in one of two symposia, organized by the SIG, to be presented at the 2009 conference in Strasbourg. This was considered an opportunity for authors to receive critical feedback from the broader EECERA audience and to strengthen the academic integrity of their work. In addition, each (second) draft chapter was sent to another contributing author to be internally peer-reviewed. These reviews, and the editors' summative comments, were presented to authors at a specifically convened meeting on the day prior to the 2009 conference. Alison Clark was invited, and attended, as an independent observer and critical friend.

The two EECERA symposia by authors of chapters from the proposed book were highly acclaimed in Strasbourg and provided a great deal of feedback to the authors. As well, an outstanding presentation outside the symposia but highly relevant to the topic of the book, resulted in a twelfth chapter being commissioned by the editors.

It was at this point that the editors approached the publisher, Routledge, with a well-developed proposal and a book that was well on its way to completion. A next (third) draft chapter was required from each of the author teams in November 2009. These were subsequently sent out to blind review to early childhood academics and researchers of international renown. Alison Clark was also invited to write a Foreword for the book, as a pre-eminent scholar and writer in the field of researching with children. In June 2010, a full manuscript that had been through thorough and complete development and review processes was submitted to the publisher.

The *Young Children's Perspectives* SIG continues to be active in publication. As a result of individual papers presented by members at the 2009 meeting in Strasbourg, a special edition of the *European Early Childhood Research Journal* was commissioned to be published in 2011 and is guest edited by the SIG co-conveners Deborah Harcourt and Jóhanna Einarsdóttir. Active membership of the SIG now sits at around 48.

Overview of the book

This book *Researching Young Children's Perspectives: Ethics and Dilemmas of Educational Research with Children* is a timely addition to a burgeoning field of great importance. It builds on the sustained, exemplary work of members of the *Young Children's Perspectives* SIG and other colleagues at a time when many people who research with children felt that it was time to pause and take stock of their work, their theoretical and practical frameworks and their ethical stances. Influenced by commitments to the recognition of children as active citizens with participation rights in all that affects them, including research (Jans 2004; United Nations 1989); strengths-based perceptions of children, where children are regarded as competent social actors who are experts on their own lives (James and Prout 1997; Mayall 2002; Rinaldi 2006); and principles of ethical symmetry (Christensen and Prout 2002), which positions all research – including that involving children – as a process of ethical practice that necessarily involves obligations and responsibilities on the part of researchers as well as the researched, this book seeks to map the current terrain, celebrate its peaks and consider its consequences. In particular, the book has the following specific aims:

1 to critically examine the challenges and complexities of rights-based, participatory research with children;
2 to provide researchers (the student, novice and experienced researcher) with points of consideration for the conceptualization of children's genuine involvement in a research enterprise;
3 to provide exemplars that identify best practice when researching with children.

As editors, we have been very fortunate to have been able to gather together chapter authors who lead the field of researching with young children. The 12 chapter author teams represent nine countries from Europe and beyond, providing a very broad coverage of the topic as well as ensuring the intellectual depth expected.

The book is divided into two complementary parts. Part I considers the ethics, methodologies and theoretical frameworks involved in researching with children while Part II provides case studies of high quality research with young children.

All chapters adhere to the theoretical foundations outlined above and address the three aims for the book.

Part I, entitled 'Ethics, methodologies and theoretical frameworks', begins with the foundational chapter 'Respecting children's rights and agency: Theoretical insights into ethical research procedures', authored by Anne B. Smith from New Zealand. Anne has used her vast knowledge and experience in this chapter which considers how Children's Rights and Childhood Studies theory inform approaches to research with young children. The links between what researchers believe about young children and how they undertake research with young children are high-lighted.

The other four chapters in Part I all consider particular aspects of the researching with children endeavour and build on the foundations set in the first chapter. Chapter 2 (Gray and Winter) and Chapter 4 (Bitou and Waller) consider researching with two groups of children which are often neglected in discussions of engagement with researchers. In Chapter 2, Colette Gray and Eileen Winter tackle the challenges involved in researching with children who have special needs (or special rights). In particular, they focus on the particular challenges around informed consent, confidentiality and the roles of gatekeepers when researching with these children. As with Smith's Chapter 1, the basis for the discussion is participatory rights-based research and, while the examples used involve children with special needs/rights, there is much that is applicable in more general settings. In Chapter 4, Angeliki Bitou and Tim Waller consider children under the age of three years and the challenges to be considered in undertaking participatory research with them. This chapter is an important inclusion in the book as it highlights specific challenges that might be met with younger children and forms a strong link with Chapter 8 (Sumsion *et al.*) concerning researching with infants and toddlers. Bitou and Waller discuss a number of possible methods of working with children under three, including video (linking again to Chapter 8 and also to Chapter 12) and consider possibilities, limitations and challenges to participatory research with such young children.

The remaining two chapters in Part I consider two separate issues that are often discussed as dichotomies or synonyms – assent and consent (Chapter 3, Harcourt and Conroy) and methods and methodologies (Chapter 5, Dockett, Einarsdóttir and Perry). Deborah Harcourt and Heather Conroy explore the challenges around informed assent/consent with young children, use examples to show how this notion may be introduced and implemented with young children and stress the assent/consent *process*. They also consider issues around children 'changing their minds' over assent/consent and the mechanisms that researchers might need to employ in order to allow withdrawal of initial assent/consent by the children involved. The challenges created through recognition of young children's rights and capabilities are highlighted in this chapter.

In their chapter, Sue Dockett, Jóhanna Einarsdóttir and Bob Perry utilize a distinction between methodology – the set of beliefs and values upon which the research endeavour is based – and methods – the techniques and approaches that are used to gather or generate data – to problematize their implementation in participatory rights-based research with young children. In particular, the authors consider the implications of such a distinction on ethical research in the early years. Practical examples of these implications are presented in this chapter and are reiterated in many of the chapters in Part II.

Part II, 'Case studies of high quality research with young children', presents exemplary case studies of researching with young children based on the theoretical foundations canvassed in Part I. Each chapter discusses particular research projects, the challenges that needed to be met in order to maintain a rights-based participatory approach, the results of the research where applicable, and the ways in which the adult and child researchers have collaborated in the projects. Readers are encouraged to peruse these chapters in any order that suits their needs and to link these readings to the more foundational chapters in Part I.

Chapter 6, by Sarah Te One, reports a study undertaken in a New Zealand preschool in which she worked with three- and four-year-old children to assist them in voicing their opinions about their rights. Using a number of interesting methods, including a mediating persona doll, she has elicited children's thinking and discourse about their rights as well as about researching with children. The context in which the children 'are' was found to be a strong mediator of the rights that were voiced.

Chapter 7 (Kupfer) and Chapter 11 (Wallerstedt, Pramling and Pramling Samuelsson) both deal with the interpretation of children's voices by researchers, but in quite different ways and different contexts. Hartmut Kupfer uses five examples drawn from German, New Zealand and US contexts to introduce a dialogic framework for understanding children's voices. He suggests to researchers in the early years that hearing a child's utterances is only part of the story and that they must also consider what, how and where children *hear*. Through the constructs of *voices of others*, *voices of place(s)* and *voices of game(s)*, Kupfer explores children's voices in everyday contexts and discusses the implications for ethical participatory research with children.

In Chapter 11, Cecilia Wallerstedt, Niklas Pramling and Ingrid Pramling Samuelsson discuss three long-standing issues confronting researchers with young children which impact on the conduct and interpretation of interviews with these children. The three issues are the situated nature of knowing, the need to consider any interview as a social practice, and the need to consider the interview not only from the researcher's perspective but also from the child's perspective. Using children's understanding of musical time as the topic for the interviews, the chapter authors have explored how the three issues can impact on analysis of children's learning and understanding.

Two research projects undertaken with school-aged children are reported in Chapter 9 (Dunphy and Farrell) and Chapter 10 (Fleet and Britt). Liz Dunphy and Thérèse Farrell consider the perspectives of children on indoor play in their classroom. While the study is well developed as rights-based participatory research using innovative methods such as video recording of children's play, it has further importance because of the position of one of the researchers as the classroom teacher. This requires that different aspects of researcher–children relationships be considered. One ramification of these relationships is the challenge that is set up when it comes time to implement the findings of the research. Another interesting aspect of this chapter is the reflection on the positions of the two authors vis-à-vis each other. Farrell was a Master's degree student being mentored by Dunphy. Many readers will have found themselves in one or both of these positions and the chapter helps explain some of the challenges involved.

Alma Fleet and Clare Britt have authored a chapter that will challenge readers in many ways. Two separate studies concerning children's perceptions of place are presented. Both are about children's recollections of experiences in the first year of school. Clare works with children in this first year, while Alma reports on conversations with children in the final year of primary school, thus introducing the notion of memoried experiences. The key in both cases is the authors' dedication to their methodology of 'listening as research' and 'research as listening'. Many innovative methods are used so that the researchers can hear what the children are telling them, and these will be of great interest to early years researchers. However, a major strength of this chapter is the weaving of stories that is undertaken and the importance given to children's agency and relationships as they inhabit their place(s).

Recalling some of the ideas on the use of video recording very young children experiences introduced in Chapter 4 by Angeliki Bitou and Tim Waller, Chapter 8 investigates the methodological and technical challenges created in wishing to research with infants. Jennifer Sumsion and her colleagues (Linda Harrison, Fran Press, Sharynne McLeod, Joy Goodfellow and Ben Bradley) introduce the *Infants' Lives in Childcare* project and explain some of the challenges they have faced in commencing this study of very young children's experiences of child care. While the study is in its early phases, the insights provided by this chapter concerning how – and even if – participatory, inclusive research is possible with such young children bring together many of the major themes of this book. Readers will be very interested not only in the technology of the 'baby cam' and the analytical tools such as *Studiocode* but will experience the many frustrations that can accompany research in this field.

The use of video data of young children and the consequent challenges concerning children's agency, ongoing assent/consent and children's rights form the subject of the final chapter in the book. In the context of the ongoing research project *The Voice of the Child: Ownership and Autonomy in Early Learning*, Sue Robson investigates the positive role that the use of video data can have as well as the challenges that creating and analyzing such data raise. Issues around who decides on the participants in a study; how consent and assent are obtained, renewed and withdrawn; how confidentiality is ensured or not, accepting that the children have opinions (and rights) about this; and what impacts the research has on the children are all canvassed. Dilemmas about the value of video in research and in practice and the place of children's rights in each case are also considered.

In many ways, this chapter reprises the key constructs introduced in Part I and provides a fitting summary of the work of all the authors.

It has been a pleasure to help create the book *Researching Young Children's Perspectives: Debating the Ethics and Dilemmas of Educational Research with Children*. Such an important book is, of course, the combined work of many people over many years. First, thanks must go to the 26 authors who have created the various chapters through careful research, reflection on research and writing. Their work has undergone numerous reviews and revisions, all in good spirit and with timely expedience. Second, we must thank the reviewers of the chapters in their various forms – initially, leaders of the author teams who considered first drafts – and then a group of independent reviewers who considered the revised drafts. Third, recognition must be given to Alison Clark, not only for her ground-breaking work in the area of researching with children, but for her encouragement in the development of the book and her willingness to pen the Foreword. Fourth, the team of professionals at Routledge are to be congratulated on their foresight in agreeing to publish the book and their expertise in doing so. Fifth, we must thank our respective families for their patience, forbearance and understanding when one or all of Mum, Dad or partner were not available to do important things because of 'the book'.

Finally, and most importantly, we thank all the children who, over many years, have taught us all what is reasonable, ethical and appropriate in researching with children. We hope that this book might repay some of the challenges that you have faced as we have tried to honour you as important people who have rights and are human beings capable of understanding, communicating and influencing your own lives and those around you.

References

Christensen, P. and Prout, A. (2002) 'Working with ethical symmetry in social research with children', *Childhood*, 9(4): 477–497.

James, A. and Prout, A. (1997) *Constructing and Reconstructing Childhood: Contemporary Issues in the Sociological Study of Childhood*, 2nd edn, London: Falmer Press.

Jans, M. (2004) 'Children as citizens: Towards a contemporary notion of child participation', *Childhood*, 11(1): 27–44.

Mayall, B. (2002) *Towards a Sociology of Childhood*, Maidenhead: Open University Press.

Rinaldi, C. (2006) *In Dialogue with Reggio Emilia: Listening, Researching and Learning*, London: Routledge.

United Nations (1989) *Convention on the Rights of the Child*, available at: http://www.unicef.org/crc/crc (accessed 30 March 2009).

Part I

Ethics, methodologies and theoretical frameworks

Chapter 1

Respecting children's rights and agency

Theoretical insights into ethical research procedures

Anne B. Smith

This chapter looks at how Children's Rights and Childhood Studies theory inform approaches to carrying out research with young children. Young children's participation rights entitle them to have their voices heard and taken into account, and to give and receive information. A recent Committee on the Rights of the Child document emphasizes that Article 12 applies equally to older and younger children. Childhood Studies theory argues that children are participating subjects rather than the mute objects of research or incompetent and immature beings. Childhood is a social construction, which influences how researchers treat children, and how children are positioned within the research process. The chapter argues that researchers should view and treat children as capable, competent people who can contribute ideas and knowledge to researchers, and who should be informed and respected. Research topics, recruitment, methodology, feedback and dissemination procedures, all reflect researchers' constructions of childhood and children, and influence whether children can be engaged in research in a way which respects their participation rights.

Introduction and theoretical framework

> Our understanding of research with children, and, indeed of ethics in research with children, are embedded within our understandings of children and childhood.
>
> (Farrell 2005a: 5)

Taking a rights perspective is a powerful way of uncovering previously unheard or hidden stories (Freeman 2007). In the past, the voices of children, particularly young children, have often been ignored or silenced in research and are the 'missing piece of the puzzle in understanding childhood' (Smith and Taylor 2000: ix). It is not that research has ignored children, because there is a huge body of research *on* children. The problem is that the dominant approach to researching children's experience has been from a 'looking down' standpoint (Alanen 1998, cited by Mayall 2002: 3), which views childhood from a large-scale and adult point of view. Performance or behaviour is measured through highly structured instruments, such as standardized tests, questionnaires and interviews, which are guided entirely by the hypotheses and questions of adult researchers, and in which there is a marked power imbalance in favour of adult dominance and control. 'Grand overarching abstract generalizations substitute for empirical studies of children in their everyday environments' (Oakley 1994: 22). An alternative approach from Children's Rights and Childhood Studies paradigms is to study childhood in a more contextualized way – by 'looking up' (Mayall 2002), trying to understand children's standpoints in the context of their own lives, and treating them as actors and knowers.

Children's rights

> Rights are claims that are justifiable on legal or moral grounds to have or obtain something, or to act in a certain way.
>
> (James and James 2008: 109)

The introduction of the United Nations Convention on the Rights of the Child (UNCRC) in 1989 helped change the dominant image of childhood and bring about a new culture in relation to children's rights and interests in many parts of the world (Karp 2008). UNCRC 'confirmed an agreement that children and young people are citizens whose entitlements straddle moral, political and social agendas' (Matthews 2005: 1) and became 'a watershed in the global articulation of children's rights as human rights' (Farrell 2005b: 167). UNCRC provides an internationally accepted standard of basic human rights for children. It is a document of reconciliation, which treats parents and children with respect, and recommends a partnership between parents, children and the institutions of the state.

The 54 Articles in the Convention are divided into three main types: (1) provision rights (to health, education, social security, physical care, play, etc.); (2) protection rights (to be safe from abuse, discrimination and injustice); and (3) participation rights (to have a say in matters which affect you, to have access to information and to be able to express an opinion) (Lansdown 1994). These rights are to apply to all children wherever they live, which has sometimes been used as a criticism that it imposes a global model of childhood, despite the different social and cultural contexts of childhood (James and James 2008). The most innovative and controversial aspect of the convention, however, has been its message that children should have agency and voice, and that they have a right to participate – to receive and give information, and to take part in decisions in matters that affect them.[1] Participation rights are particularly important when it comes to considering how research with children should be conducted, but protection rights are also relevant because they point to the importance of ensuring that the child is not subjected to discrimination, humiliation or ill-treatment. The protection rights of children, especially young children, however, are commonly given more prominence than their participation rights. Woodhead (2005) argues that the image of a child in need is associated with protection rights, while an image of a competent child is associated with participation rights.

There is no mention of early childhood in the original 1989 UNCRC document, but the Committee on the Rights of the Child remedied this omission by holding a day of discussion in 2004 about implementing children's rights in early childhood (defined as below eight years of age). This discussion resulted in General Comment No. 7, 2005 (published in September 2006) which contains a set of recommendations explicitly addressing dominant assumptions about early childhood. Section 3 of the document (page 2) explained the Committee's concern that children as rights holders were not being given sufficient attention by state parties in their laws, policies and programmes. They advocated a shift away from traditional beliefs that early childhood is a time when immature human beings are socialized towards adulthood, towards the recognition that young children have their own concerns, interests and points of view, and should have the freedom to express these from the earliest stages:

> Article 12 states that the child has a right to express his or her views freely in all matters affecting the child, and to have them taken into account. This right reinforces the status of the young child as an active participant in the promotion, protection and monitoring of their rights. Respect for the young child's agency – as a participant in family, community and society – is frequently overlooked, or rejected as inappropriate on the grounds of age and immaturity. In many countries and regions, traditional beliefs have emphasized young children's need for training and socialization. They have been regarded as undeveloped, lacking even basic capacities for understanding, voiceless and invisible within society. The Committee wishes to emphasize that *article 12 applies both to younger and older children.*
>
> (Committee on the Rights of the Child 2006:
> General Comment 7, III, 14, p. 7, my italics)

Childhood Studies

Childhood Studies is compatible with a rights-based approach towards ethical and methodological issues in research with children. It is engaged in producing new knowledge of children's experience, grounded in children's perspectives, and it has been productive in extending our understanding of childhood. Childhood Studies evolved from a critique of developmental psychology, and from the treatment of children (like women in previous years) as a social minority group lacking in independence, rationality, intelligence, autonomy and confidence (Oakley 1994). Allison James suggests that there is now a considerable body of research on childhood which challenges taken-for-granted assumptions about what children do or do not think. She defines the field of Childhood Studies as follows:

> With a commitment to interdisciplinarity at its core, and drawing on sociology, anthropology, psychology, history, geography, and law, what united this field of concern was a concern for the socially constructed character of childhood that involves the twin research foci of childhood as a sociocultural space and children's own perspectives as social actors.
>
> (James 2007: 263)

If children's 'voice' is being sought, then children have to be positioned as participating subjects, knowers and social actors, rather than objects of the researcher's gaze. The generational divide between adults and children is not unbridgeable. James (ibid., citing Alanen and Mayall) argues that it is important to acknowledge the different standpoints of adult researcher and child participant, but that good conversations are achievable within participatory dialogue. It is important, however, for researchers to be aware of power differentials in research with children. Respecting the agency of the child 'strikes at the heart of conventional authority relationships between children and the adults who regulate their lives' (Woodhead 2005: 92).

> The consensus that emerges from studies exploring children's perspectives is that the major issues of the researcher–researched relationship are *essentially the same* with children as they are with adults. These issues include the need to be aware of and respect the imbalanced *power relations* of the researcher vis-à-vis the researched, the importance of distinguishing *'private'* from *'public'* accounts and the need to handle controversial and or personal topics with sensitivity.
>
> (Oakley 1994: 26)

An interesting question is to what extent research which is not participatory can be considered to be ethical, and whether Childhood Studies itself is wide and interdisciplinary enough to encompass traditional developmental psychology approaches. It has been argued that the latter should be consigned to 'the dustbin of history' (James, Jenks, and Prout 1998, cited in Woodhead 2009: 56), but in my view it is possible to do ethical research without it always having to include children's voices. As Woodhead points out (2009: 56), Childhood Studies would 'be seen as a minority interest and not of mainstream concern and relevance' if it took such an approach. He argues that this would be throwing out the baby with the bathwater, and that it would be a mistake to discard such a wide field:

> Yet concepts and tools are still needed that acknowledge that children are, for much of the time and in many contexts, relatively more vulnerable, dependent and inexperienced. They require (and often seek) guidance, support and teaching from more experienced members of society – through enabling structures and pedagogies for participation.
>
> (ibid.: 57)

In the practical implementation of participatory principles, it is important to maintain a balance, by also recognizing children's vulnerability, 'evolving capacity' and their need for guidance and direction at times (ibid.). I am arguing in this chapter for a better balance of research that foregrounds children's perspectives, and for all research to be respectful of children's agency but also aware of their dependency. It is important, I believe, for Childhood Studies to be wide enough to encompass developmental research, which hopefully will itself evolve to fit with new constructions of childhood and consequent ethical standards.

The key contribution of Childhood Studies has been to recognize children's agency, and to emphasize that children are not just empty vessels whose development is determined by biological and psychological processes (James and James 2008), and that childhood is not a natural or universal feature of human societies, but a social construction (Prout and James 1997). Constructions of childhood have important implications for what we do as researchers. Early childhood settings and practices are also culturally constructed, and mediated by complex belief systems about the 'right' way for children to develop and be cared for (Woodhead 2005). The most significant features in children's lives are the people with whom they develop close relationships, and these people are in turn are 'a product of cultural history and circumstance, which structure their lives and gives meaning and direction to the experiences of their offspring as they introduce them to cultural practices' (ibid.: 90).

I have argued (Smith 2002) that sociocultural theory can be integrated with Childhood Studies, since it suggests that children construct their own understanding in partnership with, and with guidance from others (both adults and other children). The greater the richness of the activities and communications that children participate in, the greater will be their competence. Relationships and interactions between children and other people are a key component that can enhance children's capacity to express their feelings and articulate their experiences. In order to be able to formulate and express a view, children should receive appropriate support. They should be able to receive such guidance within a social context which is capable of communicating information effectively to them, and is receptive to hearing their voices, and supportive of their efforts to formulate their views. Hence the relationships which children have with researchers, the settings where they participate in research, how children are positioned as participants (and viewed by researchers), and how they are assessed, hold the key to advancing authentic knowledge of children and childhood.

Constructing the child participant

Developmental psychology has been a dominating influence on constructions of children and approaches to research with children (Burman 2008; James and James 2008; Woodhead 2005). Developmental psychology posits a general unitary model of development where children move inexorably from immaturity and incompetence towards rationality and competence. Childhood Studies, on the other hand, emphasizes the social construction of childhood, and its embeddedness in social and cultural contexts. What children know is, in other words, inextricably interwoven with, and inseparable from the contexts of their learning environments (Burman 2008). A Piagetian view of children suggests that they are able to succeed at certain tasks depending on their operational competence, which depends in turn on their internal cognitive structures or schema. A Vygotskian view of children implies that children are able to succeed at tasks depending on their experiences in joint activities, and co-construction of meaning in social and cultural contexts.

> The stage theorists are asking the wrong question! Respecting children's competence isn't about measuring the progress of their development, like you might measure the height of a growing tree in order to decide when it should be felled. The more useful question is 'How do children's competencies develop through appropriate levels of participation?'
>
> (Woodhead 2005: 94)

The implications of a more socioculturally based view of childhood accords with Munford and Saunders' (2001) view that it is the responsibility of researchers to find an effective way of eliciting children's voices. So when it comes to questions of informed consent, it is possible, provided appropriate guidance and support are offered, that even young children are competent to give this. They suggest that: 'The requirement that we adequately inform potential participants provides us with creative and exciting opportunities to learn new ways of talking with and listening [to children]' (ibid.: 103).

Childhood Studies emphasizes that the nature of childhood and beliefs about what children are capable of vary at different times in history and in different cultural contexts. There is no unchangeable entity called childhood. Childhood and children's needs are socially constructed – they are what we think they are. Researchers working with children often do not view them as capable, competent, responsible people who are able to contribute ideas and knowledge to researchers (Smith 2007). This is a particular problem when working with younger children, who are even more likely to be thought incompetent. It is often assumed that children below the age of seven (or even older) are not capable of forming a view or expressing it (Morrow and Richards 1996; Robinson and Kellett 2004). Beliefs about children's competence influence whether researchers make an effort to gain informed consent and to provide feedback to children (Powell and Smith 2009). An approach that assumes that children are competent, and that age is not a particularly good indicator of competence, is more respectful of children's rights and agency (Alderson 2005).

Another dominant construction of childhood, which influences ethical procedures in research, is that children are in need of protection, which is reinforced by a Piagetian view of children as dependent, irrational and vulnerable for a considerable length of time (Lloyd-Smith and Tarr 2000). Alderson (2001) points out that agency and dependency are often seen as opposites, and that if people are dependent, they do not have agency and ability to think, act and express themselves freely. She argues, on the contrary, that both agency and dependency are inherent in the relationships between individuals, and gives many examples of young children's interactions with adults demonstrating both agency and dependency. Alderson has shown, for instance, that children want to share decision-making with doctors about medical treatment, rather than take all of the responsibility themselves. The implications of Alderson's analysis is that researchers and parents should take into account children's dependency but at the same time respect their agency, and that these two are not contradictory constructions of childhood.

The research topic

A major issue in research on childhood and respect for children's participation rights is the choice of research topic and research questions. The nature of the topic is important to children as participants, for example, whether the topic is meaningful and engaging to them, and whether important aspects of children's experience are the objects of research. The choice of research topic is in itself an indicator of how researchers construct childhood. Ethical research with children should ask questions that are worth asking and use research methods which answer them effectively (Alderson 1995, cited by Thomas and O'Kane 1998). Curiosity or the desire to know is not sufficient justification for research with children (or families), according to Munford and Saunders (2001). They argue that it is incumbent on researchers to show that the research has the potential to enhance the well-being of participants. On the other hand, research projects of high quality can be borne out of simple curiosity. Nevertheless when funding for research is highly competitive, the potential enhancement of the well-being of children, in my view, ought to give such research higher priority.

Iterative email interviews with 12 participants explored the views of researchers who worked with children, on children's participation rights in research (Powell and Smith 2009). One of the themes which emerged from the study was the importance of the research topic. Some researchers said that it was crucial for a research topic to be interesting and meaningful to children, for them to engage authentically in the research. They said that chances of a participatory dialogue and of gaining an understanding of the child's standpoint were greater when the topic meant something to both child and researcher, and when the researcher positioned herself as less knowledgeable than the child. For example, in a recent study of children's learning dispositions (Smith, Duncan and Marshall 2005), showing four-year-old children digital photographs of their play and activities in their early childhood centres proved a very effective way of getting a dialogue underway, so that the children could help the adults to understand what they had been intending and feeling. In another study, focus groups of children acted as tutors (Dobbs, Smith and Taylor 2006), explaining to Splodge, a fictional alien from outer space, how parents on earth use physical punishment. This study approached an issue where adult attitudes about the value of physical punishment had totally dominated the research literature, while children had been viewed as the silent recipients of physical punishment. This novel approach opened up a way for children to talk comfortably about a sensitive topic, and opened up new insights into this aspect of their childhood.

Some research topics have been neglected because of dominant constructions of childhood. Woodhead (2005) is critical, for example, of the absence of accounts of children's economic activity in child development research. He argues that many millions of children, including very young children, contribute to economic activity by working. Yet the dominant construction of childhood by Western researchers has been of childhood as a time of innocence, play, schooling and extended economic dependency. He cites Punch's (2001) research on children in Bolivia where by three and four years of age, children are fetching water, collecting firewood, feeding animals, and picking fruit and vegetables.

> While universal accounts of normal development offer a powerful basis for realizing rights in early childhood, they also have limitations. Firstly, they tend to overlook the diversities in children's experiences, including differences in the ways children learn, play and communicate . . . Secondly any particular account of young children's development is always partial, and can never encompass the varieties of childhood. Thirdly, specific cultural patterns of early development and care risk being normalized and universalized.
>
> (Woodhead 2005: 88)

Certain topics and issues dominate the attention of Minority World researchers, as is pointed out by Pence and Hix-Small (2007). They suggest that efforts to understand child rearing and socialization on a global basis are relatively rare, and that the research literature focuses on pre-primary group care although such contexts are rare for children in most societies.

Another way in which some topics are neglected in childhood research, is when the topic is considered sensitive. A sensitive topic is one considered to be threatening, or to contain elements of risk. Research on sensitive topics can be so difficult to do that children are excluded entirely from becoming participants in such research. The majority of researchers in our study (Powell and Smith 2009) had experienced barriers to children's voices being heard in 'sensitive' research: 'Children with knowledge about sensitive topics . . . were often excluded from participation and denied this opportunity to have their voices heard because of concern for their vulnerability' (ibid.: 129).

The sensitivity about the research topic affects every aspect of the research process – from ethical approval and recruitment to research procedures. Ethical approval was a particularly arduous process involving multiple gatekeepers, when sensitive issues were being researched. The conflict between ethical concerns – to protect the children from harm, and their right to express their views and participate – is a particular concern for sensitive topics. Issues, such as the experiences of children in state care, their perspectives on parental divorce and separation, or their experience of violence, can be closed to research scrutiny, and these children's rights to be heard are not respected. Such exclusion denies policy-makers and practitioners access to knowledge, which could help them improve children's well-being in difficult circumstances.

Atwool (2008) carried out research on the use of attachment assessments to support placement decisions for children in state care, especially in conflicted situations where agreement could not be reached. Atwool's study was framed by her view that 'Children's voices are silenced by adults' certainty about their capacity to act in children's best interests combined with their absence from decision-making' (ibid.: 59). Children's views about their experience in state care had been very little researched in New Zealand, so Atwool's study aimed to remedy this neglect. Her original research plan had been to include children as participants but she was unable to proceed with it due to a number of obstacles. First, there were protracted delays in her contacts with the government agency, Child, Youth and Family (CYF, responsible for approving access to children in state care). CYF stipulated that all recruitment be negotiated through a CYF staff member, but busy CYF staff members were not necessarily supportive of or committed to the research. Second, the university ethics committee required that both parents or guardians consented to the children's involvement in the study. Atwool located 13 potential child participants, but while she gained agreement from some foster parents, most birth parents either declined, or were unable to be contacted, so the study did not include children and proceeded on the basis of interviews with social workers.

> Although the undertaking not to approach children without the consent of all of the significant adults in their lives was made in order to protect children from exposure to further conflict or pressure, it had the effect of excluding them from the research.
>
> (ibid.: 120)

Becoming a participant and the process of participating

Ethical recruitment is a difficult issue for many childhood researchers, particularly when a topic is sensitive. Developing a close relationship with gatekeepers (such as parents, early childhood teachers and social workers) and having community networks is therefore important for researchers. It is important that recruitment procedures do not make potential participants feel pressured to join in, and that they be allowed to choose freely whether or not to participate (Munford and Saunders 2001). For children, this is an especially delicate issue, when their gatekeepers (parents or teachers) are keen for them to be part of a study. Rather than assuming that children assent if their parents agree for them to be a part of a study, it is important that informed consent is gained, even from young children.

On the other hand, adults may want to discourage the recruitment of children, especially if the children are regarded as vulnerable.

Access to children to enable researchers to invite them to participate is important, and it is usually adults who open or close the doors to children's participation. Gaining access to participants can also be difficult if research focuses on children's experiences of services or interventions, when the providers of those services or interventions are the gatekeepers. Reluctance to participate may be influenced by the construction of children as vulnerable and from fears of re-traumatization, but there also may be an element of adults wanting to protect themselves from children being critical or negative about the services or interventions they experience. Adults can in some cases have an unhelpful influence on the recruitment process by eliminating particular children from an invitation to participate, or putting forward 'good' children. Not only is this unethical and disrespectful of children's participation rights, it also leads to biased and unrepresentative sample selection. Alderson and Morrow (2004) show that children themselves are aware of such inequalities.

The type of consent procedures adopted can have a big influence on recruitment. For example, there is a major debate about the age at which children can consent for themselves without parent consent, which has been discussed earlier. The type of information given is influential for successful recruitment, and it needs to be presented in a way which children (and adult participants) can understand. As soon as children are able to communicate verbally, researchers should find a way to inform children and gain their consent (Munford and Saunders 2001). Young children will be reliant on adults to truthfully explain what is involved, and this is unlikely to be achieved in one session. Munford and Saunders describe an innovative procedure, which they used to ensure that children really understood what it was they were consenting to. They showed children mock videos of a research interview to give them a concrete example of what participation in the research might be like.

For young children, it will often be parents who will explain to children about the research, but researchers too need to be sure that children are willing to participate. In our study (Carr *et al.* 2011) of four- and five-year-olds' learning dispositions, we became very aware that the initial consent process was not enough. We had to be constantly sensitive to occasions when children did not want to be observed and recorded, and be willing to remove ourselves and our recording equipment when these were not welcome. Children were aware that they could withdraw at any stage and this did happen on occasion.

An episode described by MacNaughton and Smith (2005), shows how it can be stressful at times to maintain an ethical relationship with children. Their research involved talking to children aged 3–5 years about identity construction, asking them to draw and paint images and then to explain their ideas and understanding. One child, Phoebe, talked to the researcher, describing in detail what she liked about the room she was in. She provided rich data in the form of vivid descriptions and elaborate drawings. When the researcher asked Phoebe if she could take her work home and share it with others, she said: 'Well, no. Actually, no, I need to take it home.' The researcher described her initial feeling of disappointment, but on further reflection satisfaction that Phoebe had felt confident enough to express her opinion and assert ownership of her work. Such confidence implies the child's trust in the researcher and the researcher's sensitivity to the child's wishes.

Once children have become participants in a research study and initial ethical approval has been gained, ethical issues are an ongoing issue. All of the researchers in our study (Powell and Smith 2009) argued that careful choice of research methodology was needed in order to respect children's participation rights. Children are more likely to respond openly and honestly if they feel respected and safe, and this usually depends on the skill of the researcher in putting them at ease, minimizing the distance between the adult and the child, establishing shared interests and a dialogue, and putting the child in the position of the expert (Gollop 2000). Attempts need to be made to reduce power imbalances, and time taken to build relationships (with children, parents and staff).

To return to the issue of recruitment of participants on sensitive topics, Kerryann Walsh (2005) describes the almost insurmountable barriers she faced when attempting to carry out her research. She was interested in the approaches taken by early childhood teachers working with children who had experienced abuse and neglect. Her attempts to recruit teachers for the study by mailing information to some 200 teachers resulted in a zero response rate. Walsh also experienced the stalling of approval processes by a regional authority resulting in her application for approval taking nine months to achieve a response. The teachers' reluctance to participate in this sensitive study may, she argues, have been due in part to their wariness about enquiries into their teaching and what they knew and did not know. Other factors which might have influenced gatekeepers were thought to have included fears about parent perceptions, damage to the centre's image, and loss of market share. Walsh said that one of the lessons she had learned about recruitment, was that the research aims should be expressed broadly in general terms in order to avoid dissuading potential participants. She argues that this did not involve deception, and that full explanations would have limited the research. It is clear therefore that the success of recruitment is greatly influenced by the type and nature of information that is distributed by researchers.

Our study (Powell and Smith 2009) of 12 researchers working with children showed that all of the participants, who were engaged in research on children's experiences of interventions following emotional or traumatic events, had to modify some aspect of their research design in order to be able to continue with their research. Many of them experienced a similar lack of response to Walsh (2005). According to one of the researchers:

> I was surprised at the low level of uptake by my colleagues. I believe that this was in part influenced by their not having understood the nature of the research, feelings of professional vulnerability (as the children would be

commenting on their experiences of the services they had received), attitudes towards client feedback and the status of children.

(Participant F, Powell and Smith 2009: 133)

Thomas and O'Kane (1998) were able to a large extent to overcome the barriers described by others (Atwool 2008; Powell and Smith 2009; Walsh 2005) in their research with children aged eight to twelve years in state care. They adopted a policy of requiring active consent on the part of the child and passive agreement on the part of caretakers. (It is not likely, however, that researchers working with preschool children would be permitted by ethics committees to place parental consent secondary to child consent.) Thomas and O'Kane prepared an information pack which included a leaflet or audiotape describing the research for the children as well as separate information leaflets for parents and caregivers. They viewed children's choice to participate as central to the study, and checked at every stage whether children wanted to continue with the process. Being able to offer children information about the research directly was crucial to the researchers' confidence that they were following an ethical process. Social workers were still gatekeepers and in some cases objected to children's participation on such grounds that the children had 'too much else to deal with at present' or 'wouldn't be interested' (Thomas and O'Kane 1998: 346). When adults did not want children to be invited to participate, the researchers had to accept their judgement.

Feedback and dissemination

An important and challenging part of ethical research is the fulfilment of an obligation to ensure that participants have the opportunity to hear about the findings of research. Article 13 of UNCRC states that children have the right to freedom of expression, but also the right to *receive* information and ideas, 'in writing or in print, in the form of art, or through any other media of the child's choice' (Article 13, United Nations Convention on the Rights of the Child). Research publications only reach a select few people, but the contributions which participants have made to research, should be acknowledged by allowing participants access to the research outcomes. This is related to children's ownership of research data, an issue raised by MacNaughton and Smith (2005). Children have the right to access and ownership of research outputs to which they have contributed, such as drawings, writings, photographs or interview material. They are also entitled, like adult research participants, to feedback: 'Children, like adults, should be able to comment on how their data set is interpreted and presented to others. Children, like adults, should have the research findings reported back to them' (ibid.: 116).

While research findings are often directed at adults, it is possible to provide young child participants, through their parents or teachers, with simple summaries of research findings, which can be explained to children. In our work observing young children's learning dispositions in early childhood teachers and homes (Carr *et al.* 2011), we have found photographs and copies of field notes to be a valued form of feedback for parents and teachers, which can be shown to children, incorporated into portfolios and learning stories (Carr 2001), and kept for reflection and discussion.

Conclusion

This chapter has examined the contribution that Childhood Studies and Children's Rights perspectives make to our understanding of ethical research procedures. These paradigms and perspectives foreground children's perspectives and view children as competent interpreters of their own experiences and partners in the research process, rather than the passive objects of the researcher's enquiries. Instead of assuming that children are incomplete beings on the path to adulthood, children are viewed as citizens who can help unravel knowledge about childhood. Barriers to ethical research on critical issues for children's well-being include assumptions of children's incompetence or vulnerability, fears about the sensitivity of research topics, and over-assiduous gatekeeping. The chapter concludes that children should be provided with opportunities for informed consent; respectful, reciprocal and trusting relationships with researchers; appropriate and effective methods for hearing children; and opportunities for feedback about findings and ownership of data.

Note

1   State Parties shall assure to the child who is capable of forming his or her own views the right to express those views freely in all matters affecting the child, the views of the child being given due weight in accordance with the age and maturity of the child (#1, Article 12, United Nations Convention on the Rights of the Child).

References

Alanen, L. (1998) 'Children and the family order', in I. Hutchby and J. Moran-Ellis (eds), *Children and Social Competence*, London: Falmer Press.

Alderson, P. (1995) 'Researching children's right to integrity', in B. Mayall (ed.), *Children's Childhoods: Observed and Experienced*, London: Falmer Press, pp. 45–62.

Alderson, P. (2001) 'Life and death: agency and dependency in young children's health care', *Childrenz Issues*, 5(1): 23–27.

Alderson, P. (2005) 'Designing ethical research with children', in A. Farrell (ed.), *Ethical Research with Children*, Maidenhead: Open University Press, pp. 27–36.

Alderson, P. and Morrow, V. (2004) *Ethics, Social Research and Consulting with Children and Young People*, 2nd edn, Ilford: Barnardos.

Atwool, N. (2008) 'Who cares? The role of attachment assessment in decision-making for children in care', PhD thesis, University of Otago.

Burman, E. (2008) *Deconstructing Developmental Psychology*, 2nd edn, London: Routledge.

Carr, M. (2001) *Assessment in Early Childhood Settings: Learning Stories*, London: Paul Chapman.

Carr, M., Smith, A. B., Duncan, J., Jones, C., Lee, W. and Marshall, K. (2011) *Learning in the Making: Disposition and Design in Early Education*, Rotterdam: Sense Publishers.

Committee on the Rights of the Child (2006) *General Comment No. 7 (2005): Implementing rights in early childhood*. Available at: http://www2.ohchr.org/english/bodies/crc/docs/AdvanceVersions/GeneralComment7Rev1.pdf (accessed 24 June 2009).

Dobbs, T., Smith, A. B. and Taylor, N. (2006) '"No, we don't get a say, children just suffer the consequences": Children talk about family discipline', *International Journal of Children's Rights*, 14(2): 137–156.

Farrell, A. (2005a) 'Ethics and research with children', in A. Farrell (ed.), *Ethical Research with Children*, Maidenhead: Open University Press, pp. 1–14.

Farrell, A. (2005b) 'New times in ethical research with children', in A. Farrell (ed.), *Ethical Research with Children*, Maidenhead: Open University Press, pp. 166–175.

Freeman, M. (2007) 'Why it remains important to take children's rights seriously', *International Journal of Children's Rights*, 15(1): 5–23.

Gollop, M. (2000) 'Interviewing children: A research perspective', in A. B. Smith, N. J. Taylor and M. Gollop (eds), *Children's Voices: Research, Policy and Practice*, Auckland: Pearson Education, pp. 18–36.

James, A. (2007) 'Giving voice to children's voices: Practices and problems, pitfalls and potentials', *American Anthropologist*, 109(2): 261–272.

James, A. and James, A. (2008) *Key Concepts in Childhood Studies*, Los Angeles, CA: Sage.

James, A., Jenks, C. and Prout A. (1998) *Theorizing Childhood*, Cambridge: Polity Press.

Karp, J. (2008) 'Matching human dignity with the UN Convention on the Rights of the Child', in Y. Ronen and C. W. Greenbaum (eds) *The Case for the Child: Towards A New Agenda*, Oxford: Intersentia, pp. 89–135.

Lansdown, G. (1994) 'Children's rights', in B. Mayall (ed.), *Children's Childhoods: Observed and Experienced*, London: Falmer Press, pp. 33–44.

Lloyd-Smith, M. and Tarr, J. (2000) 'Researching children's perspectives: A sociological dimension', in A. Lewis and G. Lindsay (eds), *Researching Children's Perspectives*, Buckingham: Open University Press, pp. 59–70.

MacNaughton, G. and Smith, K. (2005) 'Exploring ethics and difference: The choices and challenges of researching with children', in A. Farrell (ed.), *Exploring Ethical Research with Children*, Maidenhead: Open University Press, pp. 112–123.

Matthews, H. (2005) 'The Millennium Challenge: The disappointing geographies of children's rights', *Children's Geographies*, 3(1): 1–3.

Mayall, B. (2002) *Towards a Sociology for Childhood: Thinking from Children's Lives*, Buckingham: Open University Press.

Morrow, V. and Richards, M. (1996) 'The ethics of social research with children: An overview', *Children and Society*, 10: 90–105.

Munford, R. and Saunders, J. (2001) 'Interviewing children and their parents', in M. Tolich (ed.), *Research Ethics in Aotearoa/New Zealand*, Auckland: Pearson Education. pp. 99–111.

Oakley, A. (1994) 'Women and children first and last: Parallels and differences between children's and women's studies', in B. Mayall (ed.), *Children's Childhoods: Observed and Experienced*, London: Falmer Press, pp. 11–32.

Pence, A. and Hix-Small, H. (2007) 'Global children in the shadow of the global child', *International Critical Childhood Policy Studies Journal*, 2(1): 75–91.

Powell, M-A. and Smith, A. B. (2009) 'Children's participation rights in research', *Childhood*, 16(1): 124–142.

Prout, A. and James, A. (1997) 'A new paradigm for the sociology of childhood?', in A. James and A. Prout (eds), *Constructing and Reconstructing Childhood: Contemporary Issues in the Sociological Study of Childhood*, 2nd edn, London: Falmer Press, pp. 7–34.

Punch, S. (2001) 'Household division of labour: Generation, gender, age, birth order and sibling composition', *Work, Employment and Society*, 15(4): 803–823.

Robinson, C. and Kellett, M. (2004) 'Power', in S. Fraser, V. Lewis, S. Ding, M. Kellett and C. Robinson (eds), *Doing Research with Children and Young People*. London: Sage/Open University Press, pp. 81–96.

Smith, A. B. (2002) 'Interpreting and supporting participation rights: Contributions from sociocultural theory', *International Journal of Children's Rights*, 10: 73–88.

Smith, A. B. (2007) 'Children and young people's participation rights in education', *International Journal of Children's Rights*, 15: 147–164.

Smith, A. B. and Taylor, N. J. (2000) 'The sociocultural context of childhood: Balancing agency and dependency', in A.B. Smith, N. J. Taylor and M. M. Gollop (eds), *Children's Voices: Research, Policy and Practice*, Auckland: Pearson Education, pp. 1–17.

Smith, A. B., Duncan, J. and Marshall, K. (2005) 'Children's perspectives on their learning: Exploring methods', *Early Child Development and Care*, 17(6): 473–487.

Thomas, N. and O'Kane, C. (1998) 'The ethics of participatory research with children', *Children and Society*, 12: 336–348.

Walsh, K. (2005) 'Researching sensitive issues', in A. Farrell (ed.), *Ethical Research with Children*, Maidenhead: Open University Press, pp. 68–80.

Woodhead, M. (2005) 'Early childhood development: A question of rights', *International Journal of Early Childhood*, 37(3): 79–98.

Woodhead, M. (2009) 'Child development and the development of childhood', in J. Qvortrup, W. A. Corsaro and M-S. Honig (eds), *The Palgrave Handbook of Childhood Studies*, Basingstoke: Palgrave Macmillan, pp. 46–61.

Chapter 2

The ethics of participatory research involving young children with special needs

Colette Gray and Eileen Winter

Situated within a social constructivist framework, we draw on examples from our own, national and international research to explore the effect international policy has had on children's rights and their participation in discussions about matters that affect their lives. The chapter focuses for the most part on the ethical guidelines that inform participatory research, particularly the issues of access through gatekeepers to children with special needs, informed consent, confidentiality and anonymity. In the section on research methods, we aim to highlight areas of convergence between social constructivism and the new social studies of childhood, also referred to as the new sociology of childhood. The chapter concludes that child-centred approaches that draw on a wealth of methodological techniques from a range of cognate disciplines are well placed to facilitate the child's right of expression.

Introduction

In this chapter, we explore the ethical implications of participatory research involving young children with special needs. An important part of this task begins with an explanation of what is meant by the term 'special needs'. Rather than denote a homogenized social category, we employ the term to represent a broad spectrum of young children who have additional needs that impact upon their lives. At one end of the spectrum are the more able children, such as those with English as an additional language, whose needs might be described as mild. At the other end are the less able children who may have multiple, profound and/or complex needs. Despite their differences, they all lack presence in the ever expanding body of participatory research. In this chapter, we aim to explore some of the barriers to their inclusion in the research process and suggest how these obstacles can be overcome.

Situated within a social constructivist framework, we draw on examples from our own, national and international research to explore the effect that international policy has had on children's rights and their participation in discussions about matters that affect their lives. The chapter focuses for the most part on the ethical guidelines that inform participatory research, particularly the issues of access through gatekeepers to children with special needs, informed consent, confidentiality and anonymity. In the section on research methods, we aim to highlight areas of convergence between social constructivism and the new social studies of childhood, also referred to as the new sociology of childhood. We believe that, irrespective of scholarly differences, participatory researchers working within these disciplines have more in common than is generally acknowledged. For example, both view children as competent social actors whose lives are best understood in real-world settings. Similarly, both believe that knowledge is socially constructed and maintained and that it is a subjective and personal experience. Moreover, like proponents of the new social studies of childhood, we employ a multitude of naturalistic methodological approaches to 'give children a voice' and to include them in the research process (Clark, McQuail, and Moss 2003; Clark and Statham 2005; Hill 2006; Waller 2006). In examining some of the ethical issues involved in participatory studies, we believe the boundaries between these disciplinary approaches will seem much less important than the messages that transcend them.

Equality in action

Alluded to in the Introduction, children with special needs are not a homogenous group but are more disparate than similar. Like their typically developing peers, they differ in terms of their age, gender, race, culture, ability and life experience (Marchant and Jones 2003; Whyte 2006). Unlike their typically developing peers, children with special needs differ in terms of the severity, onset, cause, type and impact of their disorder. By way of example, Filipek *et al.* (1999) point out that the term Autistic Spectrum Disorders (ASD) refers to a wide continuum of associated cognitive and neurobehavioral disorders, including, but not limited to, three core-defining features: impairments in socialization; impairments in verbal and nonverbal communication; and restricted and repetitive patterns of behaviours. While some children with ASD have very severe communication difficulties, others with ASD are able to communicate and interact effectively with a wide range of people. Another example is the term 'Visual Impairment' which denotes a broad range of eye disorders that can exert a mild, moderate or profound effect upon a child's life (Gray 2005; 2009). Given the individual characteristics and experiences of these children, we believe it is essential that, like their non-disabled peers, they are given every opportunity to participate in the research process. This is a view endorsed in Articles 7 and 8 of the United Nations Convention on the Rights of the Child (UNCRC) (United Nations 1989), which uphold the rights of children with disabilities to express their views freely on all matters that affect them. To help them realize their rights, age-appropriate assistance is recommended for children, including very young children, with disabilities (ibid.). In essence, though their experiences may be different, enshrined in law, children with and without special needs have the same rights of expression.

The impact of policy on practice

Mentioned above, the United Nations Convention on the Rights of the Child (1989), ratified in the UK in 1999, established children's rights to provision, protection and participation and changed the way children were viewed by many social and developmental researchers (Corsaro 2004). Challenging the objectification of children, the UNCRC heralded a well-documented shift away from research being 'on' to research being conducted 'with' children (Clark and Statham 2005; Hill 2006; Porter and Lacey 2005). The passing of the Children Act (1989) and the Children Bill (2004) in the UK added further weight to government assertions that children's views and perspectives can and must be heard on issues that affect them. Reflecting international trends, the UK government's commitment to the child's right to participation produced a veritable 'torrent of initiatives' undertaken to give voice to the child (Lewis and Porter 2004: 19), and which McLeod (2008: 45) believes elevated listening to children to 'a new orthodoxy'.

Even the most cursory review of the literature lends support for this notion and reveals a significant increase in children's participation in policy and decision-making in the UK (Lewis and Porter 2004; McLeod 2008; Porter and Lacey 2005). This is particularly evident in the last decade, with policy-makers increasingly inviting children and young people to join research steering committees and asking for their feedback and advice on government policies (Brownlie, Anderson, and Ormston 2006; Kellett 2005). For example, a major survey on needs and services in Northern Ireland was informed and shaped by the views of children and young people with disabilities (Monteith, McCrystal, and Iwaniec 1997). Similarly conducted in Northern Ireland, a large-scale project on the state of children's rights, and a project on the state of the rights of the child within the framework of rights, included in the research process children from all sections of the community, with and without disabilities, between three and five years of age (Kilkelly et al. 2004; NICCY 2006). A further example of a project that actively included children with special needs in the process was the 2007 UK campaign 'Every Disabled Child Matters'. The final report from the project, the *Disabled Children's Manifesto for Change*, sought to inform the government about the needs of young people with disabilities. At the time, the launch of the report attracted a considerable amount of media attention and a delegation of young people with special needs was invited to meet the Prime Minister to talk about their needs.

Nonetheless, critics believe that participatory research has no long-term impact on children's lives (Badham 2004; Clark et al. 2003). According to Brownlie et al. (2006), many of these projects are policy-led and ignore the broader concerns that affect children's lives. Summing up the views of many, Kellett (2005) describes current efforts at participatory research as merely 'tokenistic'.

Ethical guidelines for researchers

Irrespective of these shortcomings, most would agree that the ethical rigour of research involving children with special needs and vulnerable groups should be considerably greater than research involving fully cognisant, consenting adults (Whyte 2006). In the first instance, and revisited in the following section, the choice of an appropriate methodology is crucial. To support researchers at the planning stage, drawing on a range of sources, Clark *et al.* (2003) provide a comprehensive list of conditions to aid researchers in the promotion of effective listening. For example, they remind us that we should be clear about the purpose of the research and the extent to which children's views can be incorporated. They believe it is essential for the research to be conducted in a familiar and comfortable setting by adults known to the child. To fully embrace the principles of democratic participation, they encourage researchers to set aside their adult agendas and to facilitate the children's freedom of expression by using a multi-media approach, for example, hand-held Flip video cameras, disposable cameras and tape recorders.

While these conditions are fundamental to good practice, Whyte (2006) provides a more stringent and detailed checklist for researchers working with all young children, and most especially young children with special needs. She points out that researchers should have the following qualities or qualifications:

- police clearance;
- experience of participating in a disability awareness programme;
- qualifications and experience in working with children in general and also with children with disabilities, in the age group participating in the project;
- a good information base about child development;
- the ability to communicate with the participating group;
- knowledge of physical and cognitive impairments and their likely impact on children's experiences and development at different ages;
- knowledge of previous research findings in the area;
- an awareness of their own biases, assumptions and prejudices in relation to children in general and also in relation to children with disabilities of the age of those participating in the project;
- knowledge of and familiarity with relevant ethical guidelines from professional organizations;
- access to supportive committees and a professional network of professionals and experts, including children with disabilities and their parents; and in some cases, a reference group of people/children with disabilities.

In addition to these guidelines, researchers can draw on the ethical codes of their own discipline, for example, the British Psychological Society (BPS 2009) and the British Educational Research Association (BERA 2004). We were disappointed to note that the BPS makes scant reference to the needs of children, particularly children with special needs.

Access and informed consent

According to Roberts-Holmes (2006), the power dynamics between adults and children present a significant barrier to the collection of high quality evidence from children. We believe the power differential is further increased in studies which employ the terms 'consent' to denote adult permission and 'assent' for children's permission, with the latter viewed as less important. Our solution to the perennial problem of status differences is to employ the term 'consent' with both groups. This is more than mere semantics, since, irrespective of gaining adult permission, we would never include a child in our research who showed any sign of reluctance.

Nevertheless, access to children and vulnerable groups can only be gained through adult gatekeepers such as parents, early years professionals, teachers, statutory or voluntary organizations and social workers. Interestingly, there is no statutory guidance on the issue of consent for children involved in social research studies. Before granting permission, however, the majority of funding bodies, charities and University Research and Ethics committees require documentary evidence that consent will be sought from parents or carers and, increasingly, from children.

Frequently viewed as over-protective by researchers attempting to access the views of under-represented or marginalized groups (Gray and Carville 2008; Hill 2005; Masson 2005; McLeod 2008), gatekeepers are charged with the responsibility for safeguarding and protecting children. Professional gatekeepers operate two parallel strands. First, they are legally obliged to protect the children in their care. Second, they operate to protect their agency. Those who fail to meet these demands may be subject to prosecution, disciplinary action or dismissal. In zealously guarding their young charges, gatekeepers aim to protect children who find it difficult to dissent, disagree or say something unacceptable to an adult. Conversely, in denying or withholding access, adult gatekeepers can further marginalize under-represented groups or those with low incidence disorders.

In order to address their concerns and to increase the representation of minority groups, a copy of the interview questions can be given to both the gatekeeper and the child when their permission is sought. Details about data storage and the steps taken to maintain the child's anonymity and confidentiality can also be made available. Inviting a parent or advocate to be present during an interview or observation session might also allay their concerns. We accept that having a familiar adult present might encourage some children to speak out, but believe it might silence or inhibit others. The other disadvantage of this approach is that by bringing another adult into the situation, a child used to adults taking control may view themselves as having a passive rather than active role in the process. According to Mayall (2000), status differences between adults and children are inevitable and should be acknowledged at the outset of the research. While there is some merit in this proposition, we believe it is possible to reduce the impact of the power differential between the adult and child. First, using appropriately sized furniture or working at floor level can minimize the physical space between the adult and child. In a project involving six non-verbal children with profound and complex needs, Ware, Thorpe, Gray, and Behan (2005) for example, worked from large foam floor mats. With the aid of an advocate, also positioned at floor level, each child was invited to express their views by pressing a handheld computer pad or by rolling towards or away from the researcher. When the child wished to disengage from the process they closed their eyes.

Second, the psychological space between adults and children can be reduced by respecting the child's right to either give or withhold their consent to be involved in the research. While this concept can be realized with children who can express their views verbally, it presents particular challenges for researchers working with children with multiple and profound special needs who lack the verbal skills necessary to express their opinions. Our response to this challenge was to use a mixed methods approach that was not wholly reliant on language. For example, in a small-scale participatory project with 36 preschool children, half with and half without a known disability, we used verbal explanations, play, drawings and smiley face stickers to enable the children to make choices and to express their ideas and opinions freely through a medium other than language (Gray and Winter 2009). The children's understanding was tested the next day by a playgroup assistant who asked each child individually to tell her about our discussion, what we aimed to do, and whether they wished to be involved in the study.

Since giving too much information at the start of a project may prove overwhelming and confusing, as each stage of the process unfolded, we explained what was involved and revisited the issue of consent. This process gave each child multiple opportunities to either give or withhold, and was termed 'process consent' by Dockett (2008). Mindful that children can express dissent through non-verbal cues, we remained vigilant throughout the project for changes in the children's body language, engagement, facial expressions and body movements. Perhaps because they had ownership of the process or because we were alert to subtle changes in the children's demeanour, we were able to avoid the situation observed by Skanfors (2009). Reporting evidence from an ethnographic study of two- to five-year-old children in preschool, she observed young children using their body language to convey their boredom and disenchantment with the research process. Lacking the verbal skills necessary to express their thoughts, some of the children asserted control by either moving away from the researcher, by failing to respond, by hiding from or by ignoring the researcher. Terming these approaches 'say no' and 'show no', Skanfors (ibid.: 10) concluded that researchers should employ sensitivity and their 'ethical radar' throughout the research process. Though worthy, this proposition assumes that all researchers are sensitive to the needs of children. Sharing the views of many other researchers (Dockett 2008; Flewitt 2005; McLeod 2008; Roberts-Holmes 2006), we believe that consent with children should be viewed as ongoing and warranting regular review rather than a one-off process.

Confidentiality and anonymity

Confidentiality and anonymity present considerable challenges for researchers working within a participatory framework. In the interests of transparency, it is important to brief children about the limits of confidentiality before consent is sought (Dockett 2008; McLeod 2008; Roberts-Holmes 2006). By imposing parameters on confidentiality, participatory researchers aim to protect and safeguard young children. Given the lack of definitive guidance on the subject, researchers are left to make subjective judgements about an issue of personal, social and political sensitivity. A review of the literature reveals a disappointing lack of detail on the subject, with researchers in England, Scotland and Wales having no mandatory requirement to report their concerns about child abuse or child welfare. In contrast, failure to disclose child welfare concerns is a criminal offence in a number of countries including Northern Ireland, the United States of America, Australia, Canada, Argentina, Sweden, Denmark, Finland, Israel, Kyrgyzstan, the Republic of Korea, Rwanda, Spain and Sri Lanka (Wallace and Bunting 2007). While it might be supposed that this leads to over-reporting, under-reporting is a common feature of countries with mandatory and voluntary reporting systems. Wallace and Bunting attribute under-reporting to the lack of clarity on the topic of reportable child abuse. In terms of best practice, guidelines provided by the National Children's Bureau (2002: 3) indicate that 'there where child protection is an issue, researchers have a duty to take steps to protect the child or other children'. Reflecting the sharing of power and decision-making integral to participatory research, before reporting abuse, participatory researchers generally agree that it is best to inform the child about the action being taken, to update them on the situation and to offer them continued support until an appropriately trained person can take over (Hill 2005; Masson 2005; Roberts-Holmes 2006).

The anonymity of children with special needs also warrants consideration. In contrast to quantitative data which reports evidence at the aggregate level, without careful coding, there is a greater likelihood of exposure in qualitative data. This is particularly true when the research includes children with rare or low incidence disorders (e.g. Fragile X). The issue of anonymity is further challenged when children elect to report their own results or want their contribution acknowledged. In our study the children were keen to disseminate their work as presentations, pictures or collages to staff, parents, grandparents and carers on their graduation day (Gray and Winter 2009). After some discussion it was agreed that the children would take ownership of the presentations and the pictures and drawings from the research, but that in writing up the research we would use the pseudonyms chosen by the children.

Selecting the research method

The terms 'method' and 'methodology' refer to two distinct but complementary aspects of the research, which are frequently confused. Since the distinction between them is documented elsewhere (see, for example, Bussell 2008; Connolly 2003; Gray and Carville 2008), this section provides only a brief overview of these concepts. The choice of a methodology, in our view, presents a significantly greater challenge than the selection of a method. Methodologies provide the philosophy, theory and traditions that frame the research and frequently evolve over time. For example, our own theoretical approach has been strongly influenced by the emancipatory movement. Whereas we previously included children as passive participants in the research process, now we engage them as active participants. Since much of our work is conducted with children with special needs, this challenges us to identify an appropriate range of methods. Research methods are simply the range of tools or instruments available to gather the data. While it might be supposed that all methodologies employ methods suitable for use with adults and children, this is not always the case. In attempting to make the implicit explicit, for example, a phenomenology of children relies on data derived through language and verbal expression (Danaher and Briod 2005). Although drama, drawing, singing and play have been used in studies of children by a number of phenomenologists, Danaher and Briod point out that they require a verbal interpretation.

To reduce the shortcomings of single method approaches, most participatory researchers use a mixed methods approach. Triangulated approaches offer the fidelity and rigour that are often lacking in single method studies. One of the foremost psychologists to adopt a mixed method approach in the study of early childhood was Piaget (1959). Though much maligned, Piaget was the first psychologist to eschew the experimental tradition in favour of naturalistic observations. Keeping copious and detailed notes from his observations of the everyday lives of his own children, he interviewed each child to ensure that he was accurately interpreting their experiences. Contemporaries of Piaget, Vygotsky (1978) and Bronfenbrenner (1986) argued that the child's social and cultural and ecological context plays a significant role in shaping their development. According to such a theory, researchers must consider the quality and nature of the child's environment, their age, culture and life experiences before drawing any conclusions about their development. Naturalistic observation is the preferred method of contextual theorists. Without manipulating any aspect of the child's world, this approach captures the nature and detail of children's activities in an ecologically appropriate way. Paley (1988, 1990, 1993) adopted this approach to gain an insight into young children's perceptions and experiences of play within their nursery setting. Over a five-year period, she observed and noted various aspects of children's play in several settings, made tape recordings and corroborated her findings by asking the children to explain their play through stories.

More recently, Clark and Moss (2001) and Moss, Clark, and Kjørholt (2005) coined the term the 'Mosaic approach' to describe a range of age-appropriate participatory research tools for children. Used extensively in participatory research, the Mosaic approach promotes the use of traditional verbal and non-traditional visual methods; including one-to-one interaction with children, observations, cameras, bookmaking, tours and map making. Creative and innovative approaches continue to be the hallmark of participatory research. In a study of children's experience of conflict in Rwanda, Veale (2005), for example, used workshops, community mapping, drama, storytelling and drawing. Similarly, Pascal and Bertram (2009) experimented with a variety of different strategies to stimulate children's voices and to document them accurately and authentically. Central to their study were videotapes of typical days in the lives of three- and four-year-olds in early years settings in five European countries. The video tapes were employed to generate multi-voice, intercultural discussions with the adults and children involved, and to highlight cultural similarities and differences. They also used cultural circles – akin to circle time – critical incident analysis, storytelling and naming your world, wishing trees, listening posts, map guiding, guided tours and focused observations. The innovative approaches employed by these researchers serve to highlight the efforts made by participatory researchers to give voice to the child.

Conclusion

In this chapter, we explore the ethical challenges of participatory research involving children with special needs. Some of the difficulties identified within the process include: gaining access to participant groups, status differences, ensuring children understand the concept of consent, the limits of confidentiality, identifying appropriate methods and ownership of the data. We believe these challenges are not insurmountable and can be overcome, at least to some extent, by using the strategies suggested in the chapter. A notable example concerns the two-fold strategy we use to reduce the power differential between adults and children. We describe how we crossed the invisible demarcation lines that separate disciplines to gain children's informed consent. In essence, we used the methods developed by researchers working within the new social studies of childhood, sometimes referred to as the 'Mosaic approach', to inform our work. This provided us with a toolbox of verbal and non-verbal methods which were suitable for use with young children with and without special needs. Similarly, Veale (2005) and Pascal and Bertram (2009) derived their creative and innovative approaches from the child-centred methods used by researchers in disciplines such as sociology, anthropology and psychology. Engaging children, particularly children with special needs, in the research process poses additional ethical challenges. Having thoroughly reviewed the literature, in our view, child-centred approaches that draw on a wealth of methodological techniques from a range of cognate disciplines are well placed to facilitate the child's right of expression.

References

Badham, B. (2004) 'Participation – for a change: Disabled young people lead the way', *Children and Society*, 18(2): 143–154.
British Educational Research Association (BERA) (2004) *Revised Ethical Guidelines for Educational Research*. Available at: http://www.bera.ac.uk/publications/pdfs/ETHICA1. PDF (accessed 12 August 2009).

British Psychological Society (BPS) (2009) *Code of Ethics and Conduct*. Available at: http://www.bps.org.uk/document-download-area/document-download$.cfm?restart=true andfile_uuid=E6917759-9799-434A-F313-9C35698E1864 (accessed 12 August 2009).

Bronfenbrenner, U. (1986) 'Ecology of the family as a context for human development', *Developmental Psychology*, 22: 723–742.

Brownlie, J., Anderson, S. and Ormston, R. (2006) *Children as Researchers: SEED Sponsored Research*. Available at: www.scotland.gov.uk/insight (accessed 14 November 2009).

Bussell, S. (2008) *Research with Children: Thinking about Method and Methodology: Involving Children and Young People in Research*, pp. 17–29. Compendium of papers and reflections from a Think Tank, co-hosted by the Australian Research Alliance for Children and Youth and the New South Wales Commission for Children and Young People on 11 November 2008.

Clark, A. and Moss, P. (2001) *Listening to Young Children: The Mosaic Approach*, London: National Children's Bureau for the Joseph Rowntree Foundation.

Clark, A. and Statham, J. (2005) 'Listening to young children: Experts in their own lives', *Adoption and Fostering*, 29(1): 45–56.

Clark, A., McQuail, S. and Moss, P. (2003) *Exploring the Field of Listening to and Consulting with Young Children*, Research Report 445, London: Department for Education and Skills.

Connolly, P. (2003) *Ethical Principles for Researching Vulnerable Groups*, Belfast: Office of the First Minister and Deputy First Minister.

Corsaro, W. A. (2004) *The Sociology of Childhood*, 2nd edn, Thousand Oaks, CA: Pine Forge Press.

Danaher, T. and Briod, M. (2005) 'Phenomenological approaches to research with children', in S. Greene and D. Hogan (eds), *Researching Children's Experiences: Approaches and Methods*, London: Sage Publications, pp. 217–235.

Dockett, S. (2008) *Engaging Young Children in Research*, Compendium of papers and reflections from a Think Tank co-hosted by the Australian Research Alliance for Children and Youth and the New South Wales Commission for Children and Young People on 11 November 2008, pp. 52–63.

Filipek, P. A., Accardo, P. J., Baranek, G. T., Cook Jr, G. H., Dawson, G., Gordon, B., Gravel, J. S., Johnson, C. P., Kallen, R. J., Levy, S. E., Minshew, N. M., Prizant, B. P., Rapin, I., Rogers, S. J., Stone, W. L., Teplin, S., Tuchman, R. F. and Volkmar, F. R. (1999) 'The screening and diagnosis of autistic spectrum disorders', *Journal of Autism and Developmental Disorders*, 29(6): 439–484.

Flewitt, R. (2005) 'Is every child's voice heard? Researching the different ways 3-year-old children communicate and make meaning at home and in a pre-school playgroup', *Early Years*, 25(3): 207–222.

Gray, C. (2005) 'Training and the Early Years Professional: Understanding visual impairment', *International Journal of Early Years Education*, 13(1): 1–12.

Gray, C. (2009) 'A qualitatively different experience: Mainstreaming pupils with a visual impairment in Northern Ireland', *European Journal of Special Needs Education*, 24(2): 169–172.

Gray, C. and Carville, S. (2008) 'Ethical research practices across disciplinary boundaries: The process of research involving children with a visual impairment', *Child Care in Practice*, 14(2): 217–228.

Gray, C. and Winter, E. (2009) 'Participatory research with preschool children with and without disabilities', paper presented at the European Early Childhood Education Research Association (EECERA) conference, Strasbourg, 26–29 August.

Hill, M. (2005) 'Ethical considerations in researching children's experiences', in S. Greene and D. Hogan (eds), *Researching Children's Experiences: Approaches and Methods*, London: Sage Publications, pp. 61–86.

Hill, M. (2006) 'Children's voices on ways of having a voice: Children and young people's perspectives on methods used in research and consultation', *Childhood* 13(1): 69–89.

Kellett, M. (2005) *Children as Active Researchers: A New Research Paradigm for the 21st Century*, ESRC National Centre for Research Methods. The Open University, NCRM Methods Review Paper NCRM/003.

Kilkelly, U., Kilpatrick, R., Lundy, L., Moore, L., Scraton, P., Davey, C., Dwyer, C. and McAlistair, S. (2004) *Children's Rights in Northern Ireland*, Belfast: NICCY.

Lewis, A. and Porter, J. (2004) 'Interviewing children and young people with learning disabilities: Guidelines for researchers and multi-professional practice', *British Journal of Learning Disabilities*, 32(4): 191–197.

Marchant, R. and Jones, M. (2003) *Getting It Right: Involving Disabled Children in Assessment, Planning and Review Processes*, Brighton: Triangle.

Masson, J. (2005) 'Researching children's perspectives: Legal issues', in K. Sheehy, M. Nind, J. Rix and K. Simmons (eds), *Ethics in Research in Inclusive Education: Values into Practice*, London: RoutledgeFalmer, pp. 231–241.

Mayall, B. (2000) 'Conversations with children: Working with generational issues', in P. Christensen and A. James (eds), *Research with Children: Perspectives and Practices*, London: Falmer Press, pp. 120–135.

McLeod, A. (2008) *Listening to Children: A Practitioner's Guide*, London: Jessica Kingsley Publishers.

Monteith, M., McCrystal, P. and Iwaniec, D. (1997) *Children and Young People with Disabilities in Northern Ireland. Part I: An Overview of Needs and Services*, (Report and Summary), Belfast: Centre for Child Care Research, The Queen's University of Belfast.

Moss, P., Clark, A. and Kjørholt, A. (2005) 'Introduction', in A. Clark, A. Kjørholt and P. Moss (eds), *Beyond Listening: Children's Perspectives on Early Childhood Services*, Bristol: Policy Press, pp. 1–16.

National Children's Bureau (2002) *Including Children in Social Research: Highlight, no. 193*. Available: at: http://www.ncb.org.uk/dotpdf/open%20access%20%20phase%201%20only/research_guidelines_200604.pdf (accessed 12 August 2009).

NICCY (2006) *A Northern Ireland Based Review of Children and Young People's Participation in the Care Planning Process*, Belfast: NICCY.

Paley, V. G. (1988) *Bad Guys Don't Have Birthdays: Fantasy Play at Four*, Chicago: The University of Chicago Press.

Paley, V. G. (1990) *The Boy Who Would Be a Helicopter: The Uses of Storytelling in the Classroom*, Cambridge, MA: Harvard University Press.

Paley, V. G. (1993) *You Can't Say You Can't Play*, Cambridge, MA: Harvard University Press.

Pascal, C. and Bertram, T. (2009) 'Listening to young citizens: The struggle to make real a participatory paradigm with young children', *European Early Childhood Research Journal*, 17(2): 249–262.

Piaget, J. (1959) *The Language and Thought of the Child*, London: Routledge & Kegan Paul.

Porter, J. and Lacey, P. (2005) *Researching Learning Difficulties: A Guide for Practitioners*, London: Paul Chapman Publishing.

Roberts-Holmes, G. (2006) *Doing Your Research Project: A Step-By-Step Guide*, London: Paul Chapman Publishing.

Skanfors, L. (2009) 'Ethics in child research: Children's agency and researchers "ethical radar"', *Childhoods Today*, 3(1): 1–22.

United Nations (1989) *The United Nations Convention on the Rights of the Child*, New York: UNICEF.

Veale, A. (2005) 'Creative methodologies in participatory research with children', in S. Greene and D. Hogan (eds), *Researching Children's Experiences: Approaches and Methods*, London: Sage Publications, pp. 253–272.

Vygotsky, L. (1978) *Mind in Society: The Development of Higher Psychological Processes*, Cambridge, MA: Harvard University Press.

Wallace, I. and Bunting, L. (2007) *An Examination of Local, National and International Arrangements for the Mandatory Reporting of Child Abuse: The Implications for Northern Ireland*, Belfast: NI Policy and Research Unit.

Waller, T. (2006) '"Don't come too close to my octopus tree": Recording and evaluating young children's perspectives on outdoor learning', *Children, Youth and Environments*, 16(2): 75–104.

Ware, J. Thorpe, P., Gray, C. and Behan, S. (2005) 'Developing contingency awareness in pupils with PMLD in the classroom', paper presented at ISEC (Inclusive and Supportive Education Congress), Glasgow, Scotland, 1–4 August.

Whyte, J. (2006) *Research with Children with Disabilities*, National Disability Authority. Available at: http://www.nda.ie/cntmgmtnew.nsf/0/851DE72FE32677F0802571 CB005A165B?OpenDocument (accessed 12 August 2009).

Chapter 3

Informed consent

Processes and procedures in seeking research partnerships with young children

Deborah Harcourt and Heather Conroy

There are many challenges when engaging in the process of seeking children's informed consent. It would appear that this is often a hurried process with little emphasis placed on ascertaining whether children are being empowered to make an informed decision to participate, or not to participate, in the research process. This chapter will explore, using examples from Australia and Singapore, the process of consent. Consideration will be given to how young children's competence as research participants is viewed, the intention of the research enterprise, and how this impacts on the way a researcher responds to the consent process. Finally, the chapter will explore the research relationship as it relates to consent, and reassert that informed consent by the participant is essential but that the measure of explanation regarding withdrawal of consent needs further consideration, so that children understand that their initial consent is not an on-going or final decision.

Introduction

> Many adults feel invaded by children. Adults are not always willing to welcome what the culture of childhood has to say. Some adults feel that we are seeking to allow children to have a voice that is more important than the adult voice. This shows that we still do not 'know' each other. It is not about who is more important, it is about the equity of visibility of views and opinions.
>
> (Elana Giacopini 2009)

There are many challenges for adults, both perceived and actual, when we seek to recognize, legitimate and activate the potential of children as research partners. By creating a possible reality for children as active participants in research, we cannot lose sight of the complexities that might exist as we engage in the process of seeking children's participation. However, rather than viewing these challenges as problematic, we can examine them as some of the most interesting spaces for consideration. This chapter will explore the conception of a research space being offered to children, with an emphasis on how we ensure children are being empowered to make an informed decision to participate, or not to participate, in a research enterprise. Using examples from Australia and Singapore, consideration will be given to the significance of seeing children as competent research participants in order for adults and children to work alongside each other in the construction of further knowledge about children and their childhoods.

Creating a space for children as competent research participants

Over the past decade, the fields of research that draw upon children as primary informants have seen a theoretical shift towards foregrounding a new construction of children as research participants. This shift has been particularly evident in early childhood research (Clarke 2005; Dockett and Perry 2003, 2005; Einarsdóttir 2005; Harcourt 2008). Of significance in these studies is the intention to work in *partnership* with children. Attempts are being made to accept a professional and ethical responsibility to seek meaning and understanding about children and childhood by engaging with children as an integral aspect of the research process. As researchers have begun to value this construct of building knowledge, so a new research culture is being identified. Many researchers acknowledge the United Nations Convention on the Rights of the Child (United Nations 1989) as a significant platform from which to include children's views on matters that concern them. This document has been widely regarded by the international research community as perhaps the most comprehensive statement on children's rights and a foundation for developing policy and making decisions about children. The UNCRC resonates with the emerging construction of children as active research participants and informs a new sociology of childhood where children are seen as social actors and competent contributors of valid opinions, ideas and theories (Corsaro 1997; Mayall 2002; Prout 2004). However, to be effective in upholding the possibilities offered in positioning children as researchers, a firm commitment on behalf of adults who work with and alongside children is needed, to ensure children are adequately informed and empowered to make a decision about their participation.

A commitment to involve children in the decision-making and policy environment shapes the ideas the research community develops about children. There is an opportunity to provide the structure and procedures that enable children's participation in research, from the position of the child as a competent and capable contributor. The wish to listen to and involve children originates within this context and leads to structures and procedures that can support the involvement of children (Langstead 1994). Prominent Italian researcher Rinaldi (2005) suggested that a standpoint which seeks an acknowledgement of the presence of children, and their accounts of life, is an essential element to understanding their worlds. This challenges the traditional notions of developmental psychology that children *become* someone; children *are* already someone.

Dahlberg, Moss and Pence (1999) referred to the notion of children who are worth listening to, having dialogue with and who also have the courage to think and act autonomously. Rather than children and childhood being excluded from sociological consideration (childhood as a preparatory stage rather than a participatory activity), the new sociology offers possibilities to focus on the child as an agent. This positions the child as a social actor who participates in constructing knowledge through their daily experiences and interactions. Rinaldi (2001) has argued that listening to children begins an important relationship between the child and adult. It is the on-going relationships between the protagonists that then form the corner-stone of an effective democratic community. Australian researchers Dockett and Perry (2003) remarked that including children in dialogue about their direct experience had the potential to inform adults of the implications and outcomes of these experiences for young children themselves. By engaging children in these conversations, adults are regarding children as 'competent and interpretive social participants' (Dockett and Perry 2003: 12) and 'sophisticated thinkers and communicators' (Harcourt and Conroy 2005: 567). Thorpe *et al.* (2005: 117) acknowledged children's reports of their experiences as credible information that can then 'be used to advance knowledge of children's everyday practices, relevant for policy and research directions in education and child advocacy'.

It has been proposed that significant knowledge about children's lives can result when children's active participation in the research enterprise is deliberately solicited and where their ideas, perspectives, and feelings are accepted as genuine and valid data (Prout and James 1997; Woodhead and Faulkner 2000). Castelle (1990) stated that when the researcher listens to children as part of this enterprise, it acknowledges the human rights of children to actively participate in relevant social processes. The notion of the agentic child (Danby and Baker 1998; Woodrow 1999), the competent social actor in his/her own right, is consistent with viewing the child as a reliable informant in the research process. This flies in the face of previous notions identified by Dockett and Perry (2003) that children cannot provide reliable information and invites opportunity for children to provide the 'missing perspectives of those who experience the effects of existing educational policies-in-practice' (Cook-Sather 2002: 3). According to Pence and Brenner's (2000) research, a democratic ecology involves 'doing with' rather than 'doing on', creating links not walls and engaging in dialogue that focuses on strengths and assets. If children find themselves in positions of passivity in the research process, it is questionable as to how they become active participators in matters that affect them.

Designing the research process to include children as active research participants and collaborators recognizes the inherent competence that children can offer. Children can transform and elaborate upon their experiences, through intentional symbolic representation of those experiences which support the adult researcher to generate ideas and construct theories with the child. Through making visible and communicating children's opinions, ideas and theories, the research community is provided with an opportunity to reflect and debate meaning. This is an opportunity to work together, giving value to different perspectives and an exchange of ideas which becomes reciprocal learning of great significance. Adults therefore hold the responsibility for providing children with 'respectful and legitimate opportunity for hearing of their ideas, views and opinions' (Harcourt 2009: 83). Adults also have the responsibility to engage children with research so that children are able to build competence as researchers. These responsibilities, those that position children as research partners, provide a crucial conceptual backcloth for this discussion.

Establishing a research relationship

If researchers want to work *with* children rather than *on* children, it is critical that time is dedicated to establishing a research relationship with children. Many studies are conducted over relatively short periods of time, which may impact on how meaningful the research relationship can be. Establishing trust and security are, however, important factors to consider when asking any person to agree to share their lived experiences, knowing that this sharing may then become part of a wider and more public discussion. Grover (2004) also noted the importance of establishing trusting relationships to overcome the predisposition of children to respond to adults with a 'right answer'. Harcourt and Conroy (2005) stated that the time needed to develop this relationship cannot be circumvented or overstated. However, it is not so much an issue of 'how much time', but more a commitment to the quality of the conversation in forging the partnership – quality time. Both adults and children need time to explore, reflect and understand what the complexities of working together as partners might be. Early discussion, where possibilities (and questions) are raised, by either party, support negotiation of shared meaning about what adult and child researchers will be working on together. Rinaldi (2006) identified the significance and power of the *pedagogy of listening* – listening with intentionality, creating sustained opportunities for children's thinking to become apparent. In creating opportunities for children to 'play' with the idea of being involved in the research enterprise (and what that might look like), we establish and demonstrate one of the basic ground rules of the research relationship with children, i.e. 'what you have to say' and 'what you think about' are of interest to me.

Valentine (1999) asserted that children's capacities to agree to participate in research are contextual and relational (rather than developmental). Edwards and Aldred (2000) have suggested that thoughtful consideration needs to be given to the specific context in which children are invited to participate. Familiar surroundings such as prior-to-school and school settings, or at home, may be optimal environments to initially engage with children. That these are everyday places and spaces where children live their childhoods can also give rise to opportunities for the research participants to form social solidarity or for partnerships to be established (Clark, McQuail and Moss 2003; Smith, Taylor and Gollop 2000).

Whether the time frame for the research project is short or long, it is a relationship that will potentially end once the research project is completed and this may be problematic. The tentative or temporary nature of the partnership must be discussed with the children and considered sensitively and respectfully. Thoughtful engagement with the children in regard to transiting in and out of their world, whether it be in a formal setting such as prior-to-school/school, or an informal setting such as at home, should be a significant predicator to gaining the children's consent to participate.

Informing

Integral to moving toward further developing the relationship as a research partnership is the exploration of what is expected within the partnership. The manner in which this is explored with the children will be dependent on their age and evolving capacities to make meaning of the potential partnership, and the researcher's competence as a communicator with children. Introducing the children to the concepts of a university (or the researcher's institution), the work of the adult researcher and the role and purpose of research is an important beginning point in establishing the parameters of the potential partnership. Discussions about the roles and responsibilities of those participating in the research project, how data will be gathered and analysed, and with whom they will be shared need to be undertaken. Developing an understanding of these concepts can be supported by helping the children to make connections between their own everyday experiences and the research enterprise. Rogoff (1990) saw shared understanding occurring through active communication, as participants elicit and share information with others, i.e., *negotiate* a shared meaning. Participant standpoints are adjusted as they communicate and discuss ideas, reaching common ground or mutual understanding of the experience to be shared. Principles of respect are vital. Children have the right to be spoken to as co-researchers, in language that makes connections to their prior experience. Exploring familiar terminologies provide child and adult researchers with an opportunity to acknowledge a shared understanding of the language of research and therefore tools that encourage a balance of power in decision-making, as will be demonstrated below.

Example 1: Harcourt

In a study conducted with 25 five- and six-year-old children in Singapore, Harcourt (2008) proposed an examination on children's standpoints of measuring the quality of their experiences within the children's prior-to-school settings. In proposing this study to the children, the researcher was influenced by her previous work on informed assent (Harcourt and Conroy 2005) in the context of ethical research with children. The children's parents and teachers were able to provide consent/dissent by being informed through the ethical research structures of written explanatory statements, and posing questions and raising concerns through informal and formal encounters. However, Harcourt (2008) reports it was often a struggle to ascertain whether the children were being empowered by their understanding of similar (verbal) information sessions.

Researchers may unconsciously use verbal and non-verbal languages of power, which can communicate to the child that they are expected to participate. Phrasing requests to participate such as *I have come to get your permission* or *I have come to get you to sign saying you agree to be involved in my research* may hold the intention to seek permission, but the request is posed as an already negotiated agreement (Harcourt and Conroy 2005). The perceived authority of adults can imply power and children may find it difficult or intimidating to decline the researcher's request. In an attempt to mitigate an imbalance of power, Harcourt (2008) used the initial sessions with the children to discuss the research proposal with the children as a group (12 children in Centre A and 13 in Centre B). Both groups were informed that the researcher was working with another group of children in Singapore.

Discussion then focussed on what research was and what a researcher might do. Given that both groups employed a curriculum that focussed on long-term projects, the children were familiar with the words *research* and *investigate*. This made it easier to explain the research *project* (another term familiar to the children) and to establish a shared understanding about what the adult and children might do together. Here, using a common language, that which was already part of the classroom culture, assisted in the development of a research relationship. Terms not apparent in the children's own lexicon or vocabulary were also explored. One new word introduced for consideration was *quality* (the focus of Harcourt's study), which was discussed over several sessions and one which the children decided had an association with the word *good*. This decision was made only after careful consideration by the children, who made reference to other aspects of their lives to establish its meaning (e.g., *Do you mean Singapore Quality Class? My father says that means a good place to buy things*). Attempting to bridge the semantics of the academic world and that which the children inhabited became an important step. Through these dialogues, the adult and children constructed a shared meaning about the key terms that framed the project.

With a commitment to collaborating with the children on as many aspects of the study as possible, the researcher then sought ideas on how they (the adult and child researchers) might find out about a *good school*. The adult used the provocation *I wonder how I might find out about a good school? You see, I have forgotten what it is like to go to school. Since we know each other a little bit, maybe you could help me?* Harcourt reports that many children were enthusiastic (e.g., *You need to ask lots of questions to* [sic] *us*), while others were more reticent in their responses, listening rather than contributing verbally to conversations. In later discussions, the groups talked about how the information might be collected (e.g., *Maybe we could write or draw for you?*) and what might happen to it once it was given to the adult (e.g., *I need to show it to other people at the University where I work. Sometimes I will share your ideas with other teachers who work with children or who do research like us*). A point also discussed was what a child might do if they had something to share about someone or something that was not so kind or good; when it would be OK to use it in the project or when it would not be written down, recorded or taken away.

Another complexity that provided a potential challenge in this study was the traditional conception of 'confidentiality'. Often researchers are encouraged to use pseudonyms in order to protect children's identity. In particular, many ethics committees prefer the use of pseudonyms as a safer option. In many cases this is indeed erring on the side of caution, but this should be a point of negotiated compromise with each child. For example, in Harcourt's study, the children were less concerned about confidentiality and more concerned about owning their ideas. When invited to use 'another name' the children were emphatic that this would not be an acceptable option. The children asked for their real names to be used as *it says who we really are*. Giving children the option to determine how they wish to be referenced in any written work is an important aspect of respecting children and invites them to hold a degree of control as active participants. When there is no risk involved, children should have the right to decide how they want their ideas and experiences referenced. Perhaps there is also the possibility of revisiting these decisions when the children more fully understand the purposes for which the work is being put, as they engage with the research process.

Example 2: Conroy

To establish an understanding of what the process of negotiating informed consent might look like, Conroy includes excerpts of conversations between student observer (CK), and V (4.11), which took place in the child's preschool classroom. Prior to meeting with children, student observers were asked to prepare 'scripts', outlining key aspects of what they wanted to include in their conversations. These 'scripts' were not intended to be read to the children, but served to inform and organize the observer's thinking as to how the conversation might proceed. Observers were encouraged to reflect on their participation in earlier conversations to determine how best to situate language in the child's sphere of understanding and to consider authentic strategies as to how the child's understanding of the task could be confirmed.

The observer initially introduced herself and the research task by attempting to make connections to the child's prior experience (of going to preschool and having a teacher); *I go to school just like you to study about children and to learn how children play.* The observer then shared the proposed research tools with the child; *in my bag I have all of these to help me. I have a camera, a notebook, pen and a voice recorder.* When the child asked *why do you need all of these?* the observer offered a genuine response in that she needed these tools to help her remember various aspects of their work together. Engaging with the child's questions demonstrates an essential aspect of the proposed partnership, i.e. 'how we will work together'. *The notebook is to help me remember what you said ... this* (pointing to the voice recorder) *helps me to listen to our conversations.* When the child displayed interest in the research tools (the voice recorder in particular), seeking information about its various functions and physical characteristics, the observer extended the conversation around the child's area of interest; *See this red button, when I press this, it will record our voices.* The child was then supported to record several short messages, which were then played back to her. This allocation of time, with no apparent purpose, other than to build relationship, demonstrates a commitment to the research partnership. Time creates possibilities for the observer to support the child's contribution to and shaping of the conversation. As such, the responsibility for the direction of the conversation becomes a shared responsibility.

As the conversation continued, the observer repeatedly paused to ascertain whether the child understood what was being proposed and to seek confirmation that the child was willing to proceed *when we play, I would need to use the voice recorder. Is that okay with you? Can I do that?* The intention was always to present sufficient information and opportunity to support the child in making an informed decision about her involvement in the research process.

The observer then presented another request, *Is it okay to show your work to my teacher and friends . . . can we talk about your work?* This presented a challenge to the consent process as the request moved to include players who were not known to the child (the observer's peers and lecturers). In this instance, the child initially indicated that the observer could only share her work with the child's teacher. The observer acknowledged this proposal, of sharing work with an individual of importance to the child, demonstrating her capacity to listen and take action on the child's request. The observer then made a second request which included the child's teacher; *I will show Ms X . . . My teacher and my friends will also get to see your work and we will talk about it. Is that okay with you?* When the child agreed, the observer further confirmed, *Are you sure about that?*

The following excerpt, again between observer CK and V (4.11), places emphasis on documenting the child's agreement to participate in the research process. The observer had developed a proforma with clip art images to visually represent aspects of her earlier conversation, e.g. images of a camera to represent that the child might be comfortable in being photographed. The intention was to re-visit the various images with the child to deconstruct the (abstract) visual images to further support the child in making connections about her own engagement in the proposed research task.

Initially the child had many questions about the proforma images, however, she clearly connected the clip art images with herself and the observer. *Is this you? Why are the children so small? Who are they? Are they us?* The observer (pointing to the visual image of the camera) asked, *You know what this is, right? What do you think the camera is for? For taking our pictures,* the child replied, clenching her fist, moving her right index finger and making a clicking sound, as if taking a photograph.

The observer then confirmed, by pointing to the images of the notebook (*it is for you to write notes*) and the voice recorder (*this is the voice recorder to record our voices*) that the child not only understood what the image was, but also understood what the research tools implied. *Why do you think that I show this picture of a child's drawing?* asked the observer, again requesting permission to share the child's work with others. The child made the connection to her own drawings and indicated agreement, that her work could be shared with other people.

Establishing a context for listening not only supports the adult to more fully understand the child's perspective, but also to critically reflect on how personal (subjective) understandings of the research process are presented to the child. The potential for collaboration is strengthened as both parties reflect on and together define their roles and responsibilities.

Documenting consent

Once the informing process has been carefully examined by all of the potential research participants, discussion should then move to inviting children to document their consent. It is critical at this point to reassert to children that their agreement to participate is essential but that their initial consent is not a one-off and final decision (Valentine 1999). It is equally important that children are sufficiently informed that a decision to withdraw their consent, at any point in the project, will be respected without consequence. This reassurance is not only vital for the children, but should also be reinforced by any of the consenting adults (Hurley and Underwood 2002).

At this point, the researcher must not confuse the issue of withdrawing from the research project altogether with a child's not wishing to participate at a particular time. In respecting children's decision-making, it is anticipated that there may be times when individual children do not wish to engage with the adult researcher. Given the opportunity to pursue their own interests, the child may indeed be a willing participant at a later time. Matters such as meeting times can be negotiated as part of early discussions where parties discuss responsibilities. The issue is about voluntary participation, which implies respect for children's decisions.

Supporting children in developing an understanding of documented consent follows the same premise as the informing process. Making connections to familiar practices and contextualising the importance of recording evidence of consent respects children's developing competence as partners in research. Children may be familiar with excursion permission forms as part of the ritual of going out of their school environment and could be considered as a reference point. They may be shown the forms that their parents might sign as examples of how an adult records their consent. While these provocations can be offered to children as examples of consent, the children should then be invited to think of ways that they might record their agreement to participate, in a manner they are comfortable and confident in (Harcourt and Conroy 2005). An examination might also occur on what a signature is and what that signifies in relation to consent. Clark (2007) noted that children in her studies recorded their name, initial or 'signature symbol' as a declaration or 'marker' of their presence in the study. Harcourt and Conroy (2005) reported on a range of documented agreements to participate from children, some as young as two years old, in work conducted with student teachers undertaking observational studies with children.

Initial consents given by children should be reaffirmed at the beginning of each research-focussed encounter with the children. Wertsch (2007) pointed out that remembering is a dyadic construct for children and they often need an adult to ask strategic questions in order to follow the path of their memories. In regard to giving agreement to participate as research partners, it does not necessarily follow that children's initial consent has been intended as a permanent proclamation. Children should be given the opportunity to reaffirm their agreement to participate and the adult partner will need to support the children in remembering what has occurred, and what might happen next in the project.

Example 3: Harcourt

In a study currently being proposed to three–five-year-olds in a prior-to-school setting (kindy) in Australia, children are being asked to consider the difference between lived and observed childhood. This study responds to the notion that perhaps adults and children have differing perceptions of life as it is observed and as it is experienced. At the time of writing, the adult researcher had been engaging with the children around documenting their consent. The three-year-olds decided that they could write their names on a piece of paper and then write 'OK'. Some children were able to write their names and the word 'OK'. Others dictated their names and wrote/marked 'OK'. Emily (3.9) told the adult researcher that she would need to write OK every time she *had a chat* with the adult. Another child, Andreas, came to kindy in different persona each week. On the first week he was 'Annie Apple' and documented his consent as Annie. The next week, he told the adult he would have to write a new 'permission letter' as he was now 'Astro Boy'. On the third visit, he was Andy and suggested the other two permission letters would go underneath 'Andy's permission', as that was his real name.

Over in the five-year-old room, some of the children had taken further control of the process. When invited to record his consent, Jett (4.10) said, *We need to go to the office. I need to think about this. It's too noisy in the classroom with all these kids. Let's go.* The adult and child moved to the centre's entry foyer where there is an 'office' set up for the children. Here Jett documented his consent but said, *Now, you can't have this. I need to show my mum.* The adult and child discussed this, with the child indicating that he was doing important work at kindy and wanted to share it with his mum. A compromise was reached and a photocopy was taken, with the original taken by the child. On another visit, Zara (4.0) was sitting close to the adult researcher during a circle time being conducted by the class teacher. She leant over to the researcher, by now a familiar figure in the room, and said, *I don't think I will talk to you today. I am feeling sad because I wanted to stay home with Cathy* (her visiting aunt). She turned back to the group for a few minutes and then said, *I could come but I think I might cry. If I do cry, can I come back to L* (her teacher)? The researcher responded in the affirmative. *Alright then, I will talk with you.* In these examples, it has been demonstrated how children have been empowered and respected as decision-making participants in the consent processes.

Example 4: Conroy

The conversation between CK and V (4.11) from Example 2 continues now in order to further demonstrate the observer's genuine desire to collaborate with the child and to highlight the depth of understanding that children can achieve when supported by time and adult responsiveness. This process of building meaning has great potential in terms of creating equity within the research relationship.

The intention of the observer was to address ethical issues of confidentiality within the research task. Given that conventions require, for example, the use of pseudonyms as discussed in Harcourt's example, this example highlights the research challenge when working with children of their desire to claim ownership of their participation in the research task. In posing the question, *how do you want others to know your name?* (and the child offered her full name), the observer attracted the child's curiosity by introducing the concept of an initial, to represent, or stand for a name. Writing her own full name and then the initial capital letter of her name, the observer proceeded to write the child's full name, followed by the initial capital letter of the child's name. In response to the child maintaining that she wanted people to know who she was, the observer went on to explain *sometimes people use a signature . . . a mark that we make to represent us and once we put our signature it means we agree to something. So you see,* again pointing to the paper, *this is my name; this is my initial and this is my signature. They all look different, but they represent me.* The child at this point indicated a nickname that she wished to see recorded as her name; however, we clearly see the observer's valuing of the child's contribution, rather than making assumptions about what the child might think or understand.

Partnership involves two-way communication as well as genuine respect for the other's perspective. When the observer seeks to secure the child's (documented) understanding that they will proceed to work in collaboration, she presents the question as a shared 'problem': *how do you think* (other people) *will know that you said okay and are willing to play with me? Do you have any great ideas . . . let's think together.* The child and observer thought together for some time before the child indicated that she didn't have any ideas. The observer, mindful of the overall complexity of this task provided encouragement by presenting the overall task as a smaller 'problem' of *how could we say yes on paper?* The child proposed using a *check – like this* and put a tick on the picture (of the adult and child playing together). To ensure shared meaning, the observer clarified with the child that the 'checks' (ticks) that she was placing against all of the clip art images (notebook, camera, tape recorder) meant agreement *you mean we can play together? What about your work? Can I talk about your work?*

Of significance within this conversation, is the observer's shift in language to the use of the collaborative 'we' . . . *Let's think together; how could we say yes on paper?* As the process of negotiating consent places more complex demands on the child's thinking, the observer adjusts her language to represent the construct of partnership, not to speak for the child, but to offer support to the child as she thinks. The observer makes a further adjustment to reflect the child's use of words (check instead of tick), thus ensuring that meaning remains with the child. In demonstrating respect for the child's language, the observer attempts to ensure the key value of reciprocity within their research relationship.

Conclusion

This chapter has attempted to address some of the complexities to be considered in conceptualizing a research space for children. At the risk of 'over-defending' *why* we include children in research conversations, we have nonetheless acknowledged the theoretical and sociocultural frameworks that provide the momentum for many of those who research with children. These frameworks continue to provide a significant platform for our work.

We believe, however, that our attention must now turn to ensuring that an authentic research relationship is developed through thoughtful reflection on the implications of time, respect, shared understandings about research and the tentative nature of consent. It has been asserted that quality time is crucial in developing trusting research relationships and both adults and children must be given an opportunity to explore, reflect and understand what the complexities are of working together as research partners. In addition, the notion of these relationships being temporary or transitory has been noted as potentially problematic, thus there needs to be sensitive and respectful dialogue with children around this issue.

The informed consent process has been highlighted in order to prompt researchers to give careful and considered thought to negotiating shared understandings with children about research and the research process. By engaging with these challenges we recognize, legitimate and activate the potential of children as research partners. The examples shared have been forwarded as possibilities for consideration, as child and adult co-construct the research relationship, establishing the roles and responsibilities for both partners and offer a commitment to being active contributors. The examples have also offered insight into the thought processes of both the adult researcher and the potential partners as they engaged with the complexities of understanding each other.

While we are still exploring the potential for working with children in research, we, as adults, have an opportunity to examine the challenges as vital spaces for rigorous debate and discourse. However, above all else, we must accept the ethical and moral responsibility to ensure that we invite children into research conversations with a great deal of *authentic* consideration.

Acknowledgement

The authors wish to acknowledge the contributions made by Cecilia Koh, the student teacher whose work appears in Conroy's examples.

References

Castelle, K. (1990) *In the Child's Best Interest: A Primer on the U.N. Convention on the Rights of the Child*, East Greenwich, RI: Plan International.

Clark, A. (2005) 'Through the viewfinder: Young children using cameras to explore their perspectives', paper presented to Early Childhood Education Research Committee Conference, Dublin, August.

Clark, A. (2007) 'Researching with young children: New possibilities, different challenges', paper presented at the Pre-conference Research Seminar, Annual EECERA Conference, Prague, 29 August.

Clark, A., McQuail, S. and Moss, P. (2003) *Exploring the Field of Listening to And Consulting with Young Children*, Research Report No. 45, Thomas Corman Research Unit, London: Queen's Printers.

Cook-Sather, A. (2002) 'Authorising students' perspectives: Toward trust, dialogue, and change in education', *Educational Researcher*, 31(4): 3–14.

Corsaro, W. (1997) *The Sociology of Childhood*, Thousand Oaks, CA: Pine Forge Press.

Dahlberg, G., Moss, P. and Pence, A. (1999) *Beyond Quality in Early Childhood Education and Care*, London: Falmer Press.

Danby, S. and Baker, C. D. (1998) 'What's the problem? Restoring social order in the preschool classroom', in I. Hutchby and J. Moran-Ellis (eds), *Children and Social Competence: Arenas of Action*, London: Falmer Press, pp. 157–186.

Dockett, S. and Perry, B. (2003) 'Children's views and children's voices in starting school', *Australian Journal of Early Childhood*, 28(1): 12–17.

Dockett, S. and Perry, B. (2005) '"You need to know how to play safe": Children's experiences in starting school', *Contemporary Issues in Early Childhood*, 6(1): 4–18.

Edwards, R. and Aldred, P. (2000) 'A topology of parent involvement in education centering on children and young people', *British Journal of Sociology of Education*, 21(1): 435–456.

Einarsdóttir, J. (2005) 'Playschool in pictures: Children's photographs as a research methodology', *Early Child Development and Care*, 175(6): 523–541.

Giacopini, E. (2009) Keynote address presented to REAIE Conference *Landscapes of Rights*, Adelaide, 8–11 July.

Grover, S. (2004) 'Why won't they listen to us? On giving power and voice to children participating in social research', *Childhood*, 11(1): 81–91.

Harcourt, D. (2008) 'Young children's accounts on quality in early childhood classrooms in Singapore', unpublished doctoral thesis, Queensland University of Technology.

Harcourt, D. (2009) *Standpoints on Quality: Young Children as Competent Research Participants*, NSW: Australian Research Alliance for Children and Youth, NSW Commission for Children and Young People.

Harcourt, D. and Conroy, H. (2005) 'Informed assent', *Early Child Development and Care*, 175(6) August: 567–577.

Hurley, J. C. and Underwood, M. K. (2002) 'Children's understanding of their research rights before and after debriefing: Informed assent, confidentiality and stopping participation', *Child Development*, 73(1): 132–143.

Langstead, O. (1994) 'Looking at quality from a child's perspective', in P. Moss and A. Pence (eds), *Valuing Quality in Early Childhood Services*, London: Paul Chapman, pp. 28–42.

Mayall, B. (2002) *Towards a Sociology of Childhood*, Maidenhead: Open University Press.

Pence, A. and Brenner, A. (2000) 'British Columbia's Ministry for Children and Families: A case study in progress', in J. Hayden (ed.), *Landscapes in Early Childhood Education*, New York: Peter Lang, pp. 427–441.

Prout, A. (2004) *The Future of Childhood*, London: RoutledgeFalmer.

Prout, A. and James, A. (1997) *Constructing and Reconstructing Childhood: Contemporary Issues in the Sociological Study of Childhood*, 2nd edn, London: Falmer Press.

Rinaldi, C. (2001) 'A pedagogy of listening: A perspective of listening from Reggio Emilia', *Children in Europe*, 1: 2–5.

Rinaldi, C. (2005) 'Citizenship', keynote address presented to Reggio Emilia Provocations Conference, Auckland, New Zealand, July.

Rinaldi, C. (2006) *In Dialogue with Reggio Emilia*, London: Routledge.

Rogoff, B. (1990) *Apprenticeship in Thinking: Cognitive Development in Social Context*, New York: Oxford University Press.

Smith, A., Taylor, N. and Gollop, M. (2000) *Children's Voices: Research, Policy and Practice*, Wellington, New Zealand: Pearson Education.

Thorpe, K., Tayler, C., Bridgstock, R., Greishaber, S., Skoien, P., Danby, S. and Petriwskyi, A. (2005) *Preparing for School: Report of the Queensland Preparing for School Trials 2003/2004*, School of Early Childhood: Queensland University of Technology.

United Nations (1989) *The United Nations Convention on the Rights of the Child*, New York: UNICEF.

Valentine, G. (1999) 'Being seen and heard? The ethical complexities of working with children and young people at home and at school', *Ethics, Place and Environment*, 2(2): 37–71.

Wertsch, J. (2007) 'Mediation', in H. Daniels, M. Cole and J. V. Wertsch (eds), *The Cambridge Companion to Vygotsky*, Cambridge: Cambridge University Press.

Woodhead, M. and Faulkner, D. (2000) 'Subjects, objects or participants?', in P. Christensen and A. James (eds), *Research with Children: Perspectives and Practices*, London: Falmer Press, pp. 9–35.

Woodrow, C. (1999) 'Revisiting images of the child in early childhood education: Reflections and considerations', *Australian Journal of Early Childhood*, 24(4): 7–12.

Chapter 4

Researching the rights of children under three years old to participate in the curriculum in early years education and care

Angeliki Bitou and Tim Waller

This chapter poses a number of questions about research with young children under three, with a particular focus on the opportunities for children's 'voices' to be heard and to participate in the planning of the curriculum in early years settings. The theoretical underpinning for the chapter is drawn from the work of Rogoff and Corsaro. Research focused on six children in both England and Greece who were observed during their involvement in both adult-directed and child-initiated activities in their settings. A range of 'participatory' methods were used including data gathered through video recordings made by both children and adults. Selected findings from the research are discussed in order to critically examine the challenges for participatory research with young children, particularly relating to issues of power and agency. The chapter also alludes to some of the benefits and limitations of participatory tools and highlights a number of ethical dilemmas for researchers.

Introduction

The main aim of this chapter is to report and critically discuss possible methods for researching the perspectives of young children (under three years of age) in early years' settings. Despite the recent popularity of participatory research in early childhood there is still little published research concerning the views of young children (Clark and Moss 2005), particularly in relation to their view of the curriculum and pedagogy and this chapter is written towards addressing this gap in the research literature. The research aims were to consider how the meaning of children's participation is defined in the settings in England and Greece; whether children use the resources provided according to adult expectation and initial planning and how practitioners react to children's choices by supporting, ignoring or disapproving them.

The chapter is informed by the theories of Rogoff (sociocultural) and Corsaro (sociology). The research was undertaken with 12 children aged two to three years in early years' settings in Greece and England over a three-year period. Drawing on the multi-method 'Mosaic approach' (Clark and Moss 2001, 2005), the research uses a range of participatory methods including data gathered through video recordings made by both children and adults. Selected findings from the research are illustrated and discussed in order to critically examine the main challenges for participatory research with young children, particularly relating to issues of power and agency. The chapter also alludes to some of the benefits and limitations of participatory tools and highlights a number of ethical dilemmas for researchers. The chapter concludes by arguing that there is an urgent need to promote the children's participatory rights, as adult's authority and power is generally taken for granted.

Theoretical underpinning

This chapter is both informed and underpinned by sociocultural theory (Rogoff, etc.) and recent work in sociology (particularly Corsaro). In order to develop a methodology for researching *with* young children we would wish to acknowledge two key aspects of both theories, namely, agency and voice, and briefly illuminate a theory which is a combination of both the sociocultural perspective and sociology (Smith 2007). The early years environments discussed in this chapter are seen as dynamic and evolving cultural contexts, in which it is meaningless to study the child apart from other people. Agency involves children's capacity to understand and act upon their world, thus demonstrating competence from birth (James *et al.* 1998; Mayall 2002). In addition, children are perceived as actively involved in the co-construction of their own lives. From this perspective, children are viewed as active agents who construct their own cultures (Corsaro 2005) and 'have their own activities, their own time and their own space' (Qvortrup *et al.* 1994: 4). It seeks to understand the definitions and meaning children give to their own lives and recognizes children's competence and capacity to understand and act upon their world. This perspective, therefore, sees the child as actively participating in her own childhood in accordance with Malaguzzi's (1996) concept of the 'rich child'.

Following on from the acknowledgement of the significance of children's agency is the recognition that children have the right to participate in processes and decisions that affect their lives; in other words, express their 'voice'. Children's views of their own childhood are therefore particularly significant. In the UK, the Children Act (2004) and *Every Child Matters* (DfES 2004) established the right of the child to be listened to. Corsaro (2005) uses the term 'interpretive repro-duction' to explain how children can act communally and jointly with adults to agree and generate changes in society. He argues that children do not just simplify what they have taken from adults but replicate and participate actively to produce culture and changes in the society. Simultaneously the term 'reproduction' portrays that children are already members of the society affected by the pre-existing culture and society which in turn has been affected by the historical changes. The process of participation into the cultural routines starts from the time that a child is born (Rogoff 2003; Corsaro 2005).

Smith (2007) argues that the movement of children's rights and the recognition of children as active agents are part of the sociology of childhood while sociocultural theory supports this theoretical development as 'agency arises out of the social and cultural context' (ibid.: 153). Smith states that in order for children to contribute in decision-making, they need to be fostered in a societal context that helps them to exercise their own right to participate. Here, as Smith states, is the contribution of sociocultural theory; supporting children to share with adults the co-construction of 'mature' activities. These are community activities which children attend to 'that often are not designed for their instruction, in which they may not be addressed directly. Rather they are present and expected to be alert and to pitch when ready' (Rogoff 2003: 317–318). For example, Rogoff discusses situations where infants are carried by their mother or older siblings as they go about their work and daily activities and 'from their mothers' or siblings' backs they can vicariously participate in the activities' (ibid.: 318). The role of the adult is to sustain and encourage the child's interest, to 'help focus on the goal, draw attention to critical features of the task, and reduce the complexity of the task. But there has to be social engagement before children can learn and gradually take on more responsibility' (Smith 2007: 154).

Methods

The research reported in this chapter is part of an ethnographic study that took place over six months in England and six months in Greece. Two settings were selected: a Sure Start Children's Centre in England and a nursery school in Greece belonging to the Day Care Centres of the Worker's Organisation (Organisation of Ergatiki Estia – OEE) where the researcher is a practitioner. The study involved a sample of six children from Greece and six from England aged two to three years old who were randomly selected.

Context and participants

In England, the setting was part of the Sure Start programme in a suburban part of the West Midlands which was economically deprived. Children and families could attend a range of education, care and health programmes on a drop-in, or daily basis. Generally, education and care in the setting was organised into two groups of children, the crèche where children under two could attend and the toddlers' room where children from two until four years were attending. The research took place in the group of the toddlers where, on average 15 or 20 children attended every day. There was a small group of children who attended every day, while the majority of children were different every day. The ratio between staff and children was one to four, although this was often supplemented by a range of volunteers. Each session took place from 9:30 am to 12 noon.

The Greek setting was organised and administered by the OEE organisation which provides free education and care for children aged eight months to six years old for parents who are on a low income and where both parents receive IKA insurance (the Social Security Organisation in Greece). This setting was in a city in the northern part of the country. The setting is divided into classes according to children's age: infant classes βρεφικό (eight months to two years old), toddlers classes μεταγραφικό (two to three years old), pre-kindergarten classes προνήπια (three to four years old) and kindergarten classes νηπιαγωγείο (four to six years old). The research for this project was with six children (aged 2.5 to three years old) who all attended on a daily basis from 7 am until 4 pm. In the group at the beginning of the academic year there were two practitioners and one assistant while after Christmas this changed to one practitioner and one assistant.

In both cases all the participant children had been attending the setting before the research started and had a 'joint history with the teacher' (Rutanen 2007: 65) working together more than two years. Also, the staff in the settings shared the same history in both cases. Thus the sample of this study had 'the history of co-adjustment' among children and staff, a term used by Rutanen (ibid.: 65) to emphasise the significance of both children and practitioners experiencing the same routines, habits, events and codes of communication. Also, in an ethnographic study, it was seen as essential for the researcher (who is a qualified and experienced early years practitioner) to integrate into the normal routines of the setting so that she learned the habits and the rules of the daily programme in order to limit her impact on activities and respect children's privacy.

Research design

A range of mainly qualitative data was gathered through ethnography including participant observation, video and photographic evidence and semi-structured interviews with parents and practitioners. In addition, this study draws on the framework for listening to young children – the multi-method Mosaic approach described by Clark and Moss (2001; 2005). The method uses both the traditional tools of observing children at play and a variety of 'participatory tools' with children.

The range of 'participatory' methods used included data gathered through video recordings made by both children and adults, which involved tools such as video and digital cameras and walking tours with or without video. Here cameras designed for use by children ('Digital Blue' cameras) and standard digital cameras were used – both tools facilitated the recording of video and still images. In addition, the researcher and children designed some participatory games such as the 'Guess what I like' game. Here, the researcher pretends that she is sure that the child is keen on an activity or an event and the child answers spontaneously 'yes' or 'no'. When the answer is 'no', the researcher pretends to be frustrated and she takes another chance to find the activity the child really likes. This game gives the children the opportunity to feel more expert than the researcher (adult) and when the researcher guesses correctly, they celebrate together.

Ethics

In the initial design of the project, careful reference was made to ethical guidelines (BERA 2004) to consider the balance of harm and effect on the children, confidentiality and issues of informed consent (Alderson 2005). Reference was also made to the principles and ethical guidance developed by the National Children's Bureau (2002; 2003) applying particularly to research with children. In the case of visual methods, gaining informed consent is much more sensitive and problematic. Flewitt (2006: 31) states that in research with children the participants' agreement should be 'provisional', 'provisional consent/ assent' can therefore be defined as ongoing and dependent on the long-term network of the researcher: researched and inter-participant relationships built upon sensitivity, reciprocal trust and collaboration. Particularly with visual data, the researcher's relationship with young children is a sensitive matter of respect and privacy and for the researcher to know where exactly to stop filming and which information to publish (Clark and Moss 2005; Flewitt 2006).

Informed consent was sought on three levels: the setting, the parents and the child. First, the researcher contacted the setting, gaining written permission from the manager and the practitioners for the research. Parents were initially informed about the research by the setting and, following this, a meeting was arranged with the researcher to sign the informed consent letters and give further details about the research. The last but most important part of the informed consent process involves the children. Initially a small A4 poster about the research was designed to be discussed with the child (Flewitt 2006) and to ask for permission to participate. At the bottom of the poster there was a place for the child and the researcher put their signatures. The final aspect of informed consent was an ongoing verbal process allowing the child to withdraw from some or all the research at any time. In many cases some children specifically asked for video or digital photographs not to be taken by the researcher or another child or adult and sometimes when viewing the visual data with the researcher the children declined to comment.

Results

The following examples are given to illustrate some of the findings of this study. Much of the evidence from the field notes, digital images and children's comments would suggest a categorisation in themes associated with participatory tools. However, it is possible that adults and children may have different perceptions of the events that are taking place in the settings (Waller 2007).

Using real tools

There are two noteworthy examples, one from Greece and one from England where children express their desire to use real tools in the setting in the same way they do at home.

Jennifer (2.10 years): Example with the digger:

> The children were playing outside. Jennifer was riding her scooter. Suddenly she stops. She leaves the scooter and she goes and takes a bike. She is not riding it but she is trying to pull it closer to the fence. She is climbing on the bicycle. She is looking at me and she is calling 'Look!! He is digging'. In the garden was the builder working on a new boat. I move closer to her. Jennifer raises her hands on me. I take her in my arms. She takes my camera and she takes a video. Then she stops it. 'I want to take a picture of him Now.' I turn the camera on pictures overview. She took the following picture.
>
> (Field notes 10th April)

Jennifer then looked at what the digger was doing.

> *Jennifer*: My mum is digging as well . . . at home.
> *Researcher*: Really?
> *Jennifer*: Yeah . . . and I am digging with her.

She raises her hands wanted to go closer: *mhmhmhmh!*

She takes the digital camera from the researcher and takes more photos. The digger sees us and he waves, 'Hello'. Jennifer then looks at the tools the digger

Figure 4.1 'The Digger' by Jennifer.

left on the ground. An electric saw was there. I place her down to ask the practitioners if they will let us to get into the other part of the garden. Jennifer tries to look at it through the fence. She climbs on the bike again and she takes more pictures. Other children now come to see the digger. One of the practitioners comes over and she asked them not to step on the bikes. Jennifer is trying to take a last picture through the fence and she gave me back the camera before going to play with her scooter again.

These findings demonstrate that in both countries children have restrictions on the use of real tools. This study found that in the English setting there are more opportunities for children to experience activities with real materials due to the way the pedagogical areas were equipped. Children have the opportunity to access and play with both real materials (flour, water, pasta, cereal) and plastic tools (building blocks, kitchen utensils, plastic fruit). However, what was found to be problematic are opportunities for children to participate in mature activities (discussed earlier in the theoretical section) that take place in the setting such as digging or tidying up after the snack time, especially when practitioners have not considered these activities as part of the planning. In these settings it appears that, in many cases, children are discouraged or prevented from participating in the 'mature' activities of adults. This point is further illustrated by Christos' perspectives of real tools and his mother's comments below.

Christos' (2:10): Example with the trolley (Video data, 22nd January)

(6:57sec) Christos parks the bike in the usual area. He gets off the bike, he looks around. He goes to the (pretend) grocery shop and he takes the knife. He leaves but he looks around trying to find something. He goes and takes the plastic trolley trying first to remove the guitar that was stuck on the wheels. He takes the trolley and he goes close to the bike. He turns it upside down trying to fix it with the knife. He places the knife into one of the wheels. Here he spends more than five minutes.

Christos' comments (Field notes, 22nd January)

After a practitioner asked the children to go the bathroom to wash their hands and go for snack. Christos is about to leave. On the way out of the room he found the trolley with the tools. He picks up the camera and he takes the pictures in Figure 4.2.

I grasped the chance to talk to him.

Researcher: I think you like that game.
Christos: No.
Researcher: No?
Christos: It is not ready yet . . . it is not walking.
Researcher: When are you thinking to fix it?

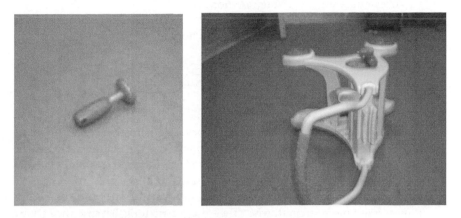

Figure 4.2 'The Plastic Tools' by Christos.

> *Christos*: I don't know . . . but look they are not real (he indicates the trolley and the tools).
> *Researcher*: But you like to build things, don't you?
> *Christos*: I like to build things but not here . . . The tools are plastic and not real.

6th February 2009 (field notes)

It was almost 12 o clock. I am preparing to leave. I am going to say goodbye to Christos.

> *Researcher*: Christos, bye . . . see you on Monday again.
> *Christos*: Where are you going?
> *Researcher*: I am leaving to go home . . . are you fixing the grocery shop with the hammer?
> *Christos*: Yeah but I don't like it.
> *Researcher*: You don't like it? ... but I thought you like to build things?
> *Christos*: I like ... but not here.
> *Researcher*: Where?
> *Christos*: In my grandfather's workshop.
> *Researcher*: There are many tools there?
> *Christos:* There are real ones . . . not fake.
> *Researcher*: And what about that plastic trolley you tried to fix with Anastasios the other day?
> *Christos*: No I don't like ... it is fake.
> *Researcher*: Well, if I was asking you where do you like to play the most, here or at home, what you would answer to me?
> *Christos*: I like to play at my grandfather's.
> *Researcher*: Here?

> *Christos*: Not here . . . they are not real.
> *Researcher*: Understood . . . OK then . . . I think today which is Friday you will go in your grandfather's house.
> *Christos*: Yeah and I will build up.
> *Researcher*: Enjoy your time then.

Mother's comments (during interview):

> I often tell teacher . . . give him scissors because otherwise he is not going to stay with you in the class and she answers me 'They will cut themselves . . . I don't want to give them' and I tell her 'He is not going to cut himself, he is even able to cut his hair by himself' . . . and I think the real tools are less dangerous than this one (meaning plastic) and he uses real tools at home. Kids exercise more strength when they use plastic tools because they try to use it as real one. But it is a matter of safety and we cannot raise up our kids in a utopia.

By simultaneously analysing the context through the personal, the interpersonal (researcher) and the institutional perspectives, a better understanding of how taken-for-granted information from the video observation may give a false impression of a child's perspective can be developed (see Table 4.1). On leaving the setting after the above incident, the researcher met Christos' mother and told her about the discussion. She told her that his grandfather has created a space for him in his house with real tools and one day he even bought him a real saw. She also said that Christos likes tractors and his other grandfather brought him a toy tractor. Christos played with the toy tractor for a couple of hours and then he told him, 'Look grandpap . . . the tractor you brought me is nice but . . . it is not a real one it is a plastic and it is better to throw it away!'

In this case because the (Greek) child has extensive experience of the use of real tools at home, he clearly does not really enjoy the toy tools at the nursery school. What is particularly problematic here is the fact that without children's comments, the researcher cannot understand a child's real experiences. Looking at the video without the child's comments, it seems that he enjoys the activity. However, according to what Christos said and his mum confirmed, the child does not enjoy the tools at the centre because they are not according to his needs and interests.

Discussion

Data are analysed and discussed through a sociocultural model focusing on shared meaning and not only on individual positions, as the isolation of specific events often leads to the alteration of their nature (Robbins 2005). The starting point for this participatory research is what the child shares with the researcher, then the researcher's observations and then discussion with parents and practitioners, which ideally is reaffirmed with the children.

Table 4.1 Mosaic of Christos' perception and use of real tools

Research instrument		
Video/digital camera	Code: MOVO 6321 Date: 22/1 Christos pretends to fix the trolley with plastic tools. He appears to enjoy this activity. [Filmed by researcher]	Code: DG 475 Date: 22/1 Photo of plastic tools in setting. [Filmed by Christos]
Field Notes	Date: 22/1 Christos says he does not like plastic tools and uses real ones at home with his grandfather.	Date: 6/2 Christos repeats that he rather prefers being in his grandfather's home to play with real tools.
Interview with parent M	Audio Code: DM 20088 Date: 22/1 Christos uses real tools at home and also does not like plastic toys.	Date: 6/2 Christos said to the other grandfather to throw away the new plastic tractor.
Interview with practitioner A	Audio Code: 20093 Date: 23/1 This is not for their age – they are too young.	Field notes: Date: 6/2 Real tools are dangerous for young children.

Children's desire for cultural membership through the use of real tools is highlighted through Jennifer's and Christos' perspectives. In the examples reported above, children and adults may have different perceptions of the use of real tools. Here there appears to be a gap between the observed (actual) lived experience. Both children used tools during their play in a manner that appeared to be different to the adult's initial expectations. For example, Christos used the doctor's and kitchen equipment as tools to fix the trolley while pretending the trolley was a car. Jennifer left aside the shape equipment provided and took the wooden digger toy to open a hole as the builder was doing on the garden. On the other hand, what was emphasised in the responses from the Greek practitioners about the use of real tools in their programmes was associated with children's age as indicated in the following interview comments:

This is not for their age.

They are too young to do that.

I am scared to give them scissors because they are still too young

I am scared they are going to harm each other and then I will have to apologise to their parents.

A number of children, however, indicated that they would like to play with real tools. Most of the parents (of the same children) confirmed that at home they involve their children in these mature activities.

Alternatively, in case of Jennifer, the practitioner did not consider in her observation the fact that the children wanted to see the digger and then included the transformation of the digger into their playdough experiences. Here Jennifer engaged actively in the situation by introducing an innovation outside the practitioner's expectation. When the practitioner did not share or reify Jennifer's meaning, the child ignored her and actually stopped the activity. With regards to Christos' use of real tools, both the practitioner and his mother were aware that he did not like playing with the plastic 'fake' tools. However, it seems that the reason why they did not respond to the child's perspective was due to the values and restrictions they met in the programme, the schedule and the regulation of the setting. As Rinaldi (2006) notes, the inside life of the setting should be connected with the outside events and the communication between them to become of great value.

With regard to children's participation in the curriculum, 'the children participate in reconstructing the adult's initial conceptions through their actions' (Rutanen 2007: 66) but it seems here that the adult's perspective and authority discourage the process. Brennan (2007: 7) contends that due to the fact that children and practitioners in settings are separated from the mature activities, the 'children demonstrate spontaneous and frequent attempts to reconnect with adults and their lives, and also with the wider social and historical community'. Thus every time a child sees an adult doing an activity, they try to find out ways to participate which may involve just observing. This is referred to by Rogoff *et al.* (2003) as intent participation, it also involves the transfer of experience into play as Christos and Jennifer, or even trying at the same moment to be involved (Jennifer's example).

A further consideration for participation here relates to the social construction of toys. For Barthes (1957), the construction of toys defines the role of the child as a consumer and not as an inventor and creator. Christos' and Jennifer's perspective of the tools as 'fake' and the lack of response to this from the practitioners also suggest a number of implications for pedagogy as it is questionable how well a child's learning and well-being can be supported effectively when the provision and materials are not valued by the children. Cannella (1997: 152) argues that professional discourses often 'silence children as they are used to create a "pretend" world for them, a world that has nothing to do with their real lives'.

Not only was this tension found in the child's perception of the curriculum but also in the use of participatory tools used in this study. Indeed, in the case of Greece, the first thing that the children did every morning as the researcher entered the setting was to grasp her notebook and write with her pens. Using a notebook and pen was not usually permitted in the classroom. Also, after a while the children demanded that the Digital Blue camera they were encouraged to use should be replaced with a camera that adults use. For example:

Panayiotis (Field notes, 1st December)

> *Panayiotis:* I don't want this camera.
> *Researcher*: Do you mean the Digital Blue camera?
> *Panayiotis:* I want the other one like yours.

Maria (Field notes, 8th December)

> *Maria*: I don't like this blue (camera) . . . it is like fake . . . give me yours, the real one!
> *Researcher*: But you can take pictures even with that one.
> *Maria*: I don't like that one. I want something like yours – can you understand what I am telling you?

Furthermore, the researcher's beliefs about the child and childhood do influence the research design (Harden *et al.* 2000; Thomson 2007). The children's comments about the Digital Blue camera reveal that the methods used in this study also appear to be influenced by the theories about age segregation. On reflection we would question why a child-friendly tool was chosen to elicit children's perceptions.

A further pitfall that Robbins (2005) has discussed in research with very young children is children's answers to adult's questions. For example, Christos' answers were not what the researcher was expecting to hear. Looking repeatedly at the videos, the researcher was convinced the child was enjoying playing with the trolley and the tools (as Table 4.1). However, in different contexts, Christos confirmed to her that it is not what he would like to do in the setting. This supports Jordan's (2004) model of 'co-construction' where children and adults share ideas, values and create meaning. This model gives the child the initiative and cultivates the idea of 'constructing with others' (Jordan 2004: 33). As Jordan points out, adults need to learn how to see unknown aspects of the child – what the child knows and thinks. As Rinaldi (2006: 101) states, researchers need to develop a 'culture of research' when they are working with children through documentation.

Another problematic area for research with young children using participatory tools concerns the interpretation of data when children decline to make a comment immediately or shortly after a video film is made. Making an assumption about Christos' perspective of the incident with the trolley without his comments would have led the researcher to misunderstanding, misinterpretation and over-simplification of the significance of the activity. Unfortunately, in doing research with young children, they very often declined to speak about the video. On other occasions the children may invite the researcher to join them, as did Jennifer and Christos, even determining rules about whether or not to use the camera (who) and put aside the notebook for collecting data (who). However, in all the above cases, the child is clearly aware of what the researcher is recording and intentionally let her participate in the activity. Thus, it could be argued that the children exercised some power and authority over the researcher's agenda and a 'reactive' (responsive) method (Corsaro 2005), may facilitate this possibility. However, the photographic and video images do not empower children on their own (Waller and Bitou forthcoming). It is the shared construction of knowledge around conversations with the children based on their photographs that can enable children's meaning to prevail. As Cook and Hess (2007: 44) argue, the danger is that

> receiving a child's commentary is the end as well as the beginning of the process. It was the end of the attempt by the adults to find out a child's understanding and the beginning of an adult interpretation of what has been revealed. Importantly, the second process was unmediated by the children.

Dahlberg *et al.* (2007) and Rinaldi (2006) argue that documentation plays an important role in understanding children, giving a starting point for dialogue and making visible aspects that were blurred. However, what it is documented and from whose perspectives is crucial. Gallacher and Gallagher (2006) assert that participatory research is not part of children's culture but an adult-constructed phenomenon. There is an uneven and interchangeable power between the adult and the child as the adult may not be certain about the response of the child. Further, it is possible that children may also exercise agency with the cameras but choose not to contribute to the research agenda (Gallacher and Gallagher 2006). It is argued here that the regular use of participatory tools in research in early years' settings can form new positions and different relations. Goldman-Segall (1998) points out that through using visual data there is an indivisible relationship between the tools, the child, the adult who conducts the research and the whole environment. If the adult researcher repositions themself into the community and becomes a member, her voice is one among the many others. In this process a 'culture for shared collaborative "authorship" and distributed co-construction is created' (Goldman-Segall 1998: 88).

Conclusion

In this chapter we have briefly reported on research aiming to elicit the perspectives of young children under three years old, with particular reference to their views of the curriculum in early years' settings. Drawing on both sociocultural theory and recent work in sociology, we argued that in order to understand the agency and voice of the child it is necessary to investigate how these are co-constructed within the context of both settings and family life.

We discussed a number of challenges relating to issues of power and agency for both research and pedagogy with young children. First, even when we are intending to seek young children's perspectives, we would wish to acknowledge the need for researchers (including ourselves) to question their own inherent beliefs about the competence of children under three and start from a position of Malaguzzi's (1996) concept of the 'rich child'. A further significant issue arising from the findings was the children's desire for cultural membership through the use of real tools that were available for pedagogy and research (highlighted through Jennifer's and Christos' perspectives). Here the importance of involving children in 'mature' activities (Rogoff 2003) is emphasised.

Second, the chapter has also alluded to some of the benefits and limitations of participatory tools and highlighted some methodological dilemmas for researchers. The starting point for this participatory research was what the child chose to share with the researcher which was triangulated. Here there appears to be a gap between the observed (actual) lived experience and the researcher's observations and discussion with parents and practitioners. Significantly, this method allowed us to develop a better understanding of how taken-for-granted assumptions about data from video material may give an ill-informed impression of a child's perspective. Here it is possible that, sometimes, the tools may inhibit mutuality and sustained engagement between children and adults. For example, how do researchers interpret data when children decline to make a comment immediately or shortly after a film is made? Thus a further problematic area for research with young children using participatory tools is raised.

As Buchwald, Schantz-Laursen and Delmar (2009) discuss, it is crucial for the researcher to search for opportunities to test what is found in the data. This may be idealistic but unfortunately when doing research with young children this does not happen all the time, simply because we are adults and can exercise power and authority over children's lives. What is important for the matter of both research and pedagogy is to find ways to gain access to children's life (Corsaro 2000, 2003, 2005) through a reactive method (Corsaro 2005; Emond 2005), based on mutual trust and respect. Thus we would argue for a balanced approach to both research and pedagogy where both adults' and children's voices influence the research design and the curriculum.

We conclude by arguing that there is an urgent need to promote very young children's participatory rights, as adults' authority and power is generally taken for granted. We feel strongly that participatory methods should be grounded within ethnographic study and not seen as a replacement for it (Gallacher and Gallagher 2006). Research design is one of the many ways that adults can direct children, as Cook and Hess (2007) point out. We would concur with Cook and Hess (2007: 43) that:

> The use of the camera may have offered a glimpse into the child's world but the construction of the camera use for research may have been so embedded in our expectations that we narrowed our lens. The children's wider stories were in danger of being framed by researcher expectations.

As Waller (2006) argues, rather than just thinking about engaging children's views to inform research (or influence curriculum planning and design), we need to rethink participation also in terms of 'spaces for childhood' within which children can exercise their agency to participate in their own decisions, actions and meaning making, which may or may not involve them engaging with adults. This possibility is clearly illustrated by the perspectives of Christos and Jennifer within this chapter.

References

Alderson, P. (2005) 'Designing ethical research with children', in A. Farrell (ed.), *Ethical Research with Children*, Maidenhead: Open University Press, pp. 27–36.

Barthes, R. (1957) *Mythologies*, London: Granada.

Brennan, M. (2007) '"Beyond the child care – how else could we do this?", Sociocultural reflections on the structural and cultural arrangements of contemporary Western child care', *Australian Journal of Early Childhood*, 32(1): 1–9.

British Educational Research Association (BERA) (2004) *Revised Ethical Guidelines for Educational Research*, Southwell: BERA.

Buchwald, D., Schantz-Laursen, B. and Delmar, C. (2009) 'Video diary data collection in research with children: An alternative method', *International Journal of Qualitative Methods*, 8(1): 11–20.

Cannella, G. S. (1997) *Deconstructing Early Childhood Education: Social Justice and Revolution*, New York: Peter Lang.

Clark, A., and Moss, P. (2001) *Listening to Young Children: The Mosaic Approach*, London: National Children's Bureau.

Clark, A., and Moss, P. (2005) *Spaces to Play: More Listening to Young Children Using the Mosaic Approach*, London: National Children's Bureau.

Cook, T. and Hess, E. (2007) 'What the camera sees and from whose perspectives: Fun methodologies for engaging children in enlightening adults', *Childhood*, 14(1): 29–45.

Corsaro, W. (2000) 'Early childhood education, children's peer cultures, and the future of childhood', *European Early Childhood Education Research Journal*, 8(2): 89–102.

Corsaro W. A. (2003) *We're Friends Right? Inside Kids' Culture*, Washington, DC: Joseph Henry Press.

Corsaro, W. A. (2005) *The Sociology of Childhood*, 2nd edn, Thousand Oaks, CA: Pine Forge Press.

Dahlberg, G., Moss, P. and Pence, A. (2007) *Beyond Quality in Early Childhood Education and Care: Languages of Evaluation*, 2nd edn, London: RoutledgeFalmer.

Department of Education and Skills (DfES) (2004) *Every Child Matters: Change for Children*, London: HMSO.

Emond, R. (2005) 'Ethnographic research methods with children and young people', in S. Greene and D. Hogan (eds), *Researching Children's Experience: Approaches and Methods*. London: Sage Publications, pp. 123–140.

Flewitt, R. (2006) 'Using video to investigate preschool classroom interaction: Education research assumptions and methodological practices', *Visual Communication*, 5(1): 25–50.

Gallacher, L. A. and Gallagher, M. (2006) 'Are participatory approaches the way forward in research with children?', paper presented at the PIER Conference: Learning from Children and Young People, University of Stirling, 24 January.

Goldman-Segall, R. (1998) *Points of Seeing Children's Thinking: A Digital Ethnographer's Journey*, Mahwah, NJ: Lawrence Erlbaum Associates.

Harden, J., Scott, S., Backett-Milburn, K. and Jackson, S. (2000) 'Can't talk, won't talk?: Methodological issues in researching children', *Sociological Research Online*, 5(2). Available at: http://www.socresonline.org.uk/5/2/harden.html (accessed 17 June 2008).

Her Majesty's Government (2004) *The Children Act*, London: The Stationery Office.

James, A., Jenks, C. and Prout, A. (1998) *Theorizing Childhood*, Cambridge: Polity Press.

Jordan, B. (2004) 'Scaffolding learning and co-constructing understandings', in A. Anning, J. Cullen and M. Fleer (eds), *Early Childhood Education*, London: Sage, pp. 31–42.

Malaguzzi, L. (1996) 'The hundred languages of children', in Reggio Children, *The Hundred Languages of Children*, Reggio Emilia: Reggio Children.

Mayall, B. (2002) *Towards a Sociology for Childhood*, Buckingham: Open University Press.

National Children's Bureau (2002) 'Including children in social research', *Highlight*, no. 193, London: National Children's Bureau.

National Children's Bureau (2003) *Guidelines for Research*, London: National Children's Bureau. Available at: http://www.ncb.org.uk/ourwork/detail.asp?PID=144 (accessed 19 July 2003).

Qvortrup, J., Bardy, M., Sgritta, G. and Wintersberger, H. (eds) (1994) *Childhood Matters: Social Theory, Practice and Politics*, Avebury: Aldershot.

Rinaldi, C. (2006) *In Dialogue with Reggio Emilia: Listening, Researching and Learning*, London: Routledge.

Robbins, J. (2005) 'Contexts, collaboration, and cultural tools: A sociocultural perspective on researching children's thinking', *Contemporary Issues in Early Childhood*, 6(2): 140–149.

Rogoff, B. (2003) *The Cultural Nature of Human Development*, Oxford: Oxford University Press.

Rogoff, B. Paradise, R. Mejia Arauz, R., Correa-Chavez, M. and Angelillo, C. (2003) 'Firsthand learning through intent participation', *Annual Review of Psychology*, 54: 175–203.

Rutanen, N. (2007) 'Two-year-old children as co-constructors of culture', *European Early Childhood Education Research Journal*, 15(1): 59–69.

Smith, A. B. (2007) 'Children and young people's participation rights in education', *International Journal of Children's Rights*, 15: 147–164.

Thomson, F. (2007) 'Are methodologies for children keeping them in their place?', *Children's Geographies*, 5(3): 207–218.

Waller, T. (2006) '"Be careful – don't come too close to my Octopus Tree". Recording and evaluating young children's perspectives of outdoor learning', *Children, Youth and Environments*, 16(2): 75–104.

Waller, T. (2007) '"The Trampoline Tree and The Swamp Monster with 18 Heads": Outdoor play in the Foundation Stage and Foundation Phase', *Education 3–13*, 35(4): 395–409.

Waller, T. and Bitou, A. (forthcoming) 'Research with children: Three challenges for participatory research in early childhood', submitted to the *European Early Childhood Education Research Association Journal*, accepted November 2009.

Chapter 5

Balancing methodologies and methods in researching with young children

Sue Dockett, Jóhanna Einarsdóttir and Bob Perry

Often used in ways that confuse their meanings, the terms 'methodology' and 'method' are critical in any discussion of researching with children. This chapter explores distinctions between method and methodology and the impact of these distinctions on ethical research with children. Using examples of researching with children in Australia and Iceland, we problematize discussion of the two concepts and examine the impact of decisions about methodologies on methods used with children.

Introduction

In recent years, as researchers we have learned much from researching with children. Focus on children's participation in research has resulted in the development and refinement of a wide range of methods to facilitate the incorporation of children's perspectives (Clark, McQuail and Moss 2003; Coad and Lewis 2004; Dockett and Perry 2005a; Einarsdóttir 2005a; Veale 2005). Such methods include the use of drawing, photography, video, conversations, tours, construction and play as means for children to actively engage in research (Clark and Moss 2001). While recognizing the importance of methods that are of interest and relevance for children (Coad and Evans 2008), we support the position adopted by Bessell (2009) and argue for the significance of a well-defined theoretical base (methodology) underpinning the use of any methods.

The terms *method* and *methodology* are often used synonymously. Bessell argues that 'the world of methods has become so fascinating and now offers such opportunity for innovation that we sometimes lose sight of *why we choose* particular methods and, more importantly, *how we use them*' (2009: 17). Using this as our starting point, this chapter explores conceptual distinctions between the terms, examines why this matters and provides some examples from our involvement in research with children.

One potential consequence of the conflation of terms is that using a particular method becomes the focus of research, rather than the focus being the underpinning theory or rationale for its use. A focus on *methodology* sits within the interpretive framework, or paradigm, that researchers bring to any research (Denzin and Lincoln 2008). This theoretical framework incorporates epistemological and ontological, as well as methodological premises. Used in this way, the term methodology refers to the ways in which we think about and seek to study social phenomena (Corbin and Strauss 2008). The theoretical framework adopted in research establishes a 'set of strategic values within which individual researchers can anchor the tactics required in their everyday practice' (Christensen and Prout 2002: 477). In research with children, these values include the range of beliefs and assumptions researchers hold in relation to children, including their competence, rights and role within the research.

Identifying and reflecting on these beliefs and assumptions provides a basis for the practice of research – including the choice of methods, data collection, approaches to analysis and reporting. Within and throughout research, the methodology provides an anchor point for decisions made and approaches adopted.

The term *method* refers to the 'techniques and procedures for gathering and analysing data' (Corbin and Strauss 2008: 1). In this way, methods are the 'practical measures and tools' (Barbour 2008: 15) of research. The choice of methods is influenced by the methodology adopted in research. Methods are important research elements, but they are not the main driver of research. Methods, and their use within research, exist within a broader theoretical framework.

This chapter explores our theoretical framework and describes how this underpins a methodology that supports the use of innovative methods in research with children. It draws on research in both Iceland and Australia where children have been actively engaged as research participants and co-researchers (for example, Dockett and Perry 2007a; Einarsdóttir 2007; Einarsdóttir, Dockett and Perry 2009).

Defining our theoretical framework

Our research draws on a theoretical base influenced by commitments to strengths-based perceptions of children, where children are regarded as competent social actors who are experts on their own lives (James and Prout 1997; Rinaldi 2006); recognition of children as active citizens with participation rights (Jans 2004; United Nations 1989); and principles of ethical symmetry (Christensen and Prout 2002), which positions all research – including that involving children – as a process of ethical practice that necessarily involves obligations and responsibilities on the part of researchers as well as the researched.

Children's agency

Our focus on the competence of children and their agency is drawn from the discourse of sociology of childhood. This discourse has provoked paradigm shifts in the ways in which researchers view children and childhood, replacing positivist images of children as needy, incompetent and vulnerable with regard for children as competent agents within social and cultural settings (Clark and Moss 2001; Moss and Petrie 2002). The focus is on children as beings rather than becomings (Qvortrup 1994), experts on their own lives (Clark and Moss 2001; Lansdown 2005), competent to share their views and opinions (James and Prout 1997) and engaging in a range of social interactions, which themselves are worthy of study (Morrow 2001).

Adopting this discourse also requires acknowledgement that neither children nor their competencies are static entities. Rather, Kesby (2007) notes that children (as all people) are constantly changing and evolving as they adapt to various contexts. Lansdown (2005) too, emphasizes the evolving capacities of children. In addition, children's exercise of competence and agency is subject to many of the same constraints as those of adults (such as gender and socioeconomic status). Recognizing children's competence and agency also requires recognition that the contexts (social, cultural and historical) in which children exist impact upon their exercise of these attributes (Qvortrup 2004).

Children's rights and citizenship

Research with young children has also been influenced by discourses of children's rights and citizenship. The United Nations Convention on the Rights of the Child (UNCRC) (United Nations 1989) and General Comment 7 (Office of the High Commissioner for Human Rights 2005), assert the rights of children, including the very young, to be consulted in matters that affect them. Citizenship discourse (Invernizzi and Milne 2005; Jans 2004) recognizes children as citizens in their own right. As well as emphasizing the rights of individual children, citizenship discourse highlights the potential collective agency of children, whereby children may offer support for other children and seek to bring about change not only for themselves, but for other children (Evans and Spicer 2008; Howe and Covell 2005) through recognition of common issues. While aware that these discourses are not without challenge (Such and Walker 2004), they underscore advocacy for the rights of children to have their voices heard and to be taken seriously, as well as the obligations of adults to listen.

Children's participation in research is one area where the discourses of children's rights and sociology of childhood overlap (Hoffman–Ekstein et al. 2008). The opportunities for, and the nature of, participation afforded children within research reflect the rights of children to have their views taken seriously (rights discourse) and respect for children's agency (sociology of childhood discourse). However, participation is itself a contested term, encompassing a broad range of activities as well as multiple rationales (Evans and Spicer 2008; Hoffman-Ekstein et al. 2008). Approaches to participation in research range from those involving consultation (seeking advice from children), to others where children are engaged in decision-making (Clark et al. 2003; Hart 1997). In addition, participatory research is underpinned by rationales which range from genuine attempts at power sharing between adults and children to tokenistic efforts of compliance (Taylor and Robinson 2009; Tisdall and Davis 2004). On the basis that participatory research is 'neither inherently neutral nor objective' (Thomson 2007: 210), promoting children's participation in research that respects agency as well as rights demands acknowledgement of competing agendas.

Ethical symmetry

Promoting children's participation *in* research, as opposed to conducting research *on* children (Woodhead and Faulkner 2008), has led to debate on how research with children is the same as – or different from – research involving adults. Punch (2002) suggests that despite children's competence, child–friendly methods are often necessary because of children's marginalized social status and consequent lack of power in interactions with adults. Others, such as Qvortrup (1994), argue that children are competent social actors and therefore do not require special methods to promote participation. This latter position is supported by Christensen and Prout's (2002: 482) notion of ethical symmetry, whereby researchers assume that 'the ethical relationship between researcher and informant is the same whether he or she conducts research with adults or with children'. However, assuming ethical symmetry does not necessarily mean that researchers regard children and adults as exactly the same. Rather, it focuses on conducting research in ways that reflect appropriate methods, emphasizing the competence and agency of all research participants.

Assuming a standpoint of ethical symmetry challenges age-based determinations of children's competence, replacing these with recognition of children's experiences and social contexts (Mason and Urquhart 2001). At the same time, it recognizes that children's social status as subordinate to adults, and the attendant power relationships associated with this, impact on the nature of research, how it is conducted with children and the exercise of research rights within this (Christensen 2004). Thomson (2007: 210) argues that participatory research with children has the potential to transform power relations, particularly through 'continual interaction and negotiation between all participants, including the researcher'. This view situates power within relationships, much as in Foucault's premise that power is dispersed and contextual (Rabinow 1984). For this potential to be realized, participation needs to be conceptualized in ways that reflect democratic and emancipatory ideals, rather than increased opportunities for the surveillance and control of children by adults (Bragg 2007).

Each of these perspectives contributes to a theoretical framework that anchors our engagement of children in research. The assumptions that follow from these commitments provide a basis for decision-making – both about the nature of the research in which children participate and the outcomes of that research. For example, regarding children as competent social actors who are experts on their own lives focuses attention to their perspectives of specific events and issues. Such perspectives are respected as valid and reliable. Regarding even the youngest of children as citizens (Office of the High Commissioner for Human Rights 2005), rather than as people who will later become citizens (Qvortrup 1994), supports notions of participatory rights and suggests that involving children in research should provide opportunities for them to exercise those rights. Further, working with notions of ethical symmetry involves ensuring that the ethical principles enshrined in research with adults (such as those relating to consent and confidentiality) have counterparts in researching with children.

Without such a theoretical framework for seeking children's involvement in research, we contend that the use of specific methods can become tokenistic. Following this argument, we propose that many methods can be used to facilitate children's engagement in research, when underpinned by appropriate methodology. However, methods alone do not facilitate children's active engagement in research (Bessell 2009).

Matching methods and methodology

The remainder of this chapter explores the ways in which this theoretical framework informs our approaches to research. We draw on examples from our own research to illustrate a range of situations and outcomes, acknowledging a range of tensions and challenges we have encountered. We offer these as examples of issues that have arisen, rather than solutions.

Designing research begins with the identification of a research area. Much educational research is guided by the prevailing research landscape, including research priorities supported at national and/or local levels, the availability of research funding, potential research outcomes, perceived need and usefulness of the research. In many current research contexts, the call for evidence-based research (Erickson and Guiterrez 2002) has been translated into calls for large-scale, randomized trials, diminishing the respect accorded to participatory research guided by children.

We were reminded of this after a recent presentation, where we had emphasized the importance of children providing informed assent throughout a project which sought their perspectives on their local communities (Dockett, Perry and Kearney 2009a). Following the presentation, a fellow researcher questioned the necessity for such an approach, arguing that one outcome was a reduced sample size, as children exercised their right to dissent, and so to disengage from the project. He commented: 'If it was really important research, you couldn't give them [children] a choice, because you would need to get some results.' The notion that it is acceptable to draw upon a participatory, rights-based framework with children in research that 'didn't really matter' presented a challenge, but also reflects a view, we suspect, that is not uncommon. Such questions raise issues of who decides what is researched, by whom and with what underlying theoretical framework.

Selecting research methods

In recent years, many exciting and innovative methods have been used to engage with children in research. Methods inviting children to draw, photograph, talk about, enact and model their experiences and expectations have been used to promote the engagement of diverse groups of children in multiple contexts (Barker and Weller 2003; Clark and Moss 2001; Clark *et al.* 2003; Fattore, Mason and Nixon 2005; Hoffman-Ekstein *et al.* 2008; Punch 2002). Often, these methods have been used in combination. The rationale for the use of these methods varies. In some research, it is related to the use of 'child–friendly' approaches – a rationale founded on the premise that children are similar to adults, but have different expertise and competencies, necessitating methods that are often based on visual, rather than text, materials (Punch 2002). Challenges with this rationale include the positioning of children as different from adults (Lahman 2008) and assumptions about what children find interesting and engaging (Kirk 2007). While there is an assumption that children like to draw, paint or play, across a number of research projects we have encountered children who have had no desire to undertake these activities, and who have preferred to engage in 'adult-friendly' methods such as structured interviews.

Another rationale for the use of specific methods with children relates to the provision of choice. Children may well be capable of responding to a range of methods. However, providing choices can set up 'opportunities for children to express themselves in a way that makes them feel empowered and capable' (Hoffman–Ekstein *et al.* 2008). Providing choices recognizes children's diverse interests and experiences and recognizes their ability to exercise choices. It also acknowledges that there is 'no one size fits all model for participatory research' (Clark *et al.* 2001: 59). However, in the drive to develop new, innovative and novel methods to promote children's participation in research, we have noted previously the 'tension between developing interesting methods [and] . . . avoiding a gimmick approach' (Dockett and Perry 2007b: 50). In the same vein, Lahman (2008: 293) notes that 'it is important for researchers to avoid getting caught up in method for method's sake'.

Exercising choice

While there are increasing efforts to engage children in all elements of the research process (Jones 2004), children are most likely to participate in some, rather than all, aspects of research (Hill *et al.* 2004). Even when children have not been involved in designing the research, there is potential for them to exert some control over the agenda when they have choices and are encouraged to exercise these (Clark and Statham 2005; Kendrick, Steckley and Lerpiniere 2008). In adopting a rights-based, participatory framework, one of the bases of our use of methods has been providing genuine choices to participants.

Informed assent

Ongoing discussions with children about their research rights, including their right to provide assent and/or dissent over the length of the project, were a feature of the investigation of children's perspectives on their communities (Dockett et al. 2009a). Children's participation choices were framed as process assent (Alderson 2005; Cocks 2007), with multiple opportunities provided for children to consider and/or reassess these choices. One consequence of this approach was that a large number of children chose not to participate. In one first-year-of-school class group (children aged five to six years), most children were eager to engage in the activities (such as drawing and photographing aspects of their communities). However, only nine of the 22 children chose to contribute their work as data for the research project. On the one hand, it was positive that children exercised their rights. On the other hand, the sample size was reduced considerably. While children's exercise of their participation rights has implications for the outcomes of the research, we are confident that the data that were contributed reflect information that children genuinely wished to share.

Providing opportunities for informed assent also presented some challenges in a project seeking children's perspectives of their early childhood settings (Einarsdóttir 2007). In this study, the overall project was not outlined in full to the children (aged two to six years) at the beginning of the research, as it was thought that they may have been overwhelmed by too much information and may not recall their participation decisions at later points. Instead, the children were asked during each data collection phase whether or not they wished to participate. In retrospect, it was noted:

> I have been wondering if this was the most appropriate method and if I shouldn't have introduced the study for the children in the beginning. If one does not introduce a study as a whole to the participants there is a danger that they feel they have been tricked into participating.
>
> (Einarsdóttir 2007: 205)

Clearly, one of our ongoing challenges relates to establishing and identifying strategies that provide children with genuine choices about participation, and opportunities to exercise these.

Choosing what data to contribute

Across several studies we have invited children to photograph aspects of their environment or experience (Dockett and Perry 2005a; Einarsdóttir 2003, 2005a). Using cameras in research with children invites them to use a mode of communication beyond written or oral language. Integral to this method has been opportunities for children to make choices about what to photograph, direct conversations about the photos and choose what photos and/or comments are contributed as data. Children's agency is also respected when they are in control of what is done with the photos and how they are presented. In a study where children were invited to take photos of what they found important in preschool using a disposable camera (Einarsdóttir 2005a) the preschool teachers sat down with them individually after the photos had been developed and talked with them about the photos, what was on them, and why they took them. The children were then given small albums in which they could put their photos to take them home. The children were given three choices about the way in which they could preserve and present the photos: they could put the photo in the album, throw it away, or hide it behind another photo in the album. One boy had been playing with the camera and he and his friend took photos of each other's behind. The preschool teacher asked him about these photos like the others: 'What can I invite you to do with these photos?' The boy answered: 'You can invite me to throw them away.' It was his choice not to let other people see those photos.

Sometimes, children's exercise of choice is constrained by the context in which the research occurs. In several studies, we have invited children to draw the impressions of their first year at school (Dockett and Perry 2005b; Einarsdóttir 2005b). The context in which this method has been introduced to children has varied; sometimes teachers have introduced the task as a class activity, other times researchers have invited small groups of children to draw and talk about their first year of school (Einarsdóttir et al. 2009). Generally, children have been willing to participate, and many have devoted a great deal of time to the task. However, we are also aware that class activities are often regarded as compulsory, academic work by children (David, Edwards and Alldred 2001), and have seen evidence of this when children's contributions have been returned to us with corrected spelling or grammar. Clearly, these data have been constructed by both children and teachers as work samples (Coates and Coates 2006). This is but one example of the same method (drawing) being used within quite different theoretical frameworks.

Data analysis

There are many ways in which the methodology adopted influences approaches to data interpretation and analysis, and the role of children within these processes (Coad and Evans 2008; Jones 2004; Kirby 1999). The following example relates to a study that incorporated two methods of photography. One method involved providing children with digital cameras to take photos in their preschool while they took the researcher on a photo tour, pointing out important places and things. Another group of children was given disposable cameras to use in an unsupervised fashion for a period of time (Einarsdóttir 2005a). The photos could have been analysed in various ways, for example, according to their aesthetic quality or the messages that the researchers assumed the children were conveying. Since the theoretical base of the study was to listen to children's voices, the children were regarded as the experts and invited to explain their photos. In other words, the children explained why they took each picture and what was in it. The conversations with the children revealed that the photos only told part of the story. In many cases, the photos were meaningless without the benefit of the explanations. For example, many children took pictures of the outdoor playground, yet their explanations for doing so varied. One boy explained that he took a picture of the playground because he liked to play outside, whereas a girl said she took a picture of the playground because she liked to play with the girl who was also in the photo. Furthermore, another boy explained his photo of the playground by saying that he was actually taking a picture of his home, which could barely be seen in the background. Many other photos were difficult to understand without the children's elaboration. For instance, a child took a photo of a door to one of the classrooms, which he later explained is where his mother works. Yet another child took a photo of a student teacher not because she particularly liked her but because that particular day was the student teacher's last at the school. Similar examples across many studies have convinced us that children have a key role in data analysis. In this sense, data analysis is not something that occurs towards the end of a project. Rather, data provide the stimulus for ongoing 'conversations and engagement with children' (Bessell 2009: 22), which in turn, emphasizes children's meaning making and interpretation.

In another study (Einarsdóttir 2005b), preschool children were asked in group interviews what they liked and did not like in preschool. Many of the children mentioned that they viewed pre-planned activities where they were required to sit still for a period of time and listen to the teacher, such as group-time, as boring. Philosophy time (when a small group of children sit together for a teacher-led discussion) was also often mentioned as difficult and uninteresting. These activities were the ones that the teachers had often put the most effort into planning and teaching. When the results of the study were presented to the preschool staff, a common reaction was to seek the explanation within particular children. Although the children were given pseudonyms to maintain confidentiality, the staff members tried to guess which children would have expressed their dislike for these activities. They attempted to explain that specific children expressed their dislike due to their personal characteristics. Although the aim of the study was to seek ways to listen to children, these reactions from the staff did not reflect a theoretical stance that respects children as experts on their own lives or having the competence to share their views.

Reporting and dissemination of research

As well as children choosing what is considered data and how it is analysed, it is important for children to have input into decisions about the reporting and dissemination of research. In our project about children's perspectives of their community (Dockett et al. 2009a), children were invited to present their perspectives at a public forum, attended by decision-makers such as members of the local council. Children determined what data would be presented and how. One issue for many children was the use of pseudonyms. Researchers discussed issues of confidentiality and privacy with the children, explaining that the use of pseudonyms meant that they could say whatever they wanted without having to worry what other people thought. However, many children were adamant that they wanted to use their actual names, noting that they were 'proud to have a say' and, in one instance, wanted to make sure their contribution 'was copyright' (Dockett, Perry and Kearney 2009b). As a result, some children's first names were included in their data and the children did demonstrate pride in these contributions. As researchers though, we reflect on the long-term consequences of this: their data was presented at a public forum and was recorded and reported by various media. Some of the reporting focused on the cute or fanciful perspectives contributed by some children. For example, several reports focused on children's calls to have a fun park or zoo in their local area and others highlighted the call for some young children to have a playground with trees of lollies (sweets). How do these brief media reports position children and how will these same children feel in the years to come when the reports remain accessible in media archives? From a participatory rights–based research perspective, how do we work with children to emphasize the value of their own interpretive frames and perspectives in ways that are respected as citizens within their communities – now and in the future?

Conclusion

Denzin and Lincoln (2008: 4–5) note that 'qualitative researchers deploy a wide range of interconnected interpretive practices, hoping always to get a better understanding of the subject matter at hand . . . each practice makes the world visible in a different way'. Likening the qualitative researcher to a quilt maker who pieces together a set of representations relevant to a specific context, they also note the need for 'different tools, methods and techniques of representation and interpretation' (ibid.: 5). As researchers seeking genuine engagement with children in research, we have used a range of innovative methods with the intent of emphasizing children's competence, agency and participation rights, as well as the need to extend to children the same ethical rights as all research participants. The methods themselves have provided the means to an end, rather than being the purpose of the research. Guiding both the choice of methods and the ways in which these have been implemented is a theoretical framework that provides an anchor for decisions about research. We note that one of the challenges with the growing popularity of children's voices within research is balancing the *how* of such research with the *why* (Rudduck and Fielding 2006).

There is no simple one-way connection between methodology and method. The same method may be used in multiple ways, guided by quite different methodologies, and the use of a particular method in a specific context will provide feedback that influences the methodology. For example, while we may employ a specific method to seek children's participation, we are aware that the nature and extent of that participation influence our assumptions about children. Where children have genuine choices about participation, they also influence the ways in which methods are employed and how these contribute to their ongoing experiences. As an example, children who participated in a method based on constructing models of their experiences extended this to include model-making as a regular feature of their preschool experiences. They not only created models related to the research project, but continued to build models related to other issues they had identified as important. As the models were constructed, ongoing and detailed conversations were generated among the children and with the adults in the setting. The model-making method was effective in representing children's perspectives, but it also provided a context for children to demonstrate a range of skills and capacities which, in turn, influenced assumptions about the nature and extent of children's participation.

Much has been written about the potential benefits of children's participation in research (Clark and Moss 2001; Hoffman-Ekstein et al. 2008). In addition to the benefits associated with acknowledging children's agency in research, and utilizing methods that recognize children's voices, we agree with a number of other researchers who promote the importance of children's participation as a means for them to develop agency, through the acquisition of a range of skills and abilities that enable them to understand research processes and opportunities to generate and lead research (Evans and Spicer 2008; Kesby 2007). These dual benefits of children's participation – acknowledgement of agency and development of agency – are most likely to ensue when there is a focus on the purposes of participation as well as the practices.

References

Alderson, P. (2005) 'Ethics', in A. Farrell (ed.), *Ethical Research with Children*, New York: Open University Press, pp. 27–36.

Barbour, R. (2008) *Introducing Qualitative Research*, London: Sage.

Barker, J. and Weller, S. (2003) '"Is it fun?"' Developing children centered research methods', *International Journal of Sociology and Social Policy*, 1(2): 33–58.

Bessell, S. (2009) 'Research with children: Thinking about method and methodology', in *Involving Children and Young People in Research*, pp.17–27. ARACY/NSW Commission for Children and Young People. Available at: http://www.aracy.org.au (accessed 10 July 2009).

Bragg, S. (2007) '"Student voice" and governmentality: The production of enterprising subjects?', *Discourse: Studies in the Cultural Politics of Education*, 28(3): 343–358.

Christensen, P. (2004) 'Children's participation in ethnographic research: Issues of power and representation', *Children and Society*, 18: 165–176.

Christensen, P. and Prout, A. (2002) 'Working with ethical symmetry in social research with children', *Childhood*, 9(4): 477–497.

Clark, A., McQuail, S. and Moss, P. (2003) *Exploring the Field of Listening to Consulting with Young Children*, Research Report RR 445, London: Department for Education and Skills.

Clark, A. and Moss, P. (2001) *Listening to Young Children: The Mosaic Approach*, London: National Children's Bureau and Joseph Rowntree Foundation.

Clark, A. and Statham, J. (2005) 'Listening to young children: Experts in their own lives', *Adoption and Fostering*, 29(1): 45–56.

Clark, J., Dyson, A., Meagher, N., Robson, E. and Wooten, M. (2001) *Young People as Researchers: Possibilities, Problems and Politics*, Leicester: National Youth Agency/Youth Work Press.

Coad J. and Evans, R. (2008) 'Reflections on practical approaches to involving children and young people in the data analysis process', *Children and Society*, 22: 41–52.

Coad, J. and Lewis, A. (2004) *Engaging Children and Young People in Research*, London: The National Evaluation of the Children's Fund.

Coates, E. and Coates, A. (2006) 'Young children talking and drawing', *International Journal of Early Years Education*, 14(3): 221–241.

Cocks, A. (2007) 'The ethical maze: Finding an inclusive path towards gaining children's agreement to research participation', *Childhood*, 13: 247–266.

Corbin J. and Strauss, A. (2008) *Basics of Qualitative Research*, 3rd edn, Thousand Oaks, CA: Sage.

David, M., Edwards, R. and Alldred, P. (2001) 'Children and school-based research: "Informed consent" or "educated consent"?', *British Educational Research Journal*, 27(3): 347–365.

Denzin, N. K. and Lincoln, Y. S. (eds) (2008) *Collecting and Interpreting Qualitative Materials*, 3rd edn, Thousand Oaks, CA: Sage.

Dockett, S. and Perry, B. (2005a) 'Researching with children: Insights from the Starting School Research Project', *Early Child Development and Care*, 175(6): 507–522.

Dockett, S. and Perry, B. (2005b) 'Children's drawings: Experiences and expectations of school', *International Journal of Innovation and Equity in Early Childhood*, 3(2): 77–89.

Dockett, S. and Perry, B. (2007a) *Transitions to School: Perceptions, Expectations and Experiences*, Sydney: University of New South Wales Press.

Dockett S. and Perry, B. (2007b) 'Trusting children's accounts in research', *Journal of Early Childhood Research*, 5(1): 47–63.

Dockett, S., Perry, B. and Kearney, E. (2009a) 'Promoting children's informed assent in research participation', paper presented at the Australian Social Policy Research annual conference, Sydney, July.

Dockett, S., Perry, B. and Kearney, E. (2009b) 'Children's perspectives of their research rights', paper presented at Children as Experts on their Own Lives: Child inclusive research symposium, Sydney, November.

Einarsdóttir, J. (2003) '"When the bell rings we have to go inside": Preschool children's views on the primary school', *European Early Childhood Educational Research Association Research Themed Monograph*, 1: 35–50.

Einarsdóttir, J. (2005a) 'Playschool in pictures: Children's photographs as a research method', *Early Child Development and Care*, 175(6): 523–541.

Einarsdóttir, J. (2005b) '"We can decide what to play!" Children's perceptions of quality in an Icelandic playschool', *Early Education and Development*, 16(4): 469–488.

Einarsdóttir, J. (2007) 'Research with children: Methodological and ethical challenges', *European Early Childhood Education Research Journal*, 15(2): 197–211.

Einarsdóttir, J., Dockett, S. and Perry, B. (2009) 'Making meaning: Children's perspectives expressed through drawings', *Early Child Development and Care*, 179(2): 217–232.

Erickson, F. and Guiterrez, K. (2002) 'Culture, rigor, and science in educational research', *Educational Researcher*, 31(8): 21–24.

Evans, R. and Spicer, N. (2008) 'Is participation prevention? A blurring of discourses in children's preventative initiatives in the UK', *Childhood*, 15(1): 50–73.

Fattore, T., Mason, J. and Nixon, D. (2005) *Participation: Count Me In!*, Sydney: NSW Commission for Children and Young People.

Hart, R. (1997) *Children's Participation: The Theory and Practice of Involving Young Citizens in Community Development and Environmental care*, London: Earthscan.

Hill, M., Davis, J., Prout, A. and Tisdall, K. (2004) 'Moving the participation agenda forward', *Children and Society*, 18(2): 77–96.

Hoffman–Ekstein, J., Michaux, A., Bessell, B., Mason, J., Watson, E. and Fox, M. (2008) *Children's Agency in Communities: A Review of Literature and the Policy and Practice Context*. Available: www.bensoc.org.au (accessed 12 February 2009).

Howe, R. B. and Covell, K. (2005) *Empowering Children: Children's Rights Education as a Pathway to Citizenship*, Toronto: University of Toronto Press.

Invernizzi, A. and Milne, B. (2005) 'Conclusion: some elements of an emergent discourse on children's right to citizenship', *Journal of Social Sciences, Special Issue*, 9: 83–99.

James, A. and Prout, A. (1997) *Constructing and Reconstructing Childhood: Contemporary Issues in the Sociological Study of Childhood*, 2nd edn, London: Falmer Press.

Jans, M. (2004) 'Children as citizens: Towards a contemporary notion of child participation', *Childhood*, 11(1): 27–44.

Jones, A. (2004) 'Involving children and young people as researcher', in S. Fraser, V. Lewis, S. Ding, M. Kellett and C. Robinson (eds), *Doing Research with Children and Young People*, London; Sage, pp. 113–130.

Kendrick, A., Steckley, L. and Lerpiniere, J. (2008) 'Ethical issues, research and vulnerability: Gaining the views of children and young people in residential care', *Children's Geographies*, 6(1): 79–93.

Kesby, M. (2007) 'Methodological insights on and from Children's Geographies', *Children's Geographies*, 5(3): 193–205.

Kirby, P. (1999) *Involving Young Researchers: How to Enable Young People to Design and Conduct Research*, York: Joseph Rowntree Foundation/Youth Work Press.

Kirk, S. (2007) 'Methodological and ethical issues in conducting qualitative research with children and young people: A literature review', *International Journal of Nursing Studies*, 44: 1250–1260.

Lahman, M. K. E. (2008) 'Always othered: Ethical research with children', *Journal of Early Childhood Research*, 6(3): 281–300.

Lansdown, G. (2005) *The Evolving Capacities of the Child*, Florence, Italy: UNICEF Innocenti Research Centre. Available at: http://www.bernardvanleer.org/files/crc/4%20Gerison_Lansdown.pdf (accessed 30 March 2009).

Mason, J. and Urquhart, R. (2001) 'Developing a model for participation by children in research on decision making', *Children Australia*, 26(4): 16–21.

Morrow, V. (2001) 'Using qualitative methods to elicit young people's perspectives on their environments: Some ideas for community health initiatives', *Health Education Research: Theory and Practice*, 16(3): 255–268.

Moss, P. and Petrie, P. (2002) *From Children's Services to Children's Spaces*, London: RoutledgeFalmer.

Office of the High Commissioner for Human Rights (2005) *General Comment No 7: Implementing Child Rights in Early Childhood*, Available at: http://www.ohchr.org/english/bodies/crc/docs/AdvanceVersions/GeneralComment7Rev1.pdf (accessed 30 March 2009).

Punch, S. (2002) 'Research with children: The same or different from research with adults?', *Childhood*, 9(3): 321–341.

Qvortrup, J. (1994) 'Childhood matters: An introduction', in J. Qvortrup, M. Bardy, G. Sgritta and H. Wintersberger (eds), *Childhood Matters: Social Theory, Practice and Politics*, Aldershot: Avebury, pp. 1–24.

Qvortrup, J. (2004) 'The waiting child', *Childhood*, 11(3): 267–273.

Rabinow, P. (ed.) (1984) *The Foucault Reader*, London: Penguin.

Rinaldi, C. (2006) *In Dialogue with Reggio Emilia: Listening, Researching and Learning*, London: Routledge.

Rudduck, J. and Fielding, M. (2006) 'Student voice and the perils of popularity', *Educational Review*, 58(2): 219–231.

Such, E. and Walker, R. (2004) 'Being responsible and responsible beings: Children's understanding of responsibility', *Children and Society*, 18: 231–242.

Taylor, C. and Robinson, C. (2009) 'Student voice: Theorising power and participation', *Pedagogy, Culture and Society*, 17(2): 161–175.

Thomson, F. (2007) 'Are methodologies for children keeping them in their place?', *Children's Geographies*, 5(3): 207–218.

Tisdall, E. K. M. and Davis, J. (2004) 'Making a difference? Bringing children and young people's views into policy-making', *Children and Society*, 18: 131–142.

United Nations (1989) *United Nations Convention on the Rights of the Child*. New York: UNICEF. Available at: http://www.unicef.org/crc/crc (accessed 30 March 2009).

Veale, A. (2005) 'Creative methodologies in participatory research with children', in S. Greene and D. Hogan (eds), *Researching Children's Experience*, Thousand Oaks, CA: Sage, pp. 253–272.

Woodhead, M. and Faulkner, D. (2008) 'Subjects, objects or participants? Dilemmas on psychological research with children', in P. Christensen and A. James (eds), *Research with Children: Perspectives and Practices*, 2nd edn, London: Falmer, pp. 10–39.

Part II

Case studies of high quality research with young children

Chapter 6

Supporting children's participation rights

Curriculum and research approaches

Sarah Te One

This chapter describes a range of research strategies used to explore children's perceptions of children's rights in a New Zealand/Aotearoa sessional, state kindergarten for three- and four-year-old children. The case study reported here was part of a wider research project investigating perceptions of children's rights in early childhood settings. A defining characteristic of this case study was that children's perspectives were sought and included. The researcher used stories, posters, conversational interviews and a persona doll to stimulate discussions, and encourage children to voice their perspectives of children's rights.

Introduction

To include young children as genuine participants in research remains a challenge for all involved in such endeavours. The extent to which this happens depends on several factors, not the least being an understanding of what Article 12 in the United Nations Convention on the Rights of Child (UNCRC) (Child Rights Information Network 2007) means in practice. Article 12 articulates children's rights to participate in decisions that affect them, but the exercising of these rights depends upon how their views are taken into account. As Moss (2006: 30) argued, 'You need to want to listen in the first place and no amount of bullet points will help you if you don't have a culture of listening' (citing a personal communication with Olé Langsted). For researchers, the challenge of listening to children is central to including their views in the research process.

Under the UNCRC, children 'are seen as future adult citizens, but, and importantly, also as existing citizens in their own right' (Howe and Covell 2005: 62). Even though young children are thought of as evolving and becoming citizens, they still have the right to participate in decisions that affect them (Smith 2007a; 2007b). Educating children about their rights increases their knowledge of basic human rights, and the corresponding social responsibilities based on principles of social justice equality, and respect for the rights of others (Lauren 2003). Through education, including early childhood education, it is possible for children to experience the fundamentals of good citizenship as they participate in 'a democratic and human-rights based culture (Howe and Covell 2005). Children's citizenship has been defined as 'an entitlement to recognition, respect and participation' (Neale 2004: 8). It is therefore an important consideration for researchers to treat children as participants in research. Fundamentally, their rights to participate (or not) must be respected, and, further, how to support and facilitate children's participation requires thoughtful appreciation of the entire research process – from design to dissemination. This chapter reports on how children were involved in a research project investigating teachers' and children's perceptions of children's rights in a New Zealand state-funded kindergarten.[1] The focus of the chapter is on how the adult researcher facilitated children's participation rights in the research, and the research strategies developed to enhance children's participation during the research process. The chapter also documents how the kindergarten setting and programme fostered respect for children's citizenship and participation rights.

The context for the research

New Zealand kindergartens traditionally cater for three- to five-year-old children and usually operate two sessions a day, although this is changing in response to local community demands. In the study kindergarten, 43 children aged three years old attended for two hours four afternoons a week and 45 children aged four and five years old were enrolled for five mornings (8.45am–12.30pm) a week. Three trained registered teachers were employed full-time, in this kindergarten. There was also a part-time administrator and a part-time special needs teacher whose role was to work with specific children. Parent volunteers were rostered on a daily basis.

The full-time teachers had one afternoon a week (in this case it was a Wednesday) where there were no children present. During this time they planned the kindergarten programme using *Te Whāriki*, the New Zealand early childhood curriculum (Ministry of Education 1996), and the accompanying *Kei tua o te Pae* (Ministry of Education 2005), a New Zealand document intended to guide teachers as they assess children's learning (Carr 2001). Both of these documents are based on principles of empowerment, relationships, family and community, and holistic development (May and Carr 2000). They acknowledge children's rights as participants in their early education, not just access rights to an early education, but specifically as actively engaged in determining the programme in their early childhood settings (May and Carr 2000; Te One 2003). Kindergarten, teachers used learning stories (Carr *et al.* 2003), a narrative assessment tool linked to *Te Whāriki*, as part of their regular professional practices, to plan for children's interests.

Understanding the overall context in which children participate is important because this influences the nature of that participation (Te One 2008). For example, the kindergarten teachers were philosophically committed to children's active participation, and used a range of strategies to support children's citizenship in the centre. At a fundamental level, this was based on the teachers' respect for children's agency within the context of the kindergarten programme. Further, *Te Whāriki* (Ministry of Education 1996) clearly informed professional teaching decisions in the kindergarten. The kindergarten teachers did not explicitly refer to the United Nations Convention on the Rights of the Child, and they did not use the term 'children's rights'. Rather, the language teachers used to describe the children's rights reflected *Te Whāriki* (Te One 2008).

To extend children's sense of belonging to a community founded on a respect for others, the teachers in this particular kindergarten intentionally developed resources with the children to support a long-term project they referred to as *Playing as a Good Friend*. The overall aim of the project was to develop social competence, or nurture emergent, responsive and respectful citizenship derived from the aspiration of *Te Whāriki*: 'To grow up as competent and confident learners and communicators, healthy in mind, body, and spirit, secure in their sense of belonging and in the knowledge that they make a valued contribution to society' (Ministry of Education 1996: 9). A further purpose was to develop a culture that supported children's social competence by providing them with opportunities to develop strategies for initiating play with each other, and sustaining interactions in appropriate ways for all. In other words, children were encouraged to act respectfully and responsibly as citizens in their kindergarten.

Nurturing relationships, by articulating to the children why these were important at kindergarten, was a strategy the teachers developed to establish a sense of belonging to the kindergarten's community of learners (Rogoff 1998). Belonging, a strand of *Te Whāriki*, emphasizes trusting relationships between teachers, children and their families, and community. *Playing as a Good Friend* was a strong message that teachers believed enhances children's sense of belonging. Professional practices, such as brainstorming, poster-making and hand-made books, offered consistent messages about the nature and purpose of friendship in this setting.

The *Playing as a Good Friend* project was based on three simple rules:

1   We are not allowed to hurt anyone or anything.
2   We use good words. This includes tone, pitch, body language.
3   We need to listen to each other.

Teachers believed that the project would enhance children's sense of belonging to the kindergarten by encouraging them to participate as a good friend; and second, the project would clarify expectations of how all the participants in the kindergarten would treat one another. An observed feature of the project was the way in which all the teachers, including the part-time staff, used a consistent set of phrases such as 'That was really kind when you . . .'; or, more specifically, encouraged children to express their point of view:

> Sharon (a teacher) is telling a small group on the veranda about how to be a good friend. You don't say: 'You're not my friend' – you say 'When you do

this or when you say that I feel [sad] or [upset].' OK? So, you need to let people know how you feel but you don't say you're not my friend. We are all friends here.

(Field notes, Day 5)

The cultural norms of the kindergarten protected children's emotional rights, and empowered them to participate. Article 19 supports 'parents and others responsible for the care of the child [to] establish appropriate social programmes' to protect children (as interpreted in Child Rights Information Network 2007: 7). Building on Lansdown's (2005) notion of protection as a route to enhancing participation rights, Lundy (2007) argues that adults have a responsibility to provide space to listen to children's voices. Children too were very clear about what the project entailed, and, as the research revealed, were remarkably consistent about their rights and responsibilities as they played as good friends at kindergarten:

> *Sam*: Well, you have to be a good friend.
> *Erika*: Yes, you have to be a good friend.
> *Henry²: Can you be my friend?*
> *Paul*: Well, he's my friend, but . . .
> *Sam*: But you aren't allowed to hit. You have to use your words.
> *Henry: I don't like hitting.*
> *Paul*: Yea, you can say 'Stop it, I don't like it', can't you?
> *Sophie*: But you can say, you can say . . .
> *Erika*: You can say 'I don't want to play just now' . . . But you can't be mean.

(Field notes, Day 14)

The *Playing as a Good Friend* project inadvertently supported the researcher's own strategies as she endeavoured to involve children in the research. The chapter concludes with the children's voices expressing their perceptions of their rights in the context of their experiences in this particular New Zealand kindergarten.

The research design

Interpretive, qualitative methods were used to investigate perceptions of children's rights in the kindergarten. Data were generated through individual and focus group interviews with the teachers, conversational interviews with children, and observational field notes and photographs. A persona doll, posters and a book of illustrations depicting children's rights were used to stimulate children's conversations about their rights in the kindergarten, as well as to support their participation in the research if they so wished. These research tools are discussed later in the chapter. A researcher journal documented insights and reflective comments.

An information sheet and consent form for parents accompanied a specially written information booklet designed for the children. This explained what the researcher would be doing, and what could be expected by children if they chose to participate in the research. The booklet included an assent form for the children. The intention was to support their agency. They had the opportunity to give their assent before their parental or caregiver consent was sought, although parents had been informed that the research was taking place (Te One 2007; 2008). The ethics requirements offered an opportunity to involve children, and support their participation rights both in the research and more generally. The researcher's white file box became the consent/assent 'posting box'. On the first day of field work, a small group of children decided to decorate the box with collage. 'It's too boring,' one said. This created an opportunity for the researcher to talk about the research with children and by the end of that particular session, the decorators had asked every parent who came in to collect their child whether or not they had filled out the forms. Interestingly, even though the assent process was intended to support children's right to choose, and the children's comments to parents indicated they understood the researcher's expectations, they still saw final consent as an adult's responsibility.

A further ethical consideration required resolving before entering the field, and this was how to position the researcher as an atypical, less powerful adult. The age and authority of adult researchers constrain their participation in a child's world (Christensen 2004; Christensen and James 2008). The power of adults in early childhood centres is difficult to minimize. Thoughtful attention was required about how to build relationships with children while at the same time building relationships with the teachers and parent community. In the first instance, children's participation rights are easily overlooked in centre-based settings, and enabling children to exercise these rights, particularly the right not to participate, requires an acute awareness on the part of a researcher:

Lulu: You mean I can choose a different name if I want?

(Field notes, Day 1)

and

Sarah (researcher): Can I come and talk to you?
Keith: Not now, but after maybe . . .
Jacob: Yea, after, coz we are too busy, aren't we? (Looks intently at Keith)

(Field notes, Day 8)

Even though children may have filled in an assent form, with parental consent, the idea of ongoing informed assent might be a more useful process than the one-off 'sign-the-form' approach. Allowing children to ask questions about the researcher (Who's mum are you?) as well as about the research questions facilitated children's participation in the research during the field work, and these interactions also heightened their awareness of their rights as participants.

Strategies to stimulate discussion about children's rights

An awareness of children's participation rights created a conceptual challenge in this research: how could the researcher as an atypical, non-authoritarian adult and the children find a mutually agreed space to discuss perceptions of children's rights (Corsaro and Molinari 2000; Davis 1998)? Before beginning the field work, the question of how to introduce the topic of children's rights to children was an issue. No assumptions could be made that children would understand what was meant by the phrase 'children's rights'. Several strategies were devised to address this challenge including using a book about children's rights; making posters; using a persona doll; and conversational interviews. Fundamentally, however, successfully encouraging children to participate depended on the quality of the relationships between the researcher and the children, and, to a large extent, on the cultural climate in the kindergarten.

Henry, the persona doll

One technique used to prompt discussions with children was a persona doll. These life-sized dolls (two- to three-year-old child-sized) are often used with children to raise an awareness of discriminatory behaviours among children and adults (Brown 2001; Derman-Sparks and the ABC Task Force 1989). The dolls have their own personality, developed by their user – in this case the researcher (Brown 2001). Henry, the persona doll created for this research, did not have a physical voice of his own, but he spoke to the children through the researcher, who asked and answered questions on his behalf. Henry's persona was developed to encourage children's participation in the research in a way that allowed for some responsive interaction through conversations about the children's perceptions of children's rights. Through him it was possible to ask naïve questions and access children's perceptions about their rights in the kindergarten. There was no doubt that Henry had an immediate impact on the children:

> The first person to actually meet Henry was Lulu who questioned his realness. I explained to her that Henry was a bit shy and that he was just wondering about who would be his friend here. 'I'll be his friend,' she said. At that point we were joined by Ashley who was really interested in Henry. I explained that he had just come to visit with me. 'Hey, I know,' says Lulu, 'I'll be his friend and then you can be his friend after, OK?' Ashley looked confused by this. 'Well,' said Lulu, 'I'll go first and then when I have had a turn, you can be his friend. So it's me and then it's you and then it's me again.' Lulu had, by this time, climbed onto the couch and was touching Henry and kissing him. She looked at Ashley who moved further away. More and more children were joining us and we were all sitting together on the couch in the book corner. Henry was on my knee and whispering his responses into my ear. 'Can you

all be friends at the same time?' he asked. 'No,' said Lulu. 'Yes,' said Ashley. At this stage Lulu tried to take Henry from my knee. She was curious about his clothes and his new gumboots and told him, and then me that she had new gumboots: 'But you shouldn't have them on inside.' She took off Henry's gumboots and put them by the door.

(Field notes, Day 8)

Towards the end of the field work Henry came to mat time with one of the teachers. It was his 'goodbye' session and, typically in the kindergarten, when a child left, their time at the centre was celebrated with special attention. During this session Henry interacted with the group to ask about important things other visitors needed to know about the kindergarten. One teacher held Henry, but the researcher interpreted and acted in the ventriloquist's role, with hands free to take notes as Henry interacted with the children:

For Ethan's turn with Henry, he told the group: 'Mine is a secret and you can't hear it, or listen to it, just Henry.' He crouched down and whispered in Henry's ear. Then he looked up at me and said: 'He's got a secret for me now.' The teacher made Henry whisper in Ethan's ear and whatever was said remains between Henry and Ethan.

(Field notes, Day 11)

A final conversation with Henry revealed how children understood their rights at kindergarten:

Liam and Eli (both 4 years) wanted to come up and see Henry together and they just giggled and said '[it is important to] be a friend' and then sat down together. Henry asked them if they would be his friend and Liam told him probably not. At that Luke and Paul (both 4 years) didn't think that they would be his friend either but Lance (4 years) told 'You aren't allowed to say it like that. You have to say it like, "I am busy doing this now and then maybe later . . ."'

(Field notes, Day 11)

Henry encouraged another level of engagement with the research questions about children's perceptions of rights. The risks here were that he became a novelty, and that could escalate his presence into an 'edutainment' type of exercise. However, Henry proved be 'a good friend' because his presence supported some children to express their perceptions of children's rights.

Books and posters

Other techniques used to support children to form a perspective on their rights in the kindergarten were books and posters. A book (Castle 2000) containing a collection of well-known children's illustrators' interpretations of various articles of the United Nations Convention on the Rights of the Child stimulated discussion. Reading to children was a natural part of everyday life in the kindergarten, and knowing this, the researcher placed the book on a shelf in the book corner before the session began. She then sat on the book corner couch, quietly waiting with Henry. Very quickly, a small group of children gathered next to her on the couch and were chatting to Henry when one of them noticed the new book. They then requested that she read to them with Henry. Because the book was not a story as such, both Henry and the children commented on the lack of usual story book words, and this offered the researcher another opportunity to invite children to participate in the research. The book was a 'research' book, with a purpose beyond telling a story and while some children may not have understood this without the researcher present, it was clear that those listening understood that it was:

> *Lulu*: This is Sarah's special book . . .
> *Liam*: Hey, hey, this is a new special book. It's got not much words?
> *Lulu*: Hey, Sharon (one of the teachers), Sarah's got a new book but it's pictures.
> *Sharon*: Where did you find that one? That looks perfect [for the research].
>
> (Field notes, Day 8)

The researcher turned the pages, and, in response to the children's reactions to the pictures, she, via Henry, either commented or asked open-ended questions to elicit what they thought about them, intentionally consulting them, and supporting them to form an opinion. Some pictures drew no comment, and others were clear favourites. Colour photocopies of the illustrations the children responded to the most were made into large, laminated posters and left in the book corner. The one reproduced in Figure 6.1 stimulated a great deal of conversation that was readily assimilated into the style of language used in the kindergarten:

> 'Are they friends?' they asked me. I said 'What do you think?' 'Yes.' they said. Henry came in at that point and asked about making a friend here. 'Well', said Lulu, 'you can be friends here, we'll be your friend.' 'Yes.' agreed Suzie, 'We'll be friends.' Henry added that he had a friend at his other kindy, but he was a bit shy here. By this time Paul had joined us . . . 'You have to say "Stop it I don't like it" and you have to learn about sharing all the things and books and trolleys and the things are for everyone here and you have to use your hands as tools and you have to be a good friend.' Paul had a great deal to say about friends and friendship.
>
> (Field notes, Day 8)

The conversation recorded here was prompted by one of the laminated posters. Throughout the field work phase of the research, children were observed referring

Figure 6.1 Example of a poster to stimulate conversation.

to the posters rather than the book, and conversations about their interpretations affirmed the kindergarten programme, and in terms of the research, focused the conversational prompts more closely on children's experiences of their rights and responsibilities in that particular context. This was largely due to the *Playing as a Good Friend* project. The characteristic principles of the *Playing as a Good Friend* project emerged as significant to the children's perceptions of themselves as rights holders, deserving of respect, and with responsibilities as citizens in the kindergarten.

Children's sense of well-being and belonging, knowing they have a place at kindergarten (both strands of *Te Whāriki*), was evident in the kindergarten community of learners where all the participants had rights and responsibilities. An example of children understanding respect for others is apparent in the next example, where a kindergarten rule, and a principle of *Playing as a Good Friend* were invoked. Phoebe, Conrad and Greg were playing with some electrical circuits. Conrad had made an electrical circuit work and Phoebe, annoyed by his success, not only refused to acknowledge it, but claimed it as her own and lashed out:

Phoebe leans over to Conrad and smacks him and pinches his hand. Conrad bursts into tears and nurses his hand. It has gone red. He is quite shocked.

> *Greg*: (To Phoebe) You don't smack. You aren't allowed to smack here. You need to say sorry and you need to tell him and look into his face and tell him.

Phoebe is very preoccupied with the alarm and fiddles self-consciously.

. . .

> *Greg*: It hurts if you hit, Phoebe, you need to say sorry and you don't hit.

Phoebe is determined to ignore both Greg and Conrad but Greg still persists with his line of argument.

> *Greg*: You shouldn't hit at kindy, eh? You need to say sorry at kindy, and you need to take turns too. You need to use your words.
> *Conrad*: Yes. You could have said 'Please' and not scratched and pinched my hand.
> *Greg*: Phoebe should tell him sorry.

Conrad nods.

> *Greg*: Yes.
> *Phoebe*: (Mumbles and fiddles with the alarm.) Sorry.
> *Greg*: Not like that – you need to look in his eyes and say sorry.

She does.

> *Conrad*: Thank you.

(Field notes, Day 7)

This upsetting incident was resolved with children, by children and for children. Arguably that could only happen in a facilitative environment which supported children's right to participate and as such is a descriptive account of how rights were enacted in the kindergarten case study. Due to the pervasiveness of the *Playing as a Good Friend* project, children accepted responsibility for not hurting one another and, consequently, nurtured an awareness of the rights of others.

As well, in this particular kindergarten, the teachers regularly produced their own books about key messages for the children. They used photographs of the children and their words to express messages, such as 'sharing at kindergarten' and 'being a good friend'. A combination of discussing the posters made from the book about rights, reading the books produced by the kindergarten, and discussing these with the children led to a shared understanding (Cullen 2004; Rogoff 2003) of the teachers' expectations about children's rights and responsibilities at kindergarten.

Conversational interviews with children

A very effective method of interviewing children was to participate as a newcomer alongside them in the daily routines and activities: 'Children, especially young children, acquire social knowledge through interaction with others as they construct meanings through a shared process' (Eder and Fingerson 2003: 35). Sitting alongside children was a deliberate strategy intended to establish a research relationship between children and the researcher, and to facilitate children's rights to participate in the research. This involved serious consideration of the children's status as regular participants in their centre, and the researcher's status as a visiting adult. Children in the kindergarten often expected all adults to arbitrate, to pro-vide solutions, and to understand the setting. Assuming the role of a naïve adult can give children a sense of empowerment: questions about their perceptions were usually regarded as genuine and generally answered conscientiously. 'Insight can also be gained from how children react to the researcher's role in their world' (Davis 1998: 330), as the following story illustrates:

> I was wondering why when I asked the groups of children 'What I could do at Kindergarten?' they came up with such sedentary and sedate options. I could paint, or do collage, or the book corner or dough. It was only after I prompted one group about the outside area ('What about the obstacle course?') that I realized they were thinking about what I, Sarah, was able to do. It was a good reality check – they saw me, quite rightly, as too big and too grown-up to play outside as they did.
>
> (Field notes, Day 12)

In context, conversations with children proved to be effective, and while inter-actions began from Day 1, conversational interviews did not take place until the final weeks of the field work. This allowed time for the participants to get to know the researcher. These were natural conversations in the field, with and without a tape recorder. In fact, the tape recorder was not successful for two reasons. First, the conversations tended to be with groups of children and the recorded sound was blurred by several voices talking at once, and, second, the microphone picked up a lot of extraneous noise beyond the immediate conversation. Despite the difficulties that this introduced for transcribing, the recorded comments were transcribed for analysis.

Children's recorded comments were played back to them at the time. Usually children requested that the recording be played several times, and this became a source of great amusement for those children. In more than one instance, a child chose to re-record what he or she had said, but this appeared to be more about gaining control of the tape recorder than it was about accurately reflecting their comments. A jointly constructed set of rules applied to using the tape recorder, and once they understood the machine's workings through a shared trial and error process, participants controlled the record button:

Erika: I know how, I know how.
Sally: I know, you push that one.
Thomas: No! No! You push them together.

There is some shoving going on here. The machine starts squealing as the play and rewind buttons are pressed together:

Alice: You need to have turns.
Thomas: That button goes it away [wipes the recording].
Sally: I know (she pushes the buttons too).
Sarah (researcher): We could have turns.
Erika: Yeah, we can. (She starts pushing all the buttons starting from the left)
   I can be next, eh?

(Field notes, Day 12)

Similar conversations were recorded sitting in the book corner of the kindergarten with Henry, the persona doll, looking at the posters. Both these research strategies enabled the researcher to prompt numerous conversations with children about their rights. Henry, rather than the researcher, facilitated children's participation, and his reactions and responses to both the posters and the conversations encouraged children to share their emerging perceptions of friendship and, at the same time, a sense of what it means to respect the rights of others. Children had their own views about friendship. Greg (four years) reflected on the nature of friendship in his conversation with Henry after the other children had left to eat morning tea:

Well, when you are a friend you have to be kind and care about it. That's about being a friend but, you know, you can have a feeling about friendship and friendships are about being kind and friendships have different feelings too. They are about being kind and you have to care about it too.

It was morning tea for the adults but Greg went off to find his friend, Lulu. As he left he said again how his friendships had 'different feelings' but he couldn't say much more than that.

(Field notes, Day 12)

Conclusion

This chapter has presented some data from a wider study investigating children's rights in early childhood settings. The theme of the chapter reflected the researcher's concern to facilitate children's rights to participate in the research, to listen to children's own perspectives of their rights in the kindergarten and to observe how participation rights were enacted in the kindergarten setting. Supported by a long-term *Playing as a Good Friend* project in the kindergarten, the strategies the researcher used enabled her to listen and observe children's experiences of their rights to participate in the kindergarten curriculum, and observe how the teachers and children developed a sense of citizenship within the context of that particular community. By using a persona doll, a book and posters, plus conversational interviews with children, the researcher included children in the research in ways that were meaningful to them. These research tools also created an awareness of what was important for the children. Clearly articulated expectations such as not hurting each other, playing as a good friend, and listening to one another, permeated all areas of the kindergarten. These three principles were observed to support children's participation rights in the kindergarten, and in the research, and at the same time, develop a respect for the rights of others.

Acknowledgements

First, I would like to thank the children, teachers and parents who participated in this research. I also wish to acknowledge the support of Associate Professor Dr Val Podmore and Dr Rob Strathdee from Victoria University of Wellington, New Zealand, and Emeritus Professor, Dr Anne Smith from Otago University. Finally, I wish to thank Margaret Bleasdale and Kirsten Prince for sharing the background information about the *Playing as a Good Friend* project.

Notes

1   The kindergarten case study was one of three used to investigate perceptions of children's rights in New Zealand early childhood settings (Te One 2008).
2   Henry was the name of the persona doll. Sarah, the researcher, spoke on his behalf.

References

Brown, B. (2001) *Combating Discrimination: Persona Dolls in Action*, Stoke on Trent: Trentham Books.

Carr, M. (2001) *Assessment in Early Childhood Settings: Learning Stories*, London: Paul Chapman.

Carr, M., Hatherly, A., Lee, W. and Ramsey, K. (2003) 'Te Whāriki and assessment: A case study of teacher change', in J. Nuttall (ed.), *Weaving Te Whāriki: Aotearoa New Zealand's Early Childhood Curriculum Document in Theory and Practice*, Wellington, NZ: NZCER, pp. 187–214.

Castle, C. (2000) *For Every Child*, London: Red Fox with UNICEF, Random House Children's Books.

Child Rights Information Network (2007) Convention on the Rights of the Child [Electronic Version]. *Children's Rights Information Network*, pp. 1–22. Available at: http://www.crin.org/docs/resources/treaties/uncrc.asp (accessed 25 June 2007).

Christensen, P. (2004) 'Children's participation in ethnographic research: Issues of power and representation', *Children and Society*, 18: 165–176.

Christensen, P. H. and James, A. (2008) 'Childhood diversity and commonality: Some methodological insights', in P. Christensen and A. James (eds), *Research with Children: Perspectives and Practices*, New York: Routledge, pp. 158–172.

Corsaro, W. A. and Molinari, L. (2000) 'Entering and observing in children's worlds: A reflection on a longitudinal ethnography of early education in Italy', in P. Christensen and A. James (eds), *Research with Children*, London: Falmer Press, pp. 179–200.

Cullen, J. (2004) 'Adults co-constructing professional knowledge', in A. Anning, J. Cullen and M. Fleer (eds), *Early Childhood Education: Society and Culture*, London: Sage, pp. 69–79.

Davis, J. M. (1998) 'Understanding the meanings of children: A reflexive process', *Children and Society*, 12: 325–335.

Derman-Sparks and the ABC Task Force (1989) *Anti-Bias Curriculum: Tools for Empowering Young Children*, Washington, DC: National Association for the Education of Young Children.

Eder, D. and Fingerson, L. (2003) 'Interviewing children and adolescents', in J. A. Holstein and J. F. Gubrium (eds), *Inside Interviewing: New Lenses, New Concerns*, Thousand Oaks: Sage, pp. 33–53.

Howe, B. and Covell, K. (2005) *Empowering Children: Children's Rights Education as a Pathway to Citizenship*, Toronto: University of Toronto Press.

Lansdown, G. (2005) *The Evolving Capacities of the Child*, Florence, Italy: UNICEF Innocenti Research Centre. Available at: http://www.bernardvanleer.org/files/crc/4%20Gerison_Lansdown.pdf (accessed 30 March 2009).

Lauren, P. G. (2003) *The Evolution of International Human Rights: Visions Seen*, 2nd edn, Philadelphia, PA: University of Pennsylvania Press.

Lundy, L. (2007) 'Voice is not enough: conceptualising Article 12 of the United Nations Convention on the Rights of the Child', *British Educational Research Journal*, 33(6): 927–942.

May, H. and Carr, M. (2000) 'Empowering children to learn and grow: Te Whariki, the New Zealand early childhood national curriculum', in J. Hayden (ed.), *Landscapes in Early Childhood Education: Cross-National Perspectives on Empowerment: A Guide for the New Millennium*, New York: Peter Lang, pp. 153–169.

Ministry of Education (1996) *Te Whāriki. He whāriki mātauranga mō ngā mokopuna o Aotearoa: Early Childhood Curriculum*, Wellington, NZ: Learning Media.

Ministry of Education (2005) *Kei tua o te pae/Assessment for Learning: Early Childhood Exemplars*, Wellington, NZ: Learning Media.

Moss, P. (2006) 'Listening to young children: Beyond rights to ethics', in Learning and Teaching Scotland, *Let's Talk about Listening to Children: Towards a Shared Understanding for Early Years Education in Scotland*, Vol. 2, Edinburgh: Learning and Teaching Scotland.

Neale, B. (2004) 'Introduction: Young children's citizenship', in B. Neale (ed.), *Young Children's Citizenship: Ideas into Practice*, York: The Joseph Rowntree Foundation, pp. 6–18.

Rogoff, B. (1998) 'Cognition as a collaborative process', in D. Kuhn and S. D. Siegler (eds), *Handbook of Child Psychology*, Vol. 2: *Cognition, Perception, and Language*, 5th edn, New York: John Wiley & Sons, Ltd, pp. 679–744.

Rogoff, B. (2003) *The Cultural Nature of Human Development*, Oxford: Oxford University Press.

Smith, A. B. (2007a) 'Children's rights and early childhood education: Links to theory and advocacy', *Australian Journal of Early Childhood*, 32(3): 1–8.

Smith, A. B. (2007b) 'Children and young people's participation rights in education', *International Journal of Children's Rights*, 15: 147–164.

Te One, S. (2003) '*Te Whāriki*: Contemporary issues of influence', in J. Nuttall (ed.), *Weaving Te Whāriki: Aotearoa New Zealand's Early Childhood Curriculum Document in Theory and in Practice*, Wellington, NZ: New Zealand Council for Educational Research Press, pp. 17–49.

Te One, S. (2007) 'Participatory-research methods with young children: Experiences from the field', *Early Childhood Folio*, 11: 21–25.

Te One, S. (2008) 'Perceptions of children's rights in three early childhood settings', unpublished PhD thesis, Victoria University of Wellington, NZ.

Chapter 7

Children's voices in early childhood settings' everyday concerts

Hartmut Kupfer

Exploring what young children say is not possible without taking into account what young children hear. Within a child's voice, many different sounds and voices might be found: those deriving from certain places, situations or actions and those connected to other people as talking individuals. In this chapter, some examples from early childhood settings are analyzed in order to develop a framework for understanding dialogical structures in young children's utterances. The notion of dialogue used here stands not only for the children's interpersonal relations, but also their connectedness with the places and things of their everyday lives. It is shown how *voices of others*, *voices of place(s)* and *voices of game(s)* may contribute to what we experience when listening to young children.

Introduction

In this chapter, I explore the notion of child's voice in the context of children's participation in the everyday events of their early childhood settings. As I work in an organization running several childcare centers in Berlin, Germany, my point of view is that of an educational practitioner trying to connect experiences from working with children and teachers with sociocultural educational theory. From my perspective, language development is closely connected with the emergence of *children's voices* as they develop in interaction and as they may grow and become powerful, or may. In particular, I am interested in the crucial processes through which children become authentic, strong and self-reliant speakers.

Five examples will be discussed in order to show important aspects of children's voices. The first two arise from the use of learning stories as an assessment approach in early childhood settings. I have been inspired by New Zealand early childhood teachers to explore the possibilities of narrative assessment. Consequently, the first example is taken from a New Zealand publication about working with learning stories (Hatherly and Sands 2002). The second comes from a project about implementing learning stories in German early childhood settings. Examples three and five come from my work with children and teachers in early childhood settings in Berlin. They were collected in the context of different language games in order to study the developing skills of immigrant children learning to speak German as their second language. Example four is taken from one of Vivian Paley's books, representing the inexhaustible treasure of children's (and other) voices collected by her (Paley 1995).

The power of children's voices

When analyzing communication processes in early childhood settings, I find it useful to begin with some ideas from a framework developed by E. Goffman. Quite diverse forms of interactions occur in early childhood settings, including diverse forms of talk (Goffman 1981). It is not often during the day that the people gathered in one room are included in a single communication process such as a single discussion actively involving all of them. More likely, there will be several simultaneous exchanges or encounters. This means that, for everyone involved, there are a lot of different possibilities including active participation, watching others and listening in to talk that is addressed to someone else. However, it is not often that these possibilities are freely accessible to each individual. They are often a result of processes of inclusion and exclusion, and of enforced engagement and disengagement, sometimes caused by social and/or physical constraints.

The result of all this is a diversity of participation formats, with many degrees of involvement, accompanied by many different affective characteristics such as joy, curiosity, satisfaction, boredom, anger or despair. Listening to children's voices is one of teachers' most important strategies (if not the most important) for recognizing what is happening for children. Besides posture, gesture and gaze, it is voice that gives access to children's feelings about themselves and about their environments. More than gaze, gesture and posture, voice is a medium that aims to make sense by not only expressing feelings but also giving value to them, and facilitating the exploration of the meaning of events from different perspectives. Donaldson (1992) discusses these questions in terms of difference and the complex relations between value judgements and value feelings. Nelson ([1989] 2006: 62) analyzes 'the transformation from nonverbal to verbal representation' and Dunn (1988) shows that children's responsivity to the feeling states of others plays a central part in their developing social understanding. Recent discussions about mentalization (e.g. Fonagy et al. 2002) have taken up the subject.

Early childhood curricula and programs have to make sense of these diverse participation formats. Learning in early childhood settings is only sometimes related to the existence of one single focus of attention shared by all participants in a social situation. This is usually intended in the language games of traditional instruction (Wertsch 1991). It can also be seen on occasions when a single event catches everyone's attention. Everyday experience tells us how fragile these moments of commonly shared attention can be. Young children will soon change their attention to watch another object, take another toy, address their neighbors verbally or non-verbally, express something that is disconnected with the commonly focused notion. However, if one's focus of attention was not shared with others, nobody would have a chance to join a social encounter or build meaningful relations with others, and learning processes would be restricted to individual learning by doing. At least from a Vygotskian point of view (Vygotsky 1978), this would make learning nearly impossible.

Voice is a basic means for directing others' attention in a social situation and establishing an encounter (Goffman 1981). From the first moments in life, a child's voice is recognized as an important attribute of a living being that informs others about where the child is – physically and mentally – and how she/he feels. From these very first utterances, a child's voice is not only a contribution to a dyadic dialogue, but a powerful event, sometimes able to be heard throughout the whole neighborhood. When one conceptualizes children's voices, not only their contributions to a given communicative setting have to be taken into account, but also their power to go beyond the limits of this situation, to send their signal to whoever will hear it. Children's voices often have the power to make people beyond the intended audience into unintended hearers.

Children's voices also have the ability to take up, sometimes even echo, other sounds and other voices:

> The word in language is half someone else's. It becomes 'one's own' only when the speaker populates it with his own intention, his own accent, when he appropriates the word, adapting it to his own semantic and expressive intention. Prior to this moment of appropriation, the word does not exist in a neutral and impersonal language (it is not, after all, out of a dictionary that the speaker gets his words!), but rather it exists in other people's mouths, in other people's concrete contexts, serving other people's intentions: it is from there that one must take the word, and make it one's own.
>
> (Bakhtin 1981, cited in Wertsch 1991: 59)

Children will try to make use of others' words, not only in situations where adults may find such use appropriate or funny, but also beyond. (Parents can tell a lot of stories about this.) Consequently, children's voices have to be regarded as means of transgressing established social situations. They can be seen as a kind of mirror that can show their partners in interaction much about themselves, provided they are willing and able to listen. So, if on one hand, children's voices are a power that has to be socialized, on the other, they can be regarded as a socializing power themselves, by producing a 'surplus' of meaning that may bring new and unexpected content into interaction routines or may open up these routines by involving outsiders.

Rogoff (2003: 78) argues in a similar way by proposing a dynamic framework to analyze cultural participation and cultural change.

> Instead of using a categorical approach to thinking about culture, I prefer to focus on people's involvement in their communities, to address the dynamic,

generative nature of both individual lives and community practices. With cultural participation as the focus, the question for examining an individual's cultural involvement becomes – What cultural practices are familiar to you? What cultural practices have you made use of?

In this chapter, I will investigate children's voices by using the dynamic approach outlined above, instead of using a rather static framework that regards children as disadvantaged, oppressed or 'silenced' (Pascal and Bertram 2009: 253). Instead of promoting special educational methods or programs to enhance children's involvement, I will focus on children's involvement in the cultural practices of their settings. In particular, I shall seek answers to questions such as: what are children's voices like? When a child is speaking, what other voices are involved? Do adults even notice when children contribute to the process of enriching and changing cultural procedures? I shall examine examples from early childhood settings in order to illustrate the many different ways in which children participate in social situations by speaking and listening.

Children appropriating others' voices

Consider the following example:

Example (1): A learning story from New Zealand

> I turned ready to free Lys from her clothing but was met by a serious attempt to remove her sweatshirt herself. Without any thought I began to aid Lys by shifting the bottom edge for her. Lys stopped, looked straight at me, making sure I was going to listen and stated boldly, 'No, Lys.' Of course I stopped immediately and was truly embarrassed by having doubted Lys's abilities. 'Sorry, Lys,' I apologised . . . She was working steadily on freeing her left arm. Her elbows had become entangled in the folds of the material, her face serious as she persisted in her struggles. My hands trembled . . . itching to help, but Lys had warned me, she could do it. I watched in awe as her gutsy persistence paid off.
>
> (Hatherly and Sands 2002: 12)

In this story an early childhood teacher tells about an event that happens often. It is about a girl who wants to achieve something and therefore uses her voice. The way her teacher reacts shows that she is successful – her intentions are noticed, recognized and responded to with respect for her autonomy (Carr 2001). In this event, Lys is not only fulfilling other's expectations, but she herself is constructing the situation in which she learns – and her voice plays the crucial part. Lys speaks out proudly, using words and attitudes that she often takes up when others speak, such as a self-confident 'No!' as well as the word through which she is addressed by other speakers: her own name. Lys is not only speaking: she makes sure that she is listened to. The story tells us about her stopping her activity and gazing at the teacher, reminding us that voice is not only *what* is said (the words), but also that intonation, gaze, gesture and posture have to be taken into account. This example can teach us about the importance of *appropriating others' voices* in order to achieve something by speaking.

The following example shows a similar situation, but in this event the child does not achieve her aim through speaking.

Example (2): A learning story from Germany

> Lilly, Samantha, Laurence, and Caroline are sitting at the kindergarten breakfast table. Lilly gets herself a slice of bread and puts plum butter onto it. Having eaten it quickly she looks around to see what she would like next. Lilly watches Samantha taking her second dish of muesli. The muesli bowl is at the opposite side of the table.
>
> 'I WANT MUESLI', Lilly says loudly.
>
> No child responds.
>
> Lilly waits . . . Lilly keeps waiting . . . Lilly still keeps waiting . . .
>
> Samantha doesn't wait. She takes the bowl, gets herself another portion and puts the bowl back to the other end of the table. After a long time Lilly jumps up and bends forward, her chair falling over. She takes the bowl and finally has got what she wanted.

In this episode, the most interesting thing perhaps is not what Lilly is doing, but what she is *not* doing. After having experienced that her utterance 'I want muesli' is ignored by the other girls, Lilly does not make another effort trying to direct an utterance to someone in particular, or to make use of any means to 'upgrade' her first utterance. Finally Lilly is successful as she gets her bowl filled with muesli, but she is not successful in getting a response from the other girls at the table.

Lilly's voice does not get into connection with others, it remains alone. This reminds us that the notion of *appropriating others' voices*: taking words and utterances 'from other people's mouths' (Bakhtin 1981, cited in Wertsch 1991: 59), may be strongly connected with the dynamics of inclusion and exclusion in social situations (see also Example (4)). We cannot tell just from a single example, but there might exist a connection between the utterances Lilly has in her 'language tool kit' (Wertsch 1991: 103) and her relations with Samantha, Laurence and Caroline. In this respect, it would have been interesting to know about these girls' responses to the way Lilly resolved her problem.

Children appropriating voices of place

Lilly's words are surely also 'half someone else's' (Bakhtin 1981, cited in Wertsch 1991: 59), in the sense that she is just beginning to put her own intentions clearly into the words she uses. However, her voice does not really move her addressees to a response. Therefore, it might have been helpful for her to draw on a routine or a script for a breakfast situation (in which, for example, everyone is obliged to respond to another's request to pass over objects that are out of reach). In other words, for any speaker it may be necessary not only to construct a meaningful utterance in order to enter into a dialogue (by appropriating *others' voices*), but also to speak with authority, to claim one's rights, to express by voice (either explicitly or implicitly) that the subject in question is not only a personal matter but it is also about how things should be handled in 'situations like this'. The following example shows clearly what it means to appropriate what I would like to call *voice of place*.

Example (3): A letter to a friend

Mustafa is a five-year-old boy from a Turkish immigrant family. In a 'book making' activity he decided to make a letter to Karl, another boy who had visited his group of five-year olds in a German kindergarten some days before. Within about 15 minutes he had drawn eight pictures, one on every side of the little book, and an adult wrote down his comments for each picture. Figure 7.1 shows four of the pictures and accompanying comments.

What is most striking is that the whole book is about rules: 'You may do this, you may not do that, you are allowed to do this only in case of . . .' and so on. Mustafa's voice hereby appropriates a *voice of place* to a degree that leaves almost no room for personal expression. But a second look shows that Mustafa's voice is clearly addressed to Karl (using third person, not second) so he is not only just retelling a place's rules. His drawings and his comments must be seen in the context of the specifically structured encounter that is very different from the encounters in the preceding examples. Mustafa does not refer to the rules of his place because he wants to claim his right, to get something done or to solve a conflict. When he is sitting in front of the blank pages, there is no special script to be realized; there are no others' voices to draw on in order to achieve something. He is exploring a new cultural practice, making a book, starting with the medium, not with content, and in order to cope with this challenge, he makes use of a well-known cultural practice of his place: teachers and children are used to negotiating what people should or should not do, drawing and writing down rules and fixing them on the wall. In this situation, he combined this format with another well-known format: writing a letter to someone who is absent.

The adult who is listening and writing down what Mustafa says has a special function in this encounter, being recipient and producer at the same time. As he writes down what Mustafa tells him, he is a kind of a mirror, and at the same time

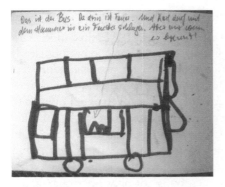

1: This is the Bus. There's fire inside. And Karl may crash a window with the hammer. But only if there is fire.

2: When there was fire, the fire brigade has come, and then Karl may come out of the fire door.

3: Karl must ask the workers if he may pass there under the site.

4: Karl may only jump onto a (one) boat all the week. He may jump into the water if he doesn't see a fish.

Figure 7.1 Karl's book.

he transforms Mustafa's utterances into a form in which they can be transmitted to the addressee, the absent friend Karl.

Voices of place are by no means confined to verbal expressions of rules and routines, as the example might suggest. In a much broader sense, they may include all the characteristic sounds that usually appear in the place, connected with other perceptions, maybe smell, visual impressions or experience of movements. We know that the distinctions that are made by adults between things and living beings as well as between human and other living beings are not so clear for young children. Therefore, children's experiences of voices speaking to them as *voices of place* may be different from adults' experiences of such voices. However, for both children and adults, experiencing and appropriating *voices of place* may have not only social, but also physical and even spiritual dimensions.

It would be interesting to discuss Example (3) from the perspective of the Bakhtinian notion of authoritative discourse as opposed to internally persuasive discourse (Wertsch 1991). In authoritative discourse there exists just a single meaning that can be accepted or rejected by the addressee; such a communication process is not open to negotiation of meanings. According to Bakhtin: '[A]uthoritative discourse cannot be represented – it is only transmitted' (1981, cited in Wertsch 1991: 79). Example (3) shows how this idea might be questioned: Members of a community might develop a sense of belonging that may lead them not only to transmit but represent their place's voices, especially when communicating from an insider position with an outsider (for further discussion of the importance of insider–outsider communication, see Rogoff 2003).

Developing a sense of belonging may be a crucial factor for children's appropriation of persons' and places' voices. This probably begins with hearing and responding to parents' voices. To start, these voices (at least mothers' voices) might be heard as voices of place rather than voices of another person. Later, when children develop a sense of belonging to individual partners and to places like their everyday environment in the family or in their kindergarten, they will explore and respond to events around them, appropriating different sounds and voices involved.

If children's sense of belonging to a place is not strong enough, their voices will not be heard so proudly and self-confidently as in Example (1). Consider another example:

Example (4): 'It didn't belong here'

In one of Vivian G. Paley's books (1995) there is a conversation between the author and a young woman, Sonya, a former pupil in her group. She asks Sonya why, as a child, she had never told the group about Kwanzaa, an African American holiday celebrated in her family:

> 'But, Sonya, why has it been such a secret? I just discovered Kwanzaa last week.'
>
> Sonya stands over me, her brows arched, her head held high . . .
>
> 'Because never once,' she measures out each word, 'did any of you teachers mention Kwanzaa. It was in the newspapers but you were not the least bit curious. We knew we'd sound ridiculous if we talked about it.'
>
> 'Why ridiculous?'
>
> 'It was too *black*, too African sounding, too pushy. It didn't belong here, which meant *we* didn't belong here. But no one said stuff like that then.'
>
> (Paley 1995: 6)

This dialogue again shows the features of *other's voices* and *voices of place* discussed above.

Children appropriating voices of game

Examples (1) to (4) demonstrate that the Bakhtinian notion of dialogicity, people talking by taking their words from other speakers and making them their own, manifests itself in different ways: there is a difference between speaking with *other's voice*, taking other persons' words into one's own utterances, and speaking with *voice of place*, taking up verbal constructions that are more than just another person's utterances, expressing the way things are (or should be) in this place. Up to now the discussion has been about children appropriating their environment's voices as they hear them. However, with this notion we have not yet reached the core of human voices' potential.

Children's voices surely can be heard not only as an echo of their partners and circumstances, but as a means of exploring who they could be, as a means of constructing identities, thus going beyond what they are hearing. In play, children not only take others' voices into their repertoire, but they also transform these voices, play with them, and explore the relations between them.

Example (3), originally introduced to illustrate the notion of *voice of place*, shows that Mustafa is not just telling Karl what are important rules in his environment. He takes Karl on a trip around his world, visiting a bus, a construction site, a boat and some other places not shown in Figure 7.1. Maybe the sequential format of the little book's empty pages leads him to this game where he is the one who decides where to go next. We feel that his statement: 'He may jump into the water if he doesn't see a fish' not only informs about how things are in this place, but also invites further negotiations: what if you don't see a fish, but there is a shark nearby?

Imagine, on the other hand, that at the same time as Lilly (in Example (2)) is pouring muesli into her bowl, one of the other girls tells her: 'Don't take too much, leave enough for others!' or the teacher says: 'Feel free to help yourself, we have got enough for all!' These utterances may be heard by Lilly as *voices of place*, providing an evaluative frame for her next action sequence, but not opening up the situation to an exploration of rules and relationships.

These examples show that it is not always clear what *voice of place* or *others' voices* mean in a certain situation – this can be subject to exploration by the participants of the conversation themselves. Using the provisional notion of *appropriating voices of game*, I shall now try to describe the possibilities of appropriating other voices by negotiating their meanings in cultural contexts.

Consider the following example:

Example (5): 'Badger needs Good Advice'

The children in this example are used to meeting a little toy animal, a badger, at some events. Before and after these events sometimes letters are exchanged. In his recent letter, Badger (B.) tells the children about how his friend Hedgehog (He.) accidently hurt Squirrel (Sq.). Sq. took away He.'s food and climbed up the tree into her nest. B. finally asks the children for ideas about a solution to this situation.

Several groups of children responded to the letter, and they did it in different ways. There were children focusing on He.'s lack of food, developing ideas to visit He. and bring some apples. Other children started to think about how an agreement between He. and Sq. could be achieved. One of these answer letters contained the following ideas:

> *Hassan*: Bird can tell Sq. that He. wants to apologize, Sq. will come down.
>
> *Mohamed*: He. can ask Cat whether he wants to climb up the tree to give a letter to Sq.
>
> *Jessica*: He. gets a present for Sq. and puts it under the tree. Then Sq. will come down.
>
> *Fatma*: The man can lift He. up and He. can apologize.
>
> *Paula*: He. tells Sq.: I will get you some food, come down.

The answer letter shows children's voices joining into what I would call *voice of game*. Although there are different individuals' ideas there is something like a common story line connecting these ideas. The children from this group join into the story told to them in the letter, and they accept its fictional character. In their individual contributions they draw on cultural properties of their environment and cultural practices of which they have made use (Rogoff 2003) such as giving presents, apologizing, sending messages. These practices are not used just when it seems appropriate to do so. They are actively represented as possibilities for action, often marked by modal verb constructions. In this context children's voices are not only agents in a given situation, but also explore different possibilities for how the story *could* continue, what a solution *could* be like. They are involved in processes of 'culture making' as Bruner (1986. 127) has suggested:

> To the extent that the materials of education are chosen for their amenableness to imaginative transformation and are presented in a light to invite negotiation and speculation, to that extent education becomes a part of what I earlier called 'culture making'.

The collaborative character of children's individual utterances taking up and contributing to a common *voice of game* appears very clearly in the content of the proposals. Sometimes new ideas enter into the story line, sometimes already existing solutions are modified. In this discourse the children usually do not explicitly refer to their antecedents, although without them, much of the meaning is lost. For instance, Paula's idea involving He. directly speaking to Sq. makes no sense without taking into account Fatma's preceding idea (He. being lifted up to Sq.'s nest). But Paula does not feel a necessity to mention Fatma's idea. Other contributions may repeat their antecedents, just fitting another subject into a 'slot' in the sentence: a bird that brings a letter may be changed by a following speaker into a cat.

Final remarks

The investigation of children's voices starting with the Bakhtinian idea of dialogicity has led to the result that a child speaking is like a musician directing a
whole orchestra rather than playing a single instrument. In this orchestra there
were to be found:

- *Voices of other(s)*: utterances children take from other people's mouths, used
  by children in order to act meaningfully in relation to other persons;
- *Voices of place(s)*: utterances (and other sounds) that represent how things are
  (or should be) in a certain place, used by children in order to connect their
  voices with some deeper understanding of the place;
- *Voices of game(s)*: utterances that construct or contribute to cultural contexts
  in which the former two kinds of voices can be negotiated, explored and
  maybe even transformed.

I am convinced that these three notions represent an appropriate answer to the
question *When a child is speaking, what other voices are involved?*

However, it is also clear that this analysis is preliminary and incomplete. It
demands complementary perspectives to be applied. First, a question has to be
raised about the individual child's capacity to appropriate others' voices. Is this
capacity, in principle, unlimited, or are there constraints that can be described on
a systematic level? While such a discussion is beyond the scope of this chapter, one
fruitful line of inquiry might be to examine links between 'voice' and 'face' (in
Goffman's sense): others' voices that cannot be appropriated will in some way
challenge or threaten a child's face and lead to special reactions, not only in voice,
but in the child's entire physical existence. Example (2) (the girls at the breakfast
table) could be read in this way – if we allow that the denial of a response
constitutes a reaction. We should always keep in mind that voices cannot exist in
a vacuum but are deeply connected with gaze, gesture and posture of bodies, and,
therefore, we do not know very much about the girls at the breakfast table when
we are only told what they *said*. Human beings' concerts involve all levels of
interaction and communication. Even the possibilities of going away, leaving or
interrupting a threatening encounter should be basic rights for everyone.

Second, the processes through which children's voices are appropriated by their
partners-in-interaction need further explanation. Questions might include how
they themselves are listened to and how their voices made others' voices, voices
of place or voices of game. For instance, in Examples (3) and (5), there are adults
carefully listening and writing down children's ideas in order to bring them into
the form of a written text that can be transmitted as a letter. These collaborative
formats surely have an effect on how the children experience themselves as
speakers. Example (4) clearly shows a situation where a child's voice has no chance
of entering into the setting's concert.

Third, it seems that the power of children's voices to go beyond a given
encounter – stressed in the introduction to this chapter – is rarely found in

descriptions of interactions in early childhood settings. The reason for this may be that there is a strong tendency to close up communicative situations, construct limited encounters, and even silence voices that may otherwise disturb the talk or play of others. However, there are some child-initiated encounters or encounters caused by a child's voice in early childhood settings. In Example (3), it was Mustafa who initiated the letter exchanging activity, a process that, however, needed some adult's scaffolding.

Finally, one of the most exciting ways of interplay among children's and adult's voices, their 'concerts' in portfolios and learning stories, was not included into the above discussions. These collaborative processes are another important subject for further examination. The concept of sociocultural assessment developed by Margaret Carr and her colleagues in New Zealand (Carr 2001; Cowie and Carr 2004) includes the idea of bringing together teachers', parents' and children's voices in a concert of dialogical meaning making. As children's voices are taken into adults' negotiations in children's environments, the new cultural tools of 'documenting' create new possibilities for how children's voices can be heard across the whole neighborhood, thus illustrating 'the dynamic, generative nature of both individual lives and community practices' (Rogoff 2003: 78).

Acknowledgements

I would like to thank colleagues from the EECERA Children's Perspectives Special Interest Group for giving me the chance to contribute to this book, and especially Bob Perry from Charles Sturt University, Australia, for his helpful comments and assistance in completing this chapter.

References

Bruner, J. (1986) 'The language of education', in J. Bruner, *Actual Minds, Possible Worlds*, Cambridge, MA: Harvard University Press, pp. 121–133.

Carr, M. (2001) *Assessment in Early Childhood Settings: Learning Stories*, London: Paul Chapman.

Cowie, B. and Carr, M. (2004) 'The consequences of socio-cultural assessment', in A. Anning, J. Cullen and M. Fleer (eds), *Early Childhood Education: Society and Culture*, London: SAGE Publications, pp. 95–106.

Donaldson, M. (1992) *Human Minds: An Exploration*, London: Penguin.

Dunn, J. (1988) *The Beginnings of Social Understanding*, Cambridge, MA: Harvard University Press.

Fonagy, P., Gergely, G., Jurist, E. L. and Target, M. (2002) *Affect Regulation, Mentalization, and the Development of the Self*, New York: Other Press.

Goffman, E. (1981) 'Footing', in E. Goffman, *Forms of Talk*, Philadelphia, PA: University of Pennsylvania Press, pp. 124–159.

Hatherly, A. and Sands, L. (2002) 'So what is different about learning stories?', *The First Years. Nga Tau Tuatahi. New Zealand Journal of Infant and Toddler Education*, 4(1): 8–12.

Nelson, K. ([1989] 2006) 'Monologue as representation of real-life experience', in K. Nelson (ed.), *Narratives from the Crib*, Cambridge, MA: Harvard University Press, pp. 284–308.

Paley, V. G. (1995) *Kwanzaa and Me: A Teacher's Story*, Cambridge, MA: Harvard University Press.

Pascal, C. and Bertram, T. (2009) 'Listening to young citizens. The struggle to make real a participatory paradigm in research with young children', *European Early Childhood Education Research Journal*, 17(2): 249–262.

Rogoff, B. (2003) *The Cultural Nature of Human Development*, Oxford: Oxford University Press.

Vygotsky, L. S. (1978) 'Tool and symbol in child development', in L. S. Vygotsky, M. Cole, V. John-Steiner, S. Scibner, and E. Souberman (eds), *Mind in Society: The Development of Higher Psychological Processes*, Cambridge, MA: Harvard University Press, pp. 19–30.

Wertsch, J. V. (1991) *Voices of the Mind: A Sociocultural Approach to Mediated Action*, Cambridge, MA: Harvard University Press.

Chapter 8

Researching infants' experiences of early childhood education and care

Jennifer Sumsion, Linda Harrison, Frances Press, Sharynne McLeod, Joy Goodfellow and Ben Bradley

This chapter reports on an Australian study that set out to investigate and illuminate what life is like for infants in early childhood education and care settings, as far as possible from the perspective of the infants themselves. We begin by describing the project. We then identify some of the many methodological and technical challenges encountered in the early phases and ethical issues that have arisen in our efforts to address them. In particular, we reflect on our use of 'baby cam', a micro video camera system comprising a video camera and sound recording equipment worn by an infant. Drawing on an adaptation of Shier's (2001) pathways to participation model for conceptualizing and enhancing children's participation in decision-making, we consider to what extent we can legitimately claim to be making progress in establishing participatory ways of researching with infants.

Introduction

In many industrialised countries, global competition, intensifying productivity agendas, labour market policies, and feminism have led to increasing demand for formal non-parental care of children younger than two years of age (OECD 2007). By age two, 48 percent of Australian children use some form of formal early years' services such as centre-based long day care, family day care, or a combination of both (Australian Bureau of Statistics 2008). Yet non-parental care for children aged younger than two, particularly the use of formal centre-based care, remains a contentious issue and the focus of considerable debate. Very rarely, however, are these debates informed by the views of the young children who experience these early years settings. Indeed, there are few reports in the research literature about infants' views of their experience of early childhood services. The United Nations Convention on the Rights of the Child (United Nations 1989), however, establishes children's rights to have their perspectives considered in matters that affect them. A key premise underpinning the research project reported in this chapter is that an understanding of the perspectives of those who experience early childhood services – especially the infants themselves – has much to offer policy debates and decision-making about non-parental care for infants, as well as professional practice with infants in early years' settings.

The *Infants' Lives in Childcare* project, undertaken by the authors of this chapter, has two primary aims. First, we aim to address the paucity of attention to infants' experience of early childhood education and care from the perspectives of infants themselves. Second, through our focus on infants who have not yet acquired the language skills to readily communicate their experiences verbally, we are also seeking to contribute new insights to the corpus of literature about researching with young children in participatory and inclusive ways. As Clark, McQuail and Moss (2003) point out, participatory research can mean children actively engaging with research activities; but in a broader sense, it can also entail their involvement in decision-making about the research. In both interpretations, developing skills in listening respectfully and actively to children to better 'recognize the many ways in which children skilfully communicate their realities to us' (Pascal and Bertram 2009: 254) is considered central. Yet with notable exceptions (e.g., Dalli 2000; Degotardi 2009; Elfer 1996; Karlsson 2007; Thyssen 2000; White 2009), there has been relatively little attention to theoretical, methodological and ethical issues associated with endeavouring to work in participatory ways with infants in research contexts to better understand their perspectives. Participatory research with infants is a recent focus for our research group and the *Infants' Lives in Childcare* project requires our sustained attention to the complex issues involved.

The chapter comprises two sections. In the first section, we describe the project. In the second section, we identify and reflect on some of the many methodological and technical challenges we are encountering in the early phases of the project, and some of the ethical issues that have arisen in our efforts to address them.

The *Infants' Lives in Childcare* project

In setting out to investigate and illuminate infants' lived experience of early years' settings, our aim is to understand what life is like for infants in long day care and family day care in Australia, as far as possible from the perspectives of the infants themselves. By 'infants', we mean children aged from birth to 18 months, a time of life in which they are not usually able to articulate their experiences readily through words. By 'lived experience', we are referring to infants making meaning of 'what is going on around and "within" them; a process that mixes memory, desire, anticipation, relations with others, cultural patterns, bodily feelings, sights, smells and sounds' (Bradley 2005: 7–8). Lived experience is also an inter-personal phenomenon; it both shapes and is shaped by families, carers and other children. In an ontological sense, we are interested in infants' experiences as ways of being within the social, cultural and physical spaces of their early years' environments.

In keeping with our intent of taking a participatory approach to researching with infants, we bring to the project a commitment to recognising and valuing infants as competent social agents, co-constructors of and active participants in their social worlds, and capable of conveying their experiences. We are mindful, for example, of their capacities to communicate their emotional states and to regulate their emotional environment through vocalisations, gaze, facial expression, eye contact, body language and gesturing (Cole, Martin and Dennis 2004). We are acutely aware, however, that if we are to be fully receptive to infants' communications, including their communications with us about their involvement in the research process, we need to further develop our capacities to become deeply attuned to infants. Attuning respectfully to infants requires us to acknowledge, with considerable humility, the impossibility of conclusively knowing their experiences and thus the need for tentative interpretations.

Humility entails for us, in part, relinquishing the certainty that can arise when working with a single theoretical perspective, or relying only on our accustomed and preferred theoretical perspectives. Humility also involves resisting our habitual reliance on researcher-mediated frames and researcher-only interpretations, and creating spaces for collaborative exploration, dialogue, and multiple perspectives, including those of the infants with whom we are seeking to collaborate. It means, as well, recognising the inherent complexity of early years' contexts, the value of multiple perspectives in generating new insights into the complex phenomena of infants' experiences in early years settings, and the limits of our abilities to fully comprehend and represent those experiences.

Accordingly, we use the Mosaic methodology, derived from the Mosaic approach (Clark, 2005; Clark and Moss 2001) to piece together fine-grained details of infants' experiences, generated from multiple sources of data and interpreted from multiple perspectives, to form what we hope will be a comprehensive picture of their lives in early years' settings. Like Pascal and Bertram (2009: 254), we see the perspectives of parents, children, practitioners and researchers as 'not in competition but standing together in the construction of dialogues, in which there is mutual respect, active participation and the negotiation and co-construction of meaning'. For this reason, our focus is on joint exploration with carers, parents, older children where feasible, and, wherever possible, the infants themselves to open up investigative spaces not otherwise available.

Our intent retains the strong philosophical and ethical commitment of the Mosaic approach to recognising that infants have valuable perspectives to contribute about their lives. At the same time, we extend the Mosaic approach by drawing on a rich diversity of theoretical perspectives in recognition that, kaleidoscope-like, each perspective can enable different and valuable insights. To us, however, the Mosaic methodology involves far more than using an array of methods and analytical or interpretive frames; rather it involves actively fostering productive dialogue across theoretical traditions. We see this theoretical eclecticism and the dialogue that it generates as a distinguishing and exciting methodological feature of the *Infants' Lives in Childcare* project. Before expanding a little further on how this works in practice, we briefly outline the project design.

Project design

The project involves a series of Australian case studies of infants in family day care homes across four family day care schemes and in four long day care centres operated by a large not-for-profit organisation. The aim of the case studies is to provide a rich picture of infants as social actors within a group. In each setting, three layers of data will be generated in consultation with carers, parents, and, as far as possible, infants and older children in the setting.

The first layer of data consists of digital video footage, digital photography, observations, and field notes, time use diaries and vocabulary records. Our emphasis is on data that can provide multiple perspectives on infants' sense of well-being, belonging, and scope for agency; engagement in experiences that support their learning and development; interactions and relationships with carers, parents, peers, other children, and with the environment. In each early years' setting, we plan to invite carers, parents, older children, and where possible, infants to share their perspectives on the data, particularly through their reflections on edited videos compiled by the researchers from key, illustrative moments in video footage.

The second layer of data encompasses contextual information relevant to the family day care schemes and the long day care centers, while the third layer pertains to the external childcare policy context that has potential to effect infants' experiences. Figure 8.1 represents the mosaic that we anticipate being able to piece together about infants' experiences of early years' settings from the data sources obtained from the three layers of data. At the time of writing this chapter, data generation has commenced in one family day care home with two participating infants: Charlie aged 14 months and Bianca aged 17 months (pseudonyms).

This chapter focuses on the methodology and methods pertaining to the first layer of data and more specifically, on issues related to the use of an innovative micro video camera system that we are colloquially terming 'baby cam'.

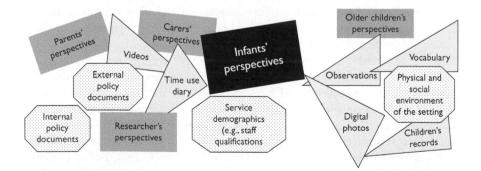

Figure 8.1 Mosaic for understanding infants' experiences: sources, contexts, and perspectives.

Theoretical eclecticism

We are actively seeking to promote dialogue between diverse theoretical approaches by making use of multiple interpretative frames from diverse knowledge bases to dislodge us from the certainties of our habitual reference points and enable greater analytic richness than would have been possible otherwise. Our eclectic set of lenses, drawn from our various theoretical and methodological expertise, includes, but is not limited to, those that have informed some of our research team's previous work with infants. They include, for example, attachment and emotional regulation (Harrison and Ungerer 2002), intersubjectivity and the babies-in-groups paradigm (Bradley 2010; Selby and Bradley 2003, 2005), policy (Press 2006), and communication (McLeod 2007). Each of these lenses is grounded in particular assumptions about infants, their experiences, and how their experiences might be understood. Bringing these lenses together requires us to articulate and at times question those assumptions. This process of destabilisation opens up new interpretive spaces in which we are hopeful of edging closer to the perspective of the infants themselves.

In conjunction with these lenses, we are using collaborative interpretative processes similar to those used by Dolby *et al.* (2006–2009) with carers and parents. Dolby *et al.* refer to seeing and guessing (i.e., saying what you see; guessing what it might mean; seeking reactions to the guess; and then coming to an agreed understanding about the meaning). Seeing and guessing involves drawing on an array of sensitising concepts and heuristic tools to inform interpretations from multiple theoretical perspectives, and seeking feedback on those interpretations from informed stakeholders.

Our sensitising questions are drawn from different theoretical perspectives. From an interpretivist perspective, we ask: what is important to these infants? Why is this important? What do they enjoy, and what bothers them? How do they manage living a life in two places (Moss 2001)? From a child development perspective, we ask: how do these infants manage their attachment needs when separating from the parent and connecting with the carer (Harrison and Ungerer 2002)? From critical theory perspectives, we ask: how are these infants enculturated into the childcare setting? What strategies of resistance do they use/ encounter? What power relations do they engage in/are they subjected to (Leavitt 1994)? From phenomenological perspectives, we ask: what do these infants direct their (conscious) behaviour/actions towards? What do their bodily actions tell us about their intent (Dalli 2000; Lindahl and Pramling Samuelson 2002)? From intersubjectivity perspectives, we ask: are these infants affected by relationships between others in their group? What 'conversations' take place among them (Selby and Bradley 2003)? From communication perspectives, we ask: what do their first words tell us about the experiences most significant to them (Hart 1991)? From sociocultural perspectives, we ask: how are these infants involved in co-constructing the culture in the setting? What culture is being constructed (Rutanen 2007)?

Likewise, heuristic tools adopted from diverse theoretical perspectives are enabling us to scaffold and extend responses to sensitising questions (see Table 8.1), although we are mindful of the need for careful attention to theoretical consistency and 'fit' between sensitising question, heuristic tool, focus of analysis, and the data.

The challenges involved in working in this theoretically eclectic way are substantial and will require ongoing and careful attention, and will become especially pertinent as the project progresses to the stage of requiring a sustained focus on analyses and interpretation of data. We anticipate reporting on these challenges in future publications.

Methodological eclecticism

We are also aiming for methodological eclecticism that goes beyond the use of heuristic tools drawn from different theoretical perspectives. For example, to enable us to analyse the video data quantitatively, as well as qualitatively, we are using *Studiocode(r)* video analysis software. *Studiocode* offers sophisticated functions including Boolean data searches, chunking data, cross-tabulation of codes, analysis of data relationships across multiple data sets that enable us to 'count', as well as interpret, data. With caregiver/infant interaction, for example, the frequency of carers' interactions with infants, the circumstances in which they interrupt infants, and infants' responses can be identified and 'counted' as one of the bases for our interpretations.

Co-constructing insights into infants' experiences with carers, parents, and, where appropriate, older children and infants adds to the eclecticism. As we jointly view, reflect on, and discuss edited videos of key segments of data, we benefit from carers' practical wisdom (Goodfellow 2003), parents' deep familiarity with their infant, and children's perspectives on what life is like for infants.

Table 8.1 Heuristic tools for guiding data analysis (examples are indicative only)

Focus	Heuristic tools
Infant–carer interactions/ relationships	Circle of security (Dolby and Swan 2002); carer sensitivity, cooperation, responsiveness [Rating scales developed by Ainsworth et al. (1978) and Biringen et al. (1998) cited in (Albers, Riksen-Walraven, and de Weerth 2007)]; improvisation (Lobman 2006)
Agency	Pathways to participation (Shier 2001); negotiations (Rutanen 2007)
Peer–peer interactions and relationships	Dimensions of supradyadic linking (i.e. two or more infants) (Selby and Bradley 2003); style (Løkken 2000)
Engagement/ learning	Enculturation, imitation, and variation (Lindahl and Pramling Samuelson 2002)

Although we are optimistic about the possibilities of the project to inform policy and practice in relation to early years education and care in ways that will benefit infants, we are more tentative about the likelihood of developing participatory ways to research with infants that enable them to be genuine co-researchers and co-constructors of new research knowledge. Indeed, we are conscious, that despite our best intentions, we could find ourselves undertaking the project in ways that revert to and perpetuate the long-standing tendency in the research literature to see infants as the objects of research, rather than as research collaborators. In the commentary that follows, we identify and reflect on some of the many methodological and associated ethical challenges that have arisen for us in the early phases of data generation in the *Infants' Lives in Childcare* project. Although these issues are far from resolved, they may be of interest to others seeking to research in participatory ways with infants.

Commentary

Our reflections are prompted by the observation by Clark *et al.* (2003: 44) that 'there is an irony that the more imaginative the methods become for listening to young children, the greater the possibility of invading their private worlds'. Invading infants' private worlds is the antithesis of our intent. Yet there are many potential ironies associated with our research design, especially in using baby cam in our endeavours to gain insight into infants' experiences, quite literally through the eyes of the infants. Because the use of baby cam is potentially controversial and because of the technical, methodological, and ethical challenges it has presented, especially in keeping to our intent of working in participatory ways with infants, we have made it the focus of this commentary.

We begin by explaining what we mean by baby cam and our reasons for using it. Using an adaptation of Shier's (2001) pathways to participation model as a scaffold, we reflect on ways in which baby cam is both enabling and constraining in engaging with infants in ways that might be considered genuinely participatory. As illustration, we refer to some of the challenges that have arisen and our endeavours to address them.

The baby cam

By baby cam, we mean a micro video camera system, comprising a video camera and sound recording equipment attached to or worn by an infant. Our intent is to generate video images that enable us to see what the infant is seeing, in the hope of gaining some insights into the infant's experiences, from the perspective of the infant. Our interest in using baby cam stems from two quite separate lines of investigation.

The first is encapsulated by Clark *et al.* (2003) in their extensive review of methods for listening to and consulting with young children. The review confirms that observation remains a foundational method for listening to young children, especially those who, like infants, cannot yet communicate their experiences in elaborated ways. Unlike in much traditional research on infants, however, in this line of investigation, observation is not for diagnostic purposes, but rather to develop an understanding of children's perspectives on their experiences and on 'the conditions for their endeavours' (Warming 2003: 64). The focus is on 'what is important for the child: what does the child want, what does the child do and say, and how are these ideas met?' (Hedegaard 1994, 1996, cited in Warming 2003: 64).

To paraphrase Stainton Rogers and Stainton Rogers (1992), observation can only provide insights into infants' experiences in a very limited and restricted sense – that which observers, using their accustomed understandings of infants, say the infants are experiencing. Whilst we do not believe that experience is ever transparently revealed (Hollway and Jefferson 2000), this problem is especially acute in the study of infants, where observers' 'accounting vocabularies and working hypotheses' (Stainton Rogers and Stainton Rogers 1992: 18) may easily divert attempts to grapple with how infants experience their worlds. By providing a visual perspective that we can rarely access, baby cam potentially offers an innovative way to further destabilise our accustomed researcher frames of reference and elicit and learn from the perspectives of others who know the infants well (i.e. their carers, siblings, and parents).

Data captured by the baby cam is entered into *Studiocode*. *Studiocode*'s split screen function enables viewing of footage of the infant taken with a conventional video camera, alongside simultaneous footage from the baby cam. In other words, we can see the infant, as well as what the infant is seeing. Philosophically, we would like to be able to argue that, from a participatory perspective, baby cam potentially enables even very young infants who are not mobile to make an active contribution to the project by generating their own data that enables us to observe, as near as possible, what the infants observe. This is a contestable argument, however, and invokes issues of intention, agency, power, and representation with which we continue to grapple.

The second line of investigation had a more technical focus on experimental studies of visual attention and gaze. As Aslin (2008) explains, the direction of one's gaze is a well-established measure of what one is attending to visually. Head direction is a less accurate measure because even when the head is stationary, the eyes can move through a 90-degree sweep. Measuring gaze direction through head-mounted eye trackers is intrusive and impractical, especially with infants, because of the weight of the eye-tracking devices, the need for the head to be held relatively immobile and/or the disconcerting use of mirrors directly in front of one's eyes (Aslin 2008; Yoshida and Smith 2008). These constraints limit the use of eye-tracking devices in naturalistic settings.

The effort of maintaining eccentric gaze (i.e., when gaze direction is not aligned with head direction) is considerable, however. Experimental studies have shown that gaze tends to return to a central position following every eye movement greater than plus or minus ten degrees (Aslin 2008). In their study involving

18–24-month-old children wearing a video camera mounted on a headband and placed centrally on their foreheads, Yoshida and Smith (2008) found sufficient alignment of head and eye movement to conclude that head direction provides a useful, although not definitive, proxy for gaze direction. When reviewing relevant literature, they identified reports of similarly close alignment of head and eye movements in two- to four-month-old infants and nine- to ten-month-old infants. Given that once the headband-mounted cameras were in place, all the infants in their study appeared to forget about them, Yoshida and Smith concluded that the use of such devices hold considerable promise of offering unobtrusive new ways of viewing infants' visual experiences. Viewing infants' experiences in new ways, we speculated, potentially offers new ways to attempt to understand their experiences from their perspectives.

Pathways to participation as a tool for reflection

Bringing together two very different but possibly complementary lines of investigation presents technical, methodological, and arguably ethical challenges. In the remainder of this commentary, we identify some of those challenges and discuss how we are attempting to address them. In reflecting on our progress in establishing ways to research with infants in participatory ways, we draw on an adaptation of Shier's (2001) pathways to participation model for conceptualising and enhancing children's participation in decision-making. Shier (2001) outlines five levels of participation in decision-making. The text in brackets constitutes our adaptation to the research context for infants:

- *Level 1*: Children are listened to (as research participants and co-researchers).
- *Level 2*: Children are supported in expressing their views (as research participants and co-researchers).
- *Level 3*: Children's views (as research participants and co-researchers) are taken into account.
- *Level 4*: Children are involved in decision-making processes (about the research project and their participation in it, ideally in ways that will be conducive to them having a voice in their own care).
- *Level 5*: Children share power and responsibility for decision-making (as co-researchers).

According to Shier (2001), at each level of participation, individuals, and organisations – and research teams – might have differing degrees of commitment. Shier identifies three stages of commitment: openings, opportunities, and obligations. An intent to work in a particular way (in our case, in as a participatory way as possible with infants) constitutes an opening. An opening becomes an opportunity when whatever is needed to work in that way (e.g., in terms of knowledge, skills, resources, approaches, policies) is available. Opportunities become obligations when that particular way of working is required.

Shier's model has a number of limitations, including its seemingly linear, hier-archical, and uni-directional stages. When Layland (2009) analysed the ways in which two home-based educators in Aotearoa/New Zealand afforded young children participation rights, she found that both educators operated across all the levels described by Shier. To address this limitation of Shier's model, Layland also drew on a typology developed by Kirby and Gibbs (2006), derived in turn from Klein (2001). The typology outlines a continuum of adult facilitation roles within participatory projects involving children and, in contrast to Shier's pathways, explicitly allows for flexibility in moving across those roles. The roles range from abstainer (leaving children alone to undertake activities, develop ideas and produce materials with no adult intervention) to doer (taking action on children's behalf). Again, Layland (2009) found that both educators in her study took on a variety of facilitation roles in supporting children's participation. As we continue to reflect on and address the issues raised in this chapter, we anticipate that, like Layland, we too will turn to additional heuristic devices, such as Kirby and Gibb's (2006) typology. As we illustrate below, however, our adaptation of Shier's (2001) model is proving a useful starting point in scaffolding our thinking about the extent to which we can justifiably claim to be involving infants in participatory ways.

From the outset, our intent has been to listen in the sense of attuning as deeply as we can to infants and to what they are telling us (Moss, Clark and Kjørholt 2005), as research participants and co-researchers, about their experiences of their early childhood setting (Level 1). We bring knowledge, skills, and resources to support us in doing so and see this commitment as a fundamental obligation. We are equally committed, in intent and in our stated obligations as a research team, to supporting infants in expressing their views as research participants and co-researchers and are developing approaches and strategies to enable us to meet our obligations (Level 2). We can fairly legitimately, albeit tentatively, make similar claims about taking infants' views into account in our decision-making (Level 3), at least with our two infant participants and co-researchers thus far. That is likely to become more difficult, however, with younger infants. We also believe that our explicit intent to understand the experience of child care from the infant's perspective foregrounds the agency of the infant in a way that can inform policy and practice.

Technical and other challenges

To support our claims, we return to our use of baby cam and reflect on the issues that are arising and our endeavours to address them. Our reflections are informed by discussions in our team meetings and from a meeting involving one of the authors of this chapter, a research assistant and a parent of a six-month-old infant to discuss issues that might concern parents (and infants) about the use of video data and especially baby cam. The parent had a professional background in video and documentary work. She was invited in her own right, because of her professional expertise and her ability to provide a parent's perspective, but also in another sense, as her infant's proxy, to convey, based on her deep familiarity with her infant, her interpretation of her infant's likely response to using baby cam, had she been a participant in the research project. In informal ways such as these, we have tried to consult with infants and to gain their perspectives about our plans before entering research sites.

Getting to the point where we can begin to explore with our infant co-researchers the potential of baby cam has involved considerable investigative work and much trial and error. To date, we have been able to locate little relevant research literature to which we can turn for guidance. By outlining the nature of the difficulties we have encountered, we hope to prompt further reports of ways in which other researchers have grappled with similar challenges.

The first technical challenge was sourcing a suitable camera. We experimented initially with buttonhole cameras sold by suppliers to personal investigation agencies. These cameras look like a small black button slightly larger than the size of a shirt button. They come with a separate but quite small microphone that can be placed in a sweatband-style headband or on a small fitted cap so that the camera can be positioned on the infants' forehead. They are attached to a cord that transfers the video images to a receiver, which can be placed in an apron-style vest worn by the infant.

The advantage of buttonhole cameras is that they can be easily disguised. To this end, we envisaged making headbands and caps with a number of flowers with each having a matching button (which was supplied with the camera) at the centre of the flower. Only the flower positioned on the forehead when the infant was wearing the cap would contain the camera. Our intent in disguising the camera was not to deceive, but to minimise the likelihood that adults interacting with the infant wearing the camera would be psychologically intimidated by the camera and that other children's interactions with the infant would be distorted. On methodological and ethical grounds, we considered it crucial to avoid, as far as we possibly could, the presence of a camera interrupting natural and spontaneous interactions that are essential to fostering relationships and trust between carer and infant, and between the infant and other children. An infant and a toddler, who were not participants in the project but who acted as our consultants and who were accustomed to wearing hats and headbands, did not seem to object to wearing the headband containing the camera. The camera became quite hot after being worn by our consultants for approximately ten minutes and left a red mark on their skin; hence we were unable to continue using it. Additionally, the quality of sound was relatively poor.

We then trialled a number of small, directional lipstick size cameras (Figure 8.2), typically worn on the side of the head, and frequently used by sportspeople to assist in analysing technique and performance, as well as security personnel and police. Like the buttonhole cameras, lipstick cameras are attached by a cord to a recording device. We have mounted the lipstick camera we are currently using to

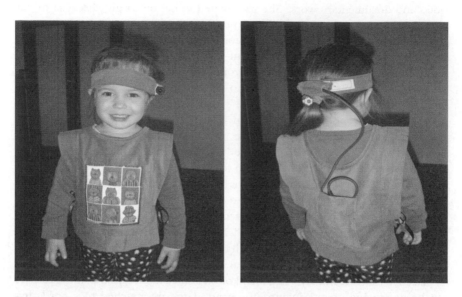

Figure 8.2 A toddler consultant trialling and providing feedback on a 'lipstick' camera-style baby cam.

a headband that is adjustable with velcro so that it can be used without a hat or over the hat if the infant is outside. Wide elastic sewn into the side of the headband enables the camera head to fit in firmly and be angled down slightly so that it points generally in the right direction. It also has a built-in conduit to direct the cord from the camera head inside the headband around to the back of the head where it comes back out of the headband and goes down into the recording device. This keeps the cord away from the side of the head and also helps to support the weight of the camera and cord. The two infants participating in the study to date seem to prefer having the camera attached permanently to an adjustable headband to an earlier system we devised that involved using velcro to fasten the camera to a non-adjustable elastic headband. The earlier system enabled the angle of the camera head to be adjusted after the headband was on the infant's head; however, this made fitting the headband to the infant more time-consuming and therefore unnecessarily distracting for the infant. Nor did the infants seem to like the sound of the velcro being adjusted close to their ear or the sensation of the tight elastic headband being pulled down over their heads.

While we are getting closer to resolving, with the assistance of the participating infants, some of the technical issues associated with the use of baby cam, we have not yet made much headway with some of the bigger, and we anticipate, more enduring methodological and ethical issues, particularly arising from participatory research perspectives. For example, how do we weigh up the possible benefits, opportunities and 'voice' that baby cam potentially offers infants by enabling them to generate data, and in that sense arguably participate as co-researchers, with the ethical implications of involving infants, especially younger infants, who are likely to have little or no awareness of understandings of their contribution or role? Do the potential advantages associated with possibly learning more about infants' worlds outweigh the possibility that we might be indeed invading their worlds? Other than trying to be as attuned as possible to the infants' responses, should we be doing more to safeguard their right to be silent and their right to privacy?

Conclusion

As Barker and Weller (2003: 8) point out, 'There is no universal truth of children's experiences to be uncovered. Rather, through child centred research methods, we can offer partial glimpses that reflect in one form the complexity and diversity of children's lives.' The implication is that the best we can hope for is a partial, tentative and imperfect understanding of children's, and especially infants', experiences. Perhaps we will find, as the *Infants' Lives in Childcare* project progresses, that we will only manage to engage with infants in participatory research in partial, tentative and imperfect ways. Given the potential benefits to infants that seem likely to arise if researchers, policy-makers, practitioners and families can gain deeper insights into infants' experiences and perspectives of ECEC, we believe the challenges associated with gaining these insights must be taken up.

Acknowledgements

The project reported in this chapter is funded by the Australian Research Council (LP 0883913) and Industry Partners, Family Day Care Australia and KU Children's Services. We would also like to acknowledge the invaluable contribution of Tina Stratigos, research assistant, and her daughter Phoebe, our toddler 'consultant' to the project.

References

Albers, E., Riksen-Walraven, J. M. and de Weerth, C. (2007) 'Infant interactions with professional caregivers at 3 and 6 months of age: A longitudinal study', *Infant Behavior and Development*, 30: 631–640.

Aslin, R. (2008) 'Headed in the right direction: A commentary on Yoshida and Smith', *Infancy*, 13(3): 275–278.

Australian Bureau of Statistics (2008) *Childhood Education and Care, Australia*, June 2008. Available at: http://www.abs.gov.au/ausstats/abs@.nsf/mf/4402.0 (accessed 11 November 2009).

Barker, J. and Weller, S. (2003) '"Is it fun?" Developing children centered research methods' *International Journal of Sociology and Social Policy*, 1(2): 33–58.

Bradley, B. S. (2005) *Psychology and Experience*, Cambridge: Cambridge University Press.

Bradley, B. S. (2010) 'Jealousy in infant-peer triads', in M. Legerstee and S. Hart (eds), *Handbook of Jealousy: Theories, Principles, and Multidisciplinary Approaches*, Hoboken, NJ: Wiley-Blackwell, pp. 192–234.

Clark, A. (2005) 'Ways of seeing: Using the Mosaic approach to listen to young children's perspectives', in A. Clark, A. T. Kjørholt and P. Moss (eds), *Beyond Listening: Children's Perspectives on Early Childhood Services*, Bristol: Policy Press, pp. 29–49.

Clark, A., McQuail, S. and Moss, P. (2003) *Exploring the Field of Listening to and Consulting with Young Children* (No. RR 445), London: Department for Education and Skills.

Clark, A. and Moss, P. (2001) *Listening to Young Children: The Mosaic Approach*, London: Joseph Rowntree Foundation.

Cole, P. N., Martin, S. E. and Dennis, T. A. (2004) 'Emotion regulation a scientific construct: Methodological challenges and directions for child development research', *Child Development*, 75(2): 317–334.

Dalli, C. (2000) 'Starting child care: What young children learn about relating to adults in the first weeks of starting child care', *Early Childhood Research and Practice*, 2(2): no page numbers.

Degotardi, S. (2009) 'Looking out and looking in: Reflecting on conducting observational research in a child-care nursery', unpublished paper.

Dolby, R. and Swan, B. (2003) 'Strengthening relationships between early childhood staff, high needs children and their families in the preschool setting', *Developing Practice: The Child, Youth and Family Work Journal*, 6: 18–23.

Dolby, R., Ungerer, J. A., Harrison, L. J., Cooper, G. and Aarts, M. (2006–2009) *Attachment Matters: From Relationships to Learning at Preschool Research Project*, Christie Foundation and KU Children's Services.

Elfer, P. (1996) 'Building intimacy in relationships with young children in nurseries', *Early Years*, 16(2): 30–34.

Goodfellow, J. (2003) 'Practical wisdom in professional practice: The person in the process', *Contemporary Issues in Early Childhood*, 4(1): 48–63.

Harrison, L. J. and Ungerer, J. A. (2002) 'Maternal employment predictors of infant–mother attachment security at 12 months postpartum', *Developmental Psychology*, 38: 758–773.

Hart, B. (1991) 'Input frequency and children's first words', *First Language*, 11(32): 289–300.

Hollway, W. and Jefferson, T. (2000) *Doing Qualitative Research Differently: Free Association, Narrative and the Interview Method*, London: Sage.

Karlsson, M. (2007) 'Viewing the world from the children's perspective: About family day care seen with the eyes of the children', *LOCUS, Magazine for Research on Children and Youths*, 1–2.

Kirby, P. and Gibbs, S. (2006) 'Facilitating participation: Adults' caring support roles within child-to-child projects in schools and after school settings', *Children and Society*, 20: 209–222.

Klein, R. (2001) *Citizens by Right: Citizenship Education in Primary Schools*, London: Save the Children and Trentham Books.

Layland, J. (2009) 'Affordance of participation rights for children in home-based education and care: An interactive process model of participation – 2007', *Children and Society*, 10.1111/j.1099-0860.2009.00254.x

Leavitt, R. L. (1994) *Power and Emotion in Infant-Toddler Day Care*, Albany, NY: State University of New York Press.

Lindahl, M. and Pramling Samuelson, I. (2002) 'Imitation and variation: Reflections on toddlers' strategies for learning', *Scandinavian Journal of Educational Research*, 46(1): 25–45.

Lobman, C. L. (2006) 'Improvisation: An analytic tool for examining teacher–child interactions in the early childhood classroom', *Early Childhood Research Quarterly*, 21: 455–470.

Løkken, G. (2000) 'Tracing the social style of toddler peers', *Scandinavian Journal of Educational Research*, 44(2): 163–174.

McLeod, S. (ed.) (2007) *The International Guide to Speech Acquisition*, Clifton Park, NY: Thomson Delmar Learning.

Moss, P. (2001) 'Listen in', *Nursery World*, July, 5.

Moss, P., Clark, A. and Kjørholt, A. T. (2005) 'Introduction', in A. Clark, A. T. Kjørholt and P. Moss (eds), *Beyond Listening: Children's Perspectives on Early Childhood services*, Bristol: Policy Press, pp. 1–16.

OECD (2007) *Babies and Bosses: Reconciling Work and Family Life: A Synthesis of Findings from OECD Countries*, Paris: OECD Publishing.

Pascal, C. and Bertram, T. (2009) 'Listening to young citizens: The struggle to make real a participatory paradigm in research with young children', *European Early Childhood Education Research Journal*, 17(2): 249–262.

Press, F. (2006) *What about the Kids? Policy Directions for Improving the Experiences of Infants and Young Children in a Changing World*, NSW: Commission for Children and Young People, NSW; Commission for Children and Young People, Queensland, National Investment for the Early Years.

Rutanen, N. (2007) 'Two-year-old children as co-constructors of culture', *European Early Childhood Education Research Journal*, 15(1): 59–69.

Selby, J. M. and Bradley, B. S. (2003) 'Infants in groups: A paradigm for the study of early social experience', *Human Development*, 46(4): 197–221.

Selby, J. M. and Bradley, B. S. (2005) 'Psychologist as moral agent: Negotiating praxis-oriented knowledge in infancy', in A. Gülerce, A. Hofmeister, I. Staeuble, G. Saunders and J. Kaye (eds), *Contemporary Theorizing in Psychology: Global Perspectives*, New York: Captus Press, pp. 242–250.

Shier, H. (2001) 'Pathways to participation: Openings opportunities and obligations', *Children and Society*, 15: 107–117.

Stainton Rogers, R. and Stainton Rogers, W. (1992) *Stories of Childhood: Shifting Agendas of Child Concern*, New York: Harvester Wheatsheaf.

Studiocode (n.d.) *Studiocode Business Group*. Available at: http://www.studiocodegroup.com (accessed 11 February 2009).

Thyssen, S. (2000) 'The child's start in day care', *Early Child Development and Care*, 161: 33–46.

United Nations (1989) *Convention on the Rights of the Child*. Document A/RES/44/25 with annex. Available at: http://www.wunrn.com/reference/pdf/Convention_Rights_Child.PDF (accessed 20 June 2009).

Warming, H. (2003) 'Appendix C Literature review on listening to young children: Views and experiences of childcare, education and services for families', in A. Clark, S. McQuail and P. Moss (eds), *Exploring the Field of Listening to and Consulting with Young Children*. London: Department for Education and Skills, pp. 62–79.

White, E. J. (2009) 'Assessment in New Zealand early childhood education: A Bakhtinian analysis of toddler metaphoricity', unpublished PhD thesis, Monash University.

Yoshida, H. and Smith, L. (2008) 'What's in view for toddlers? Using a head camera to study visual experience', *Infancy*, 13(3): 229–248.

Chapter 9

Eliciting young children's perspectives on indoor play provision in their classroom

Reflections and challenges

Liz Dunphy and Thérèse Farrell

This chapter is based on the study carried out by the second author for her Master's in Education degree at St Patrick's College, Dublin. The research investigated the perspectives of young children in relation to aspects of the indoor play provision in their classroom. One aim of this chapter is to provide a reflexive account of the study. A second aim is to illustrate the complex nature of considering how to act on children's perspectives.

Introduction

The reader should note current provision in Ireland in relation to early education and care. Although the statutory school starting age in Ireland is six, historically, many children between the ages of four and six years have attended primary school, and they continue to do so. Currently about half of all four-year-old children and nearly all five-year-olds are in infant classes in primary schools. As a result, some of what is considered preschool education in other countries is carried out within the primary education system in Ireland. This is due to the fact that the Irish preschool system is relatively underdeveloped and was, until very recently, mainly privately funded. A recent initiative by government has resulted in some limited funding for universal preschool provision for children in the year before they attend school.

It is important for the reader to understand the emphases in the course work which preceded the research study. In the context of considering issues related to quality in early childhood education, students consider a wide range of arguments for reflecting on children's perspectives in relation to the provision of school-based learning. For instance, the importance of including a 'bottom-up' approach to quality is considered, i.e. that the subjective experiences of children are essential elements in reflecting on quality (Katz 1994). They are introduced to transformational and interpretivist theories of childhood (MacNaughton and Williams 2004) and they consider the arguments that children can transform their world through the expression of their views. In particular, children's views on aspects of their learning are posited as central to teachers' efforts to maximize learning possibilities (Dunphy 2005; Pramling Samuelsson and Pramling 2009). Students engage through reading, reflection, and discussion with ideas related to the inseparable nature of eliciting children's perspectives and the establishment of mutual understanding and reciprocity between teacher and individual learners (Carr 2000).

The belief that play can be a powerful tool for promoting children's learning and holistic development is a key theme explored in the Master's in Education course. In the case of the second author, one child's comments gave cause for reflection and provided an impetus for her research on play. His teacher (the researcher) had noticed that he always withdrew from make-believe play activities and when questioned about this, he responded: 'I always have to play in here . . . I don't like it' (Daniel, five years six months). A review of the range of perspectives on play provided a starting point for the research. The early pioneers (e.g. Froebel and Montessori, as cited in Wood and Attfield 2005) offered arguments about the value and potential of play in young children's holistic development. Theorists such as Vygotsky (1978) and Piaget (1951) offered perspectives of how play relates to cognitive development. More recently, in seeking to justify play as a vehicle for learning, experts in the area of early learning argue that it leads towards increasingly mature forms of knowledge, skills and learning (Anning 2009; Broadhead 2004; Moyles 2005). Among all of these perspectives the absence of children's voices in relation to play in the classroom was striking. This absence provided the rationale for the study. The aim of the study was to increase the possibility that the play provided in the classroom did actually engage, stimulate and challenge the children by building on their interests, motives and interpretations. As the research developed and the findings emerged, ascertaining children's views on play also provided an important opportunity to review a number of issues pertaining to the pedagogy of play that prevailed in the classroom under study.

Research context

The research reported here was carried out in a senior infant classroom (the children are aged between five and six years of age) in an Educate Together primary school, located in a suburb of Dublin. The Educate Together Movement was established in the early 1980s to meet a growing need in Irish society to establish multi-denominational co-educational schools that recognized the diversity of Irish society (Educate Together Charter 1990). Today there are 56 Educate Together schools out of a total of 3,200 primary schools and the movement is growing rapidly, mainly due to the huge increase in immigration. It is claimed that an important feature that distinguishes Educate Together schools is their culturally inclusive and democratic ethos (ibid. 1990). For instance, one feature of these schools is that the children address staff members on a first name basis. This practice is unusual in the context of primary schools in Ireland. The Educate Together philosophy can be linked to that of the United Nations Convention on the Rights of the Child (International Child Development Centre 1991). The

Convention, which was ratified by the Irish Government in 1992, attests to children's rights to agency and a voice in all matters affecting them. The National Children's Strategy (Government of Ireland 2000) affords further prominence in Irish society to children's rights by recognizing that children have an active contribution to make in shaping their own lives and the lives of those around them. It states as a key goal that children be afforded a voice in matters affecting them. In the Educate Together framework, children's abilities to be active participants and decision-makers is promoted, thus highlighting their status as valued citizens and their role as equal participants in society, with the right to be heard. Children are encouraged to use their voices through activities such as circle time, debates, discussion and through taking an active role on the student council. One possibility offered by the research was the extension of the concept of 'voice' of the youngest children as it related to issues not previously addressed in this particular school.

The research site was a spacious, modern school which accommodates over 400 children aged between four and twelve years and a staff of some 40 teachers and classroom assistants. Half of the school population have an international background. The class in which the study was carried out consisted of 28 children (nineteen boys and nine girls) from different social and cultural backgrounds, including six children who spoke English as a second language and two children with special educational needs. A special needs assistant worked alongside the teacher (researcher) in the classroom. The Primary School Curriculum (Government of Ireland 1999) encompasses six areas including Language; Mathematics; Social, Environmental and Scientific Education; Social, Personal and Health Education; Physical Education and Arts Education, and this shaped much of the provision. The children in the study engaged in free play every morning for 30–40 minutes. This was generally a busy, active, creative, colourful, energetic, engaging time for the children. They had the autonomy to choose their activity (from a range of activities, including sand and water play, dress up box, a variety of construction equipment, playdough, equipment for drawing/writing, etc). They also chose their play partner(s). The researcher (teacher) routinely sought to engage with the children and support and extend their learning as opportunities arose. Children also had play opportunities intermittently throughout the day, but these tended to be more structured and generally sought to orient children towards specific curriculum objectives.

Research study

Research questions

The research explored children's perspectives of their indoor play provision. The research questions were as follows:

- What aspects of the play provision appealed to the children?
- What aspects of the play provision impeded children's enjoyment?
- What were children's perceptions of the purposes of playtime in the classroom?

Ethics and methodology

Prior to the fieldwork for the study, the researchers discussed a number of important methodological issues related to how the research was to be conducted. In particular we discussed questions related to the issues of informed assent; power relations; and the difficulty and necessity of constructing a 'true' account of children's views and ideas. It was essential that the research adhered to some important general principles. For instance, doing research 'with' children, means that they are involved as part of the research process (Christensen and James 2008); teacher and children collaborate, they work together on the research (Conroy and Harcourt 2009); the conversations are structured in such a way that the children are comfortable with the process; and useful data are generated (e.g. Punch 2002). Also, given the particular demographic profile of the school in which the research was to be carried out, a culturally sensitive research approach was essential (Grieshaber and Ryan 2006). Some ethical questions presented themselves at the outset and it was important to discuss and resolve these. For instance, were the research questions asked serious ones? Were they meaningful to children? From our shared perspective, the answer to both these questions was affirmative. Given the seriousness with which the question of play and learning is treated in early education, any new insights here are of interest and importance. Also, since children were offered play opportunities in the classroom, then research questions related to their perspectives on these can be considered meaningful for them.

Methods

The methods employed included video-recording the children during play sessions and audio-recording discussions with the children afterwards. The issue of whether the research questions were capable of being answered with the kind of research methods proposed i.e. discussion and reflection on video-tape footage, was central. We considered the methods appropriate and generally in line with, and reflective of, children's experiences, interests and everyday routines (Christensen 2004). The video-taping was not a routine activity but was introduced because of the possibilities it offered in terms of making transparent to children the aspect of learning under focus and also the possibilities it offered in supporting reflective discussion with the children. The methods chosen also appeared to provide 'a respectful and legitimate context' (Conroy and Harcourt 2009: 159) within which to carry out the research. A purposive sampling strategy was utilized to ensure the sample reflected the general population of the class. The sample comprised of ten children, six boys and four girls, including a mixture of ages, gender, ethnicity, children from higher and lower attainment groups as well as children with special educational needs.

After obtaining ethical clearance from the Board of Management, consent was sought from the parents to audio record children's responses during discussions about play and to video-record children during play sessions. Parents were assured on issues such as anonymity and confidentiality. The children were fully informed about the research and their participation was sought, thus helping to ensure that children could give their fully informed assent (Coady 2001; Conroy and Harcourt 2009). According to legal definitions, children cannot give consent (Coady 2001); rather the researcher sought the children's permission, or assent, to record their ideas. The researcher explained the purpose of the research: her interest in listening to their ideas of play and the importance of these in improving play in their classroom and in other classrooms also: 'I'd like to hear your ideas about playtime to help make playtime in our classroom and other children's classrooms a better time' (Farrell 2008).

At the outset, children had frequent opportunities to familiarize themselves with the equipment, to watch recordings of themselves during play activities and to listen to their own audio recordings. This enabled them to become comfortable with the equipment and to understand its purposes. For instance, the children enjoyed recording their play sessions and then reviewing their play, while providing a running commentary: 'Look, there I am . . . that's me (while pointing at the screen) . . . I'm playing with the Lego' (ibid.). This was a significant aspect of the research as it positioned the children as acknowledged research participants (Conroy and Harcourt 2009).

As the focused discussion was the central vehicle for children's voices to be heard, the researcher (teacher) assured the children that their ideas on play were important to her. She also sought to assure them that any ideas or opinions expressed would not result in any negative consequences: 'I'm really looking forward to hearing your ideas about playtime and whatever you say to me today whether it's a good thing or a bad thing about playtime it won't matter . . . it's just important that you tell me how you really feel' (Farrell 2008). The children were also assured that their assent could be withdrawn at any stage: 'and if you don't want to talk about playtime at any stage that's OK too' (ibid.). One example of how the researcher (teacher) sought to ensure that the children were genuinely involved throughout the process was in giving them a choice as to where the conversation should be held. Some children chose the classroom as the location for the discussion; others chose the library, which they deemed to be quieter. Thus, the children expressed their entitlement as collaborators in research conversations (Conroy and Harcourt 2009).

Due to the democratic nature of the setting, traditional hierarchical images of the power and control which encompass teacher student relationships were already reduced. To further help reduce power imbalances, the researcher engaged in discussion with the children listening to their ideas and providing the children with opportunities to be heard as opposed to carrying out conventional question-and-answer style interviews. Listening included noting other aspects of expression including facial expression, tone of voice, body language and silences also. In one instance, towards the end of the conversation, the researcher (teacher) noted that 'Barry appears tired and he has nodded in response to the last few questions so I decide to conclude the interview and thank him for his contributions' (Farrell

2008). Other measures taken were to ensure that children had sufficient thinking time when responding to questions and encouragement to elaborate and extend their views.

The visual recordings of their play were used to enable the children to engage critically and relate to the issues raised in conversation. In this way, the video camera worked by providing the researcher (teacher) with prompts for questioning the children and simultaneously allowing the children the opportunity for revisiting, reflecting and interpreting their play activities. It supported the children's memory, thereby allowing them to retrace their learning processes (Forman 1999). In response to watching the video-footage, one child comments: 'Oh yeah . . . I remember . . . I was making a fire engine and used that yoke (he points to a piece of Mobilo on the screen) for the ladder . . . 'cause it was long' (Farrell 2008). As children viewed the footage they often commented on aspects of the play such as the activity or their play partner(s); 'Here I am . . . and there's Bella, Tom and Natalie (pointing to the screen) . . . we were playing in the shop . . . Look . . . I'm the shopkeeper' (ibid.). Additional information was elicited by encouraging the children to describe their actions. In listening to individual children as she and they reviewed the tapes together, the researcher (teacher) gained rich insights into the children's perspectives on their indoor play experiences. Not only did the reviewing of the video-tapes draw on their personal experiences, it also provided the context for the children to discuss, debate and to think critically about their play. Hviid (2008) argues for the importance of negotiating and achieving shared meaning, i.e. intersubjectivity, in discussions such as the ones here. We consider that the shared viewing and discussion of the video-records of the play enhanced the level of intersubjectivity achieved between the researcher (teacher) and individual children.

Selected findings

One of the overwhelming findings to emerge from the data (transcripts, field notes and observations from the video-footage) was the enjoyment the children experienced during play activities. All of the children explicitly expressed having fun during playtime: 'The most important thing about playtime is to have fun' (Dylan, six years), 'I have great fun with a bit of everyone' (Tom, six years six months). The children also expressed views that playtime was important for social reasons. From the children's perspectives, the leading function of play was for social interactions as play provided them with opportunities to form, renegotiate and maintain friendships (Farrell 2008). All of the children mentioned special friends that they had in the class: 'Playtime helps us because . . . we play nice together' (Natalie, five years eleven months) and 'We have fun and we meet new people' (Zack, six years eight months). It appeared that children's choice of activity was influenced by who was involved rather than the activity itself, supporting the idea that children's desire to associate with others often takes precedence over the content and the nature of the play (Rogers and Evans 2006). Creating and maintaining friendships proved to be the primary motivating factor for children's engagement in play activities. This supports Broadhead's (2004) findings that children are continuously building the concept of friendship and they do not separate friendship from ongoing daily activities.

The 'surprise' finding (MacNaughton and Smith 2005), from our perspective, was that nine out of the ten participants favoured construction activities over any other type of play. They expressed their preferences in comments such as: 'I just don't like playing with still toys, I like moving toys' (Holly, six years six months); 'Lego is my favourite thing 'cause I like to build stuff' (Natalie, five years eleven months); 'I like to build things with it [Mobilo] . . . you can make a helicopter or an aeroplane' (Tom, six years six months). The children's ideas were supported by the field notes:

> Bella, Holly and Zack are working co-operatively with the Lego to construct a bridge; Tom and Natalie are working together with the Mobilo, 'Use this piece' Natalie says to Zack and she gives him a piece of Mobilo, 'It's too small . . . we need a bigger piece . . . like this one for the wing' as he finds a longer piece in the box.
>
> (Farrell 2008)

The children articulated their frustration regarding broken, damaged and immobile toys. 'Loads of them [the octagons] are broken . . . and em . . . when you see a little piece of the broken one . . . you go "oh no!" 'cause, say, if you are doing the bike it's really hard 'cause you need to find two perfect ones (for the wheels)' (John, six years three months).

The children also highlighted the importance of choice during playtime and the importance of having the autonomy to play to their own agenda. Six of the ten children stressed the importance of being able to choose their activity or their play partner(s). Speaking about choice, John (six years three months) comments: 'It's good 'cause, say, if you didn't like the thing on your table and all the other tables had really fun stuff, you could pick to go to that team.' The researcher's observations sustain this idea:

> When John comes into the classroom he sits down on his chair, he notices that the animals are on his table, he stands up and walks over to Zack and Holly who are playing with the Lego and he starts to play with them.
>
> (Farrell 2008)

The opportunity to choose provided a context within which children could exercise their autonomy.

Reflexive comments

From the researcher (teacher) perspective

A major challenge in carrying out this research was occupying the dual role of teacher and researcher. It was essential to maintain an environment in which the children felt uninhibited in expressing their ideas on play. It was important that my role as researcher created no confusion for the children. It was desirable that it should not result in children feeling that they had to adjust their responses in any way. There was also the challenge of incorporating the children's individual needs into the research design. Flexibility was needed to elicit ideas from children who lacked the language or the ability to articulate their ideas on play. In one instance I had an adult family member of the child assist by translating during the discussion. In another instance, one child's ideas were elucidated by reference to the field notes. The child who had special educational needs found it difficult to articulate his ideas or enter into discussions about play. During conversation he remarked: 'I don't know . . . I'm not sure . . . I don't know how I feel' (Tom, six years six months). Even though he was unable to articulate his ideas on play, it was possible to discern Tom's thoughts by consulting the field note record:

> His resource teacher comes to take him out of the class setting. He appears disappointed to be leaving the constructive activities as he is building an aeroplane with a friend. On his return to the classroom he goes straight over to his friend and starts examining the aeroplane.
>
> (Farrell 2008)

This, of course, subjects Tom's ideas to adult gloss and interpretation.

Previous evidence suggests that play in schools is typically structured and often constrained by contextual influences and the need to provide evidence of learning in measurable outcomes (Bennett, Wood and Rogers 1997). By giving prominence to children's voices and by utilizing a child-oriented, multi-faceted approach to gathering data, this study gave children the means to justify play in their own terms. The challenge that arises from this study is how best to use children's perspectives to help plan for, and shape, the provision for play in the classroom.

From the mentor/supervisor position

Arising from her position as teacher in an Educate Together School, Thérèse had a personal and passionate interest in children's rights, and in particular in their active participation in issues related to their everyday lives. She had established excellent relationships with the children she was teaching. During her course-work she demonstrated, at various times, a well-developed sensitivity to children's ideas and views and an ability to listen closely and hear their views and ideas, both necessary preconditions for the type of study she was planning (Pramling

Samuelsson and Pramling 2009). It appeared to me that she was engaged in developing a 'pedagogy of relationships and listening' (Rinaldi 2006: 113), and as such, she was ideally placed to conduct this study. However, it was important that we established a 'trusting' relationship and from my perspective as mentor I needed to be reassured that Thérèse was very well aware of the ethical considerations pertaining to eliciting children's perspectives. Through reading and discussion, Thérèse developed an acute awareness of the issues involved in researching with children. We discussed her plans to enable the participation of all children in the group and ensure that all of their voices were heard. A significant moment was when she outlined her plans to facilitate the participation of children who did not yet use English to communicate with her. From that point on, I felt that she demonstrated the level of awareness and sensitivity needed to research children's perspectives in an ethical way. I was aware of the power relations arising from our relative positions of mentor and student researcher. However, the initial asymmetrical nature of the relationship changed somewhat as the findings emerged and as we examined, discussed and reflected on their meaning and importance together. While my task as mentor was to ensure that the findings were problematized as far as possible, Thérèse's knowledge of the classroom and of the children enabled her to have a potentially richer understanding of the children's perspectives since she had first-hand knowledge of many of the issues they raised. She was then able to expand our sense-making efforts using contextual knowledge, as required.

Discussion

Children's perspectives on indoor play

Children's perspectives provided some important insights which complement some of those derived from the literature. For instance, children's ideas as evidenced in discussion clearly reflected the holistic learning experiences they derived from their play. Also, the value that children in the study placed on socially constructed play is fully coherent with sociocultural theories on learning and development and the kinds of learning opportunities that theory suggests should be afforded to young children.

Insights gained from the study

The discourse of quality in provision is constructed on the notion that children should be enabled to engage in a range of play opportunities in classrooms (Edgington 2008). Consequently, institutionally common practice in many classrooms is to provide a range of different types of play materials. For organizational purposes, Irish teachers often guide children through these on a rotational basis. In the discipline of early childhood education, social pretend play is considered by many as 'the paradigm case of play' for young children below six years of age

(Pellegrini 1998: 222). In stating a preference for construction play, children expressed views and wishes that appear inconsistent with the general orthodoxy related to the need to provide a range of play materials/opportunities for young children at school. This is not a novel finding. In a review of a number of play studies carried out three decades ago, using objects to create or construct, i.e. construction play, was found to be the most common form of play in over half of preschools and kindergartens (Rubin, Fein and Vandenberg 1983). In that study, the ecological setting (school/non school, indoor/outdoor) was seen to be highly relevant and appeared to determine play behaviour and influence children's preferences. Gender differences were also noted at this time, with boys of this age preferring blocks, construction toys and vehicles more than girls. In relation to the research reported in this chapter, it is important to consider the possibility that there were particular contextual factors operating that influenced children's preferences for construction play above other types. For instance, were some of the resources new or novel, and so temporarily more attractive to the children? Was the teacher more often present and participating in one type of play as opposed to others? If so, how might this have affected children's interests? Could there be other more complex possibilities that might help to account for the findings? We considered whether children's preferences for construction play might have arisen from the reification of specific learning in the classroom wherein children are oriented towards predictable, outcome-led activity. During our reflective discussions, one particular practice in the classroom in which the research was carried out emerged as potentially significant. At the end of the school day, children were routinely encouraged to invite their parents into the classroom to admire the various pieces they had made from construction materials. For children, then, the approval and admiration of their parents/guardians for their work when they collected the children, were associated with having engaged in construction play. It is possible that one of the unintended consequences of that particular practice was to enhance the importance of construction play in the minds of the children. The affective consequences of such a practice on play preferences may be significant here.

From a post-modern perspective, Dahlberg, Moss and Pence argue that uncertainty and indeterminacy are accepted as unavoidable. They speak of 'personal agency and responsibility to produce or construct meaning and deepen understanding about pedagogical work' (1999: 113). It seems then that arising from the findings presented here, there are in fact two related issues to problematize: first, the children's preference for construction play, but also their apparent lack of interest in some other types of play, in particular, social pretend play. Since children in the study had clearly indicated their interest in socially constructed construction play with their peers, we should consider whether thinking and talking about social pretend play raises difficulties for some children who may be unsure of the teacher's expectations of them in that context (Wood 2008a).

Possible implications

This research sought children's perspectives on play provision, and a logical implication and expectation are that the findings will influence provision in the future. Certainly this idea was explicit in discussions with the children about the purposes of the research. It has been observed that studies such as the one reported here are potentially very important since they illustrate 'opportunities for the intermingling between theory and practice . . . and for the actions of children . . . to make theoretical contributions to the education of young children' (Grieshaber and Ryan 2006: 548).

The *Primary School Curriculum* (Government of Ireland, 1999), in its current presentation, offers no guidance on play as a discrete activity for young children. Given the findings arising from the study here, and indeed the general consensus on the role of play in early learning, this omission should be examined and an appropriate review of guidance for teachers should be undertaken.

The children expressed clear views and preferences in relation to aspects of the play in the classroom and some of these, for instance, in relation to the replacement of equipment and increasing opportunities for free choice, are non-problematic. Others need to be problematized at a deeper level.

The finding that the children prefer construction play is challenging in terms of considering how to act. This is complex, particularly if critical perspectives are applied. For instance, teachers in the school may well ask whether there should be more provision for construction play and less for other types of play. Arising from this study, it is suggested that the issues that now arise both for Thérèse and her colleagues revolve around some difficult questions. For instance, do they accept the validity of the children's views? How might these voices be 'honoured' (MacNaughton and Smith 2005: 132)? Are other views also important? Whose? Why? How might tensions between the views be reconciled? What might be the consequences of any decisions made? The tension that arises here between 'given' practice and practice informed by children's preferences and interests suggests the need for reflective consideration by teachers. Findings related to children's preferences for construction play introduce tensions and dilemmas for teachers as to how best to structure their play provision and to implement a pedagogy of play. Decisions about what is educationally desirable require value judgements. This in turn raises questions about which values should dominate. The dilemma for teachers is how they can meet children's interests and at the same time implement a curriculum that they believe is in children's best interests. To what extent should the children's preference for construction play actually shape the provision in the classroom? This is not a simple question. Roberts has argued that, 'It is clear that listening to children, hearing children and acting on what they say are three very different activities, although they are frequently elided as if this were not the case' (2008: 273).

Wood (2008b) cautions that while the idea 'that curriculum content arises through needs and interests may be ideologically seductive . . . showing an interest is not the same as making meaningful connections between the areas of learning and experience'. She further suggests that some children may shy away from social pretend play in the school setting:

> Some forms of play, particularly role play, involve quite complex skills and processes which may not be easily understood by all children. Therefore some children may be excluded from the full range of play provision on the basis of their cultural heritage, home practices and individual differences.
>
> (ibid.: 314)

She also cautions that children's free choices have their own power effects. If children were to choose, for whatever reason, to consistently spend time on construction play to the exclusion of other forms of play, they could be disadvantaged in relation to opportunities to develop certain skills, attitudes, dispositions or knowledge more easily derived from other forms of play. Mannion raises the question of the need to 'attend to the on-going tension around children's participatory rights on the one hand, and their right to have their needs met, on the other' (2007: 407). He argues strongly that we as adults have to take account of the fact that children's capacities to make decisions are not fully developed. It seems then that 'acting on' what children say in this instance, and in others also, involves deep reflection on children's perspectives and on what these might actually mean in relation to provision and other aspects of pedagogy. It seems to us, then, that what children prefer in play terms is as much about what we don't do pedagogically, as it is about what we actually do in that respect. Here children's statements of preference for one type of play can be considered as a statement about pedagogy and about how we might unconsciously, in our practices, be promoting and supporting one type of play above others.

Conclusion

Considering children's perspectives provides an impetus to critique and develop aspects of pedagogy. The finding related to children's preference for construction play prompted both of us, in our respective roles as researcher (teacher) and mentor, towards the consideration of new ideas, new explanations, new ways to understand children, learning and play. For us, the study raises more questions than answers but a key insight gained from this research is that any consideration of children's perspectives and their implications for teachers' work in classrooms involves deep reflection on pedagogy. We strongly believe that this research was worth doing from both the children's perspective and ours. It prompted deep reflection, on both our parts, on the pedagogy of the classroom in which it was carried out and a deepened awareness of the implications of any and every action in the classroom. By listening to and valuing children's opinions, we now have a clearer understanding of how they make sense of play at school. Through engaging with children's perspectives the teacher (researcher) established a more positive, meaningful relationship with the children. In conversations with the children, open communication was developed and relationships based on mutual respect and warmth were enhanced. This is important since research suggests that children with more positive teacher–child relationships appear to exploit the learning opportunities in the classroom and construct more positive peer relations (Bowman, Donovan and Burns 2001).

References

Anning, A. (2009) 'The co-construction of an early childhood curriculum', in A. Anning, J. Cullen, and M. Fleer (eds), *Early Childhood Education: Society and Culture*, 2nd edn, London: Sage Publications, pp. 67–79.

Bennett, N., Wood, E. and Rogers, S. (1997) *Teaching Through Play: Teachers' Thinking and Classroom Practice*, Buckingham: Open University Press.

Bowman, B., Donovan, S. and Burns, M. (2001) *Eager to Learn: Educating Our Preschoolers*, Washington, DC: National Academy Press.

Broadhead, P. (2004) *Early Years Play and Learning: Developing Social Skills and Cooperation*, London: RoutledgeFalmer.

Carr, M. (2000) 'Seeking children's perspectives about their learning', in A. Smith and N. Taylor (eds), *Children's Voices: Research, Policy and Practice*, Wellington, NZ: Pearson Education, pp. 37–54.

Christensen, P. (2004) 'Children's participation in ethnographic research: Issues of power and representation', *Children and Society*, 18(2): 165–176.

Christensen, P. and James, A. (2008) *Research with Children*, 2nd edn, London: Routledge.

Coady, M. (2001) 'Ethics in early childhood research', in G. MacNaughton, S.A. Rolfe and I. Siraj-Blatchford (eds), *Doing Early Childhood Research: International Perspectives on Theory and Practice*, Buckingham: Open University Press, pp. 64–75.

Conroy, H. and Harcourt, D. (2009) 'Informed agreement to participate: Beginning the partnership with children in research', *Early Child Development and Care*, 179(2): 157–165.

Dahlberg, G., Moss, P. and Pence, A. (1999) *Beyond Quality in Early Childhood Education and Care: Postmodern Perspectives*, London: Falmer Press.

Dunphy, E. (2005) 'Children's perceptions of number and of learning about number as they enter primary school', *European Early Childhood Education Research Journal*, 12(2): 103–118.

Edgington, M. (2008) *The Foundation Stage Teacher in Action: Teaching 3, 4 and 5 Year Olds*, 3rd edn, London: Paul Chapman.

Educate Together Charter (1990) University College Galway, Ireland. Available at: http://www.educatetigether.ie/_educate_together/charter.html on 04-06-09 (accessed 19 January 2009).

Farrell, T. (2008) 'Children's perspectives of their indoor play provision in an infant classroom', thesis submitted in partial fulfilment of the requirements for the Masters in Education, St. Patrick's College, Dublin City University.

Forman, G. (1999) 'Instant video revisiting: The video camera as a "tool of the mind" for young children', *Early Childhood Research and Practice*, 1(2): 1–7. Available at: www.http://ecrp.uiuc.edu/v1n2/for4man.html on 03/12/08 (accessed 14 March 2009).

Government of Ireland (1999) *Primary School Curriculum: Introduction*, Dublin: Stationery Office.

Government of Ireland (2000) *Our Children – Their Lives: The National Children's Strategy*, Dublin: Stationery Office.

Grieshaber, S. and Ryan, S. (2006) 'Beyond certainties: Postmodern perspectives, research, and the education of young children', in B. Spodek and O. Saracho (eds), *Handbook of Research on the Education of Young Children*, 2nd edn, Mahwah, NJ: Lawrence Erlbaum and Associates, pp. 533–554.

Hviid, P. (2008) 'Interviewing using a cultural-historical approach', in M. Hedegaard and M. Fleer with J. Bang and P. Hviid (eds), *Studying Children: A Cultural-historical Approach*, London: Open University Press, pp. 139–156.

International Child Development Centre (1991) *The Convention: Child Rights and UNICEF Experience at the Country Level, Innocenti Studies*, 91(3), Florence: UNICEF Innocenti Research Centre.

Katz, L. (1994) 'Perspectives on the quality of early childhood programmes', *Phi Delta Kappa*, 75(Nov.): 200–205.

MacNaughton, G. and Smith, K. (2005) 'Transforming research ethics: The choices and challenges of researching with children', in A. Farrell (ed.), *Ethical Research with Children*, London: Open University Press, pp. 112–123.

MacNaughton, G. and Williams, G. (2004) *Techniques for Teaching Young Children: Choices in Theory and Practice*, Sydney: Pearson Education Australia.

Mannion, G. (2007) 'Going spatial, going relational: Why "listening to children" and other participation needs reframing', *Discourse: Studies in the Cultural Politics of Education*, 28(3): 405–420.

Moyles, J. (ed.) (2005) *The Excellence of Play*, 2nd edn, Maidenhead: Open University Press.

Pellegrini, A. (1998) 'Play and the assessment of young children', in O. Saracho and B. Spodek (eds), *Multiple Perspectives on Play in Early Childhood Education*, Albany, NY: State University of New York Press, pp. 220–239.

Piaget, J. (1951) *Play, Dreams and Imitation in Childhood*, London: Routledge & Kegan Paul.

Pramling Samuelsson, I. and Pramling, N. (2009) 'Children's perspectives as "touch downs" in time: Assessing and developing children's understanding simultaneously', *Early Child Development and Care*, 179(2): 205–216.

Punch, S. (2002) 'Research with children: The same or different from research with adults?', *Childhood*, 9(3): 321–341.

Rinaldi, C. (2006) *In Dialogue with Reggio Emilia: Listening, Researching and Learning*, London: Routledge.

Roberts, H. (2008) 'Listening to children: And hearing them', in P. Christensen and A. James (eds), *Research with Children*, 2nd edn, London: Routledge, pp. 260–275.

Rogers, S., and Evans, J. (2006) 'Playing the game? Exploring role play from children's perspectives', *European Early Childhood Education Research Journal*, 14(1): 43–55.

Rubin, K., Fein, G. and Vandenberg, B. (1983) 'Play', in P. Mussen (ed.), *Handbook of Child Psychology*. Vol. 1: *Socialization, Personality and Social Development*, 4th edn, E. Mavis Hetherington vol. ed., New York: Wiley, pp. 693–774.

Vygotsky, L. (1978) *Mind in Society: Development of Higher Psychological Processes*, eds and trans. M. Cole, V. John-Steiner, S. Scriber and E. Souberman, Cambridge: Cambridge University Press.

Wood, E. (2008a) 'Listening to young children: Multiple voices, meanings and under-standings', in A. Paige-Smith and A. Craft (eds), *Developing Reflective Practice in the Early Years*, Maidenhead: Open University Press, pp. 108–121.

Wood, E. (2008b) 'New directions in play: Consensus or collision?', *Education 3-13*, 35(4): 309–320.

Wood, E. and Attfield, J. (2005) *Play, Learning and the Early Childhood Curriculum*, 2nd edn, London: Paul Chapman.

Chapter 10

Seeing spaces, inhabiting places

Hearing school beginners

Alma Fleet and Clare Britt

Children are often the most silenced participants in the educative process. While being asked to write, read, draw, group, regroup, line up, pack up and otherwise conform to institutional expectations, their perceptions of schooling are often missing from considerations of optimal school environments. This chapter explores researching with children as germane to understanding not only perspectives of particular children, but the potency of the research methods employed. Findings from two studies reported here reveal children's interest in place as sensitive, thoughtful and often idiosyncratic. *Agency* (in the context of nature) and *relationships* are foregrounded with greater emotional power than teaching routines or instructional spaces. The studies discussed here contribute to conversations about this rich terrain, and the value of sharing both lived and memoried experiences with children to assist in adult understanding.

Introduction

In this chapter, we address the importance of acknowledging the interconnectedness between space and place (as embodied, lived, shared and remembered) for young children – the 'cognitive and embodied intersubjective experience' (McKenzie 2008: 2) of learning in place, and place in learning. We ask: what are the significant places within schools from the perspectives of children in the early years of primary school? We illuminate our understandings of the often surprising nature of listening seriously to children and draw together shared thematic threads across two studies, focusing particularly on children's sense of *place*. Hearing children enables us to understand the impact of place on early learners, and to share rich data from listening in unexpected ways.

The chapter considers points of intersection within and between two case studies involving the seeking of understanding through researching with children. Approaches to, and methods of data collection in both studies have been informed by the Mosaic approach (Clark and Moss 2001) and arts-informed inquiry (Cole, Neilsen, Knowles and Luciani 2004). Sensitivities between these approaches enable potent integration of research strategies.

Jalongo (2007: 114) stated: 'Children know when we are not really listening to them, just like they know when we skip pages while reading their favourite picture book.' As Malaz (aged seven) commented:

> It's good to be listened to, because you get some more ideas from people if you're talking about something in your project. And listening's a part of learning . . . we need to listen. That's how we get ideas.

Voices like this from Clare's study explore shared understandings of a group of children in the early years of school around the place of their school – specifically, the places that are significant to them. The voices from Alma's study offer a further layer, as children in their final year of primary school reflect on their memories of place in their Kindergarten year. While there are differences between memoried and lived experiences, overlapping themes from these studies suggest that by listening to children, potentialities may be offered in ways of imagining and enacting the *space and place* of primary school differently.

Theorizing place

> Place cannot be seen as a static construct; it is fluid and alive . . . often filled with tension and controversy as it assists in a very difficult process of simultaneously remaining and becoming for the individuals living within its boundaries.
> (Glasman and Crowson 2001: 6)

Within the field of education, there is often a focus on the *space* of schools – the architecture and physical organization of buildings, layout of classrooms, availability of playgrounds. It is important, however, to remember the interrelatedness and interdependence of space and place (Agnew 2005), and that while 'place as a site in space can be charted in a mathematical sense, . . . it is the human relationship with, and within a place that makes it stand apart' (Miles 2008: 4). Place becomes more than physical location, including arenas of complex memory, interaction and relationships.

Interestingly, research that does consider children's perspectives on the space and place of schools is primarily concerned with (usually older) students' overwhelmingly negative perceptions of physical spaces, in particular, the 'limited autonomy experienced by them in relation to space and body use at schools' (Gordon and Lahelma 1996: 303). Indeed, the literature (e.g. McKenzie 2008) suggests that physical spaces in many primary schools are perceived as places of adult control over children's experiences, bodies and movement; of surveillance and regulation, informed by discourses of suspicion, supervision, protection and normalization (see, e.g., MacNaughton 2005; Moss and Petrie 2002). Organization of space in schools has been identified as the area that children themselves are most aware of in separating them from (and constructing them as 'other' to) adults, symbolizing to children how they have been positioned well below adults within a hierarchy of power (Devine 2003).

Adding to this construction of schooling is the fact that pedagogy and possibility are inextricably linked, but often do not include a consideration of the spirit of place:

> A building marks a location in space. Together, the buildings and its surroundings create a 'place' with a particular identity. However, the true spirit of places resides not only in their physical parameters, but also in the symbolic meanings that grow up around them as a result of the history, participation and belonging of the people who use them.
>
> (Olds 2001: 25)

We ask here, then: What can we learn from listening to the voices of children as they illuminate special, significant and important places within the early years of school?

Listening as research

Our research approaches reflect interconnectedness between *research* and *listening*. We are influenced by Rinaldi's (2006) ideas of a pedagogy of listening, and draw on her theorizing regarding political and ethical implications of listening. From the perspective of educators in Reggio Emilia, Italy, Rinaldi reminds us that, 'Listening is not easy. It requires a deep awareness and, at the same time, a suspension of our judgments and above all our prejudices; it requires openness to change' (ibid.: 65).

We are influenced further by these Italian educators in seeking to acknowledge and find ways to listen to the hundred languages of children. Thus, within this notion of Research as Listening (and Listening as Research), we understand listening to involve listening not only to verbal/written/word communication, but also to as many other languages, expressions of meaning and experience as possible. In these studies, we emphasize the importance of not privileging one language (words) over others, deliberately seeking out greater possibilities of richness, authenticity and depth through varied means of expression (Lind 2005; Richardson 1997).

Listening thoughtfully and hearing the unexpected implies openness to uncertainty. We as researchers (along with the participants) were often moved by moments of surprise, risk, trust and joy. We find Somerville's work regarding research as a 'process that cannot begin with logic, but comes from a place of not knowing, informed by intuition and responsiveness' (2008: 210) intersecting in helpful ways with Rinaldi's theorizing around a pedagogy of listening.

Listening to children in the first years of school: two case studies

This section offers context for our studies. Alma describes the memory work that she facilitated, then Clare outlines processes of mapping place in the research that she undertook. We then draw together and analyse overlapping threads from both studies to explore questions around children's shared constructions of the place of their school.

Alma: a story

Clutching disposable cameras, six pairs of youngsters in their last weeks of primary school explored memories of Kindergarten through the cinematic lens. They chattered, ran, laughed, sketched and stepped back through time to re-inhabit themselves as Kindergarten children.

Philosophical and physical contexts

Set in the Australian state of New South Wales, this project invited Grade Six (12-year-old) children to revisit memories of their first year of formal schooling using strategies loaned by arts-based inquiry (Creates 1992; Knowles and Thomas 2002) to help identify salient features of their Kindergarten experience. This journey of memory reflected my desire to give voice to one of the silent spaces of schooling: children's perspectives in debates about core curricula, about what matters in experiences of school.

This study is located in a research frame that values relationships. As the researcher, I was a familiar, though distanced figure for the children. For their first two years of school, I had been a regular visitor to their class, working with their teacher on several initiatives, including the use of my own children's puppets (a cat and a kangaroo) to encourage early writers with purposeful correspondence. The puppets made an indelible impression, contributing an end-of-year gift to all families of letter exchanges between each child and the puppets. I reasoned that, as the children had valued puppet time, they would be open in sharing their memories. Indeed, in their last weeks of primary school, the chance to be involved in a special project with 'the puppet lady' was enough incentive to gain enthusiastic participation, from both children who were invited and their friends. Members of the children's families also shared memories of their children beginning school, but that data is not included here. The Kindergarten teacher who had taught ten of the children also contributed to initial stages of the research, adding to familiarity of context for these 12-year-olds.

The children reflect the varied economic and cultural backgrounds in a school of about 360 students. There can be considerable population turnover, reflecting local employment and a nearby women's refuge. Initial criteria for inclusion in the study was membership of the Kindergarten who were still at the school in Grade Six (less than half the original class). These ten children were joined by another two who had been in the school's other Kindergarten; while not part of the puppet project, one was the twin of a child in the project and the other had a parent actively involved in a related project at the time. So, more by accident than design, the group included six girls and six boys, a set of twins, the least and most academically able children from the Kindergarten (two of the 12 were still in Grade Five, having repeated a grade). Children's families included Chinese, Irish, Polish, Armenian and Korean backgrounds. Both children and participating family members gave consent through standard ethics procedures, although gaining informed consent from children is problematic (Greene and Hogan 2005). While the children signed permission forms (as did their parents), they were most likely expressing trust in a respectful relationship and pleasure at being involved.

The method of investigation was chosen to honor the complexity of the enquiry, to recognize that different approaches to meaning-making would be necessary to help illuminate the past. The logic underlying the study was that, in the hazy glimpses of years past, moments and spaces that emerged with clarity would be those that made a lasting impression. This goal resonated with Gahan's (2009) historical study of remembered experiences of young children in a Queensland (Australia) preschool/nursery setting in the last century, a study which 'uncovered a "secret culture" of childhood experiences at kindergarten, disclosed through often previously unspoken stories and memories' (ibid.: 4). Such narratives also emerged from this study in the context of remembering special places.

The research approach was inspired by installations of Marlene Creates (1991), a Newfoundland artist. In a 1997 Artist's Statement, she wrote: 'I am interested in the multiple realities and different, often contradictory, layers of history and memory and language hovering over and infused in places. My works are not answers, they are questions.' The methodology included, therefore, an invitation to participants to consider a place of personal relevance and to explore their relationship with that space through photography, drawing and narrative. I was interested to know, from the perspective of children who were leaving primary school, what was foregrounded for them in their Kindergarten experience. Logically, whatever might be highlighted at this distance, two thirds of their lifetime ago, would be salient to the construct of Kindergarten, and important to early years' educators.

The children were told about the project and offered disposable cameras in pairs to take pictures of each other, a special place they associated with their time in Kindergarten and a picture of themselves in that special place. These instructions reflect Creates' methodologies (1992), in a compacted time frame, with reliance on children's perspectives. Having taken their photographs, they then drew their special place and wrote about it, enabling multiple forms of meaning-making to be evidenced. While respecting the Creates' frame, these elements also reflect inspiration from educators in Reggio Emilia (Edwards, Gandini and Forman 1998).

As transition to school was a focus of earlier research, data was available from these children beginning school. These data were revisited to help inform understandings of the children's current perspectives. For example, when she was interviewed at the end of her second month in Kindergarten, Isabelle chatted about a range of things. When asked what she liked about Kindergarten, she said: 'I like afternoon because I get to do lots of exciting things, like play in the Wendy House and do messy things.'

Six years later, Isabelle was asked to reflect on what she remembered about Kindergarten. With another Grade Six student and a disposable camera, she was invited to have a portrait taken of her now (which she chose to have hanging upside down on the climbing bars), to think of a place that had particular meaning or importance to her when she thought about that time, to take a picture of that place and a picture of herself in that place. The picture that she had taken was of herself dressed up in role play, talking on the phone in 'the house corner' (the Wendy House mentioned in her Kindergarten interview). From her Grade Six perspective, Isabelle wrote:

> I liked the house corner because I enjoyed playing mums and dads. Once Louie (a boy in my class) put the milk carton in the washing machine! . . . One other thing that I remember was when the fridge fell over and all the food toys got into a huge mess. I enjoyed pretending to cook too with the pots and pans and plastic food!

Intersections of cognition, emotion and environmental embeddedness permeate the range of pieces contributed by these 12-year-olds. The elements of long-lasting emotion (playful fun) and shared narratives are typical of the writing the group contributed. All the children's writing was spontaneous, with no editing, discussion or rewriting. As a visitor, I was grateful to take small moments from the final chaotic weeks of school to gather these reflections.

Clare: mapping place

The data that I present here is a fragment of a larger study within my doctoral research, which aimed to do the following:

- illuminate what is possible in the early years of primary school when time, space/place, knowledge and relationships are imagined and enacted differently;
- investigate how this school community positions themselves, and within what discourses;
- explore how children experience this alternative positioning of teaching/ learning/school;
- analyze what hope this school offers in terms of opening up new ways/ multiple possibilities of imagining and enacting schooling.

The research that I place alongside Alma's focuses on disrupting dominant understandings of the spaces and places of school (as predominantly dehumanized, institutionalized, standardized, normalized) and further explores what it might mean when children create and inhabit places that are special and significant to them. Ultimately, I suggest that hope for new potentialities may be offered through imagining and enacting the *space and place* of the early years of primary school differently. This is why the research sought to illuminate hopeful possibilities offered by a primary school 'where alternatives are demonstrated and viable options promoted' (Cannella 2000: 217) – to locate disruptions in the regime of truth that create new trajectories, and to identify lines of flight (Deleuze and Guattari 1987) that have potential to open up spaces of freedom (Foucault 1988).

The school community

The case for this study was defined as a primary school that had different or alternative ways of thinking about and enacting time, place/space, knowledge and relationships that had potential to open up alternative discourses of education for schooling. The school was within mainstream educational systems in Australia. Figure 10.1 summarizes key demographic information about the school community, in the state of Victoria, with which I researched over six months in 2008.

Members of this community who participated in the research included ten students (aged between five and eight, from the prep – Grade Two class); five teachers; six parents; and the Leader/Administrator (junior school principal). The children reflected the diverse wider school community, speaking a range of languages including Arabic, English, Vietnamese, Tamil, Swahili, Indonesian and Amharic. This diversity in languages and literacies highlighted again the

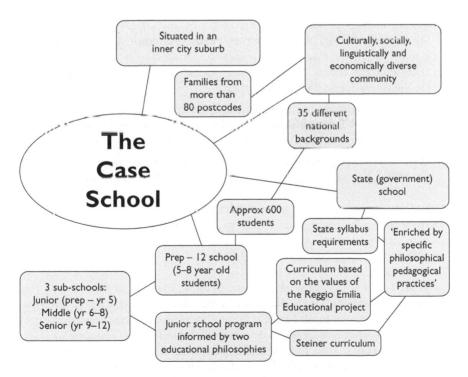

Figure 10.1 The Case School: an overview of context.

importance of engaging with arts-informed research methodologies that have the potential to harness 'the importance of diverse languages for gaining insights into the complexities of the human condition' (Cole and Knowles 2008: 59) by engaging with 'forms of representation [that] give us access to expressive possibilities that would not be possible without their presence' (Eisner 2008: 5).

An early provocation: 'mapping' the school

In my first weeks with the school community, I asked participants (children, teachers and parents – but in this chapter, I focus on the children) to help me gain an understanding of the *place* of the school from their perspectives: to each map the school for me. My interest in mapping as a method of data creation was inspired by Clark and Moss' (2001) research with young children in prior to school settings, as well as the work of others who have used various forms of mapping to explore complexities of place through arts-informed research (such as Somerville 2008; Noone 2006; Bown and Sumsion 2007).

As a provocation before mapping, I posed three questions: 'What places are important to know about in the school? What places are significant or special to you? Why?' Prior to designing the processes and creation of their mapping, I also asked participants to think about:

> **What** you might decide to represent. (What places/areas/spaces do you think are important or significant? Are they in the classroom? Are they across the school? Are they physical areas, or areas constructed by what happens within them at certain times? Where are these places? Who/what are they for? How do the places connect with each other?)
>
> **How** you might choose to represent these areas. (Drawing a map/visual representation? Taking photographs? Writing narratives? Filming? Taking me to places and telling me about them? A combination of these methods?)
>
> **Why** you have chosen to represent these areas. (Why are these significant to you? Why do you think it's important to show/tell me about these areas?)

While all the participants were given a sheet with these prompts and questions, I also spent time talking with each group, to explain more about mapping in ways that didn't rely on written words. For example, when mapping with Thara, Fergus, Dharani and Xander, I initially said to them:

> What I wanted to know about was, because I'm new at the school, I'm wondering about what the places are in the school that are important to you, or special that you think I should know about? So . . . in the classroom or in the school, what sorts of places do you think I should know about or are really special to you? . . . So I was thinking you could tell me about them, or you could draw them or we could go and take photos of them?
>
> (Transcript, 11 June 2008)

Thus, by mapping, I did not mean only drawing a map from an aerial perspective (although some participants did represent their map in this way), but mapping could also mean many forms of representation: some children drew pictures and diagrams, others took me physically around spaces and talked to me about places of significance to them, wrote prose or poetry, used photography (Figure 10.2) or collage, told me a story about a place, or something that had happened in that place. Each participant later spent time with me describing and explaining their maps, both individually and in small groups.

In describing these research processes, I am struck by the way in which written down in a linear, structured, certain way, the strategies perhaps also take on a linear, certain tone. This was far from the case. The research processes were often unexpected, joyful and emergent (Somerville 2008). What is described here in general terms was personal, relational, complex and lived.

Interestingly, while different participants chose differing forms of representation, *every* child who participated also chose to represent their mapping of place through digital photography. What was intended as an initial introduction to a case study, to assist me in gaining understanding of the significance of the place of the school from various perspectives, ultimately became, for the children, an extended photographic project. This project enabled a complex exploration of relationships between the spaces of schooling and the construction of shared understandings of connected, inhabited and embodied *places* by these children.

Figure 10.2 Mapping the school.

Hearing voices from the two case studies: seeing spaces and inhabiting places

Here we draw together thematic threads shared across both studies, focusing particularly on ideas around the *place* of school from the perspectives of children. Themes relating to the centrality for children of inhabiting place – and the key roles that both *agency* and *relationships* play in inhabiting place – are explored below.

Creative agency: high places, hidden spaces and children's places

The construct of children's agency has emerged through the data in both studies. Agency here is defined in terms of shaping place through creative decision-making and the taking of ownership of space. This creative agency is integral in the possibilities of children *inhabiting* place – as an active element in transitioning institutional space to personal place. This conceptual thread is strong across both the lived data and the memoried data from the two studies.

Many significant places selected by children were physically built or furnished spaces designed for purposes of designated (adult) functions (containment, surveillance) – spaces such as boundary walls, metal seats for sitting and eating lunch. The purposes of these functional spaces were creatively inverted, inhabited and owned by the children, often through imaginative play narratives, and through the use of these constructed spaces in unexpected (and often slightly 'forbidden' or 'secret') ways to create a special place.

Alma's story of seeking agency: looking back

One way to conceptualize this notion of agency is to examine a remembered instance where it was denied, where boundaries were adult-imposed. When asked to consider important Kindergarten places from her Grade Six perspective, Theresa had a picture of herself taken on the verandah outside the Kindergarten classroom, a space where children were kept for the first weeks of school to avoid being overwhelmed on a large playground. After showing considerable familiarity with research procedures by asking me if two children in the study were being included from the other Kindergarten as 'a control group', she wrote:

> The verandah is important to me, because there are a lot of memories surrounding it. My first memory is the annoyance of having to sit there and eat while all of the others were on the silver seats. I hated feeling isolated and different. I also remember everyone calling recess 'little lunch' and lunch 'big lunch', and wishing that I was old enough to call them 'lunch' and 'recess'. I was giving myself boundaries that weren't really there by saying that I wasn't able to call them the names that the older kids called them. I was really happy when we were finally allowed to eat outside.

This sophisticated response gives insight to Theresa's perceptions and probably to discussions which took place in her home, as well as to the tangible frustration of watching her seven-year-old sister in the lunch space reserved for those farther up the school hierarchy.

The request to think of a place that was important to these children in Kindergarten did not evoke (initially) memories of sitting, listening to the teacher read (although I know they enjoyed that) or working at a table (Figure 10.3). The children acknowledged these activities when asked to remember what they did in a typical day, but the spontaneously remembered places that had emotional resonance were places where they could interact with the environment in their own ways. Salient sites evoked detailed and often emotional reflections. In addition to the stories above, four boys wrote about climbing on playground equipment and two referred to the tree roots where they played with Matchbox cars. Of the girls, one also wrote about the House corner (like Isabelle). Another wrote about the silver benches so envied by Theresa, one talked about being with her friend and another wrote about one of the brick playing walls (the end of neighboring classrooms, with painted bright circles, inviting ball play), incorporating her friends and teacher into a fantasy future.

Each of the children's chosen sites reflects intense engagement. These are memories about open-ended opportunities where children had agency; they remembered places where they could initiate and problem-solve, talk, laugh and set their own agendas. Their schemas for inhabiting spaces created personally significant places. Perhaps we need to think more about how places and spaces

Figure 10.3 Explaining photographic 'maps'.

that matter to children can be included in activities required within societal expectations of schooling.

Clare's story of seeking agency: lived experience

Many places identified by children as being particularly important to them had elements of being secret, risky or private. Special places that children wanted me to know about were high or hidden: the bunk, climbing frame, tunnel, behind the water tank. These were spaces that acquired special significance when used creatively by the children to construct places of agency and ownership. And importantly, perhaps, these were spaces where adults do not want to (or sometimes physically cannot) go.

On the day that children started mapping the school, we went outside with clipboards, pens, paper, digital and video cameras. Fergus (aged six) and Xander (aged seven) went immediately to the high orange brick wall that ran around the school boundary, climbed up on it (each helping the other by holding clipboards and pens while the other hoisted themselves up) and sat high on the wall to draw their maps (Figure 10.4). The wall was the first thing that both Fergus and Xander drew. The first photograph that Fergus took was of the wall (Figure 10.5, Figure 10.6). I was intrigued – what was it about this brick wall, which – to me – was

Figure 10.4
Fergus' map.

Figure 10.5 Climbing the wall.

invisible, a non-place, a space important only in that it created a boundary line around school grounds, dividing it from the streets? I asked about the wall:

> *Fergus*: I've drawn the brick wall, and the oval.
> *Xander*: . . . and I have been drawing the three levels of the school, the brick wall and the garden.
> *Clare*: Have you? So what is it about the brick wall that's special? Cause I noticed that you came and sat straight on it, too.
> *Fergus*: (laughs) It's good for playing tiggy, and also it leads to the garden and the climbing frame.
> *Xander*: (at the same time as Fergus) It's nice and warm.
> *Clare:* So it's like a path?
> *Fergus*: And it's also good for sitting on.
> *Xander*: (at the same time) And we can see better on it. We like the wall because it's nice and warm . . . and you can see better on it.

Figure 10.6 The wall.

It is interesting to reflect on the wall as a place highly valued by the children. This is a space designed by adults as a boundary – a symbolic and physical barrier between inside and outside to provide containment, separation and regulation. As Olds states, 'Concepts such as ownership, exclusion, access, and control become part of a child's identity as they are learned in relationship to particular spaces' (2001: 26). In climbing the wall, and creating new play narratives around the significance of the wall (as an exclusively children's place for sitting, playing, keeping warm, seeing better, following as a path), the children seem to have subverted adult narratives of safety and surveillance, and imagined the wall as a place of freedom and wonder (with perhaps an underlying secretive element of risk).

Relationships: friendships shaping place

The second strong theme threading through both studies is the importance of relationships: the significance of places shaped by relationships and relationships shaped by places. In both the lived and memoried data, participants revealed that places were important to them because of who they played with in those places. In conversations about school spaces, most participants in both studies identified relationships with friends – within a space – as being an important foundation for the formation of that *place*. Friendships are thus seen as constituted within place, and places are constructed through relationships created within them.

Alma's story of intersections of place and friendship: looking back

Two-thirds of the places identified by the Sixth graders as special to them included play with friends. While others did not foreground friends, they embraced a sense of belonging, as in Theresa's narratives below.

When Theresa was in Kindergarten and asked to draw herself at school, she was thoughtful and drew for a while, looking up to comment, 'I drew what I was being – you know what I was being? I was being a cat!' When asked for more information, Theresa volunteered that she was 'a bit sad' when she started school, but that after that, she played with a few of her friends who lived down the street. Theresa was probably not aware that she was rapidly developing into the most able reader and writer in the class. When asked if there was anything that worried her, she said, 'Yes, if there's no-one I know here, but there's lots of people.' In fact, her seven-year-old sister was at the same school.

As a Sixth grader, when asked what she remembered about starting school, Theresa replied: 'I remember being relaxed in a big room with a lot of children, I also remember most of them. It was very different 'cos there were so many more people than when I was in preschool.' I asked for clarification, 'What do you mean by different?' and she replied: 'Lots of different personalities, 'cos the younger (preschool) children didn't show their personalities as much as the Kindergartners, I don't think.'

Clare's story of intersections of place and friendship: lived experience

In the lived data, many drawings and photographs that mapped significant places in the school drew attention to the importance of relationships – particularly the friendships – that occurred within these places.

Anike drew a map of the school depicting the places she plays with different people: hopscotch, chickens, basketball courts, climbing frame, vegetable garden, as well as arrows to show how she moves between these places. Anike pointed to different parts of her map as she explained to me the significance of what she had drawn:

> The basketball court. And the girls and the boys. Yesterday we was playing basketball and we was on girls' team and boys' team. So the girls scored one goal, and the boy had two. After that, we was playing hide and seek, so we hide in the flowers and the tree, we was hiding behind that, and then we played tiggy in the climbing frame, then we come inside to go to the library, after that the bell went and we went back the class, and the lunchtime, at lunchtime we saw this birdie, and then after we saw the bird we played basketball again, and then we played tiggy, hide and seek at the tree, then we

went back to the library, and after that we went to see upstairs class and played in there for a little bit.

Similarly, Dharani's map (Figure 10.7) shows the places she likes to be with her friends – in particular, the tree on the far right, with the wooden bench she can sit on with her friends, that she identifies as her favourite place. As she drew the map, Dharani explained:

> I'm going to draw me and my friends playing in the garden. This is my favourite thing in the school. It's like a wooden bench around a tree, and it's like that (showing drawing), and the tree's very big, and there, I'm going to do it.

These themes of relationships and agency extend a consideration of schooling from the shaping of space to the inhabiting of place.

Figure 10.7
Dharani's map.

Final considerations

Reflecting on what we have learnt from considering threads across these two studies, we find richness and complexity. Clare's study explored shared understandings of a group of young children around the place of their school – specifically, places that were significant to them – through creative mapping. Voices from Alma's study offered a further layer to these understandings, through photographic, sketched and told stories collected in another Australian public school. These remembered and imagined glimpses illustrate an inquiry with a group of young people who had been in the same small school for seven years. Asked to think about special places from their Kindergarten year, this group did not immediately bring to mind the desks, gym or library; they remembered play spaces – indoors and out – and their friends.

We have explored thematic links across these studies – in particular, the importance of *creative agency* and *relationships* in constructing and inhabiting place. This notion of children inhabiting the place of their schools in authentic ways is especially noteworthy when we consider Gruenewald's warning that: 'in place of actual experience with the phenomenal world, educators are handed, and largely accept, the mandates of a standardized, "placeless" curriculum and settle for the abstractions and simulations of classroom learning' (2003: 8).

We have also drawn links across our methodological approaches, crucially, the importance of listening to children through eyes and ears, giving time to seek children's perspectives regarding their learning environments. As the ideas around place are complex, gathering data in a range of ways throws light on more facets of the constructions of shared understandings of place than may be apparent through linear strategies. In these studies, multiple forms of representation have enabled children of varying ages, abilities and backgrounds to contribute their ideas in ways that might not be as accessible through English written text.

In focusing on children's shared understandings of space and place in the first years of school, we hope to add to the conversation that Soja refers to, when he suggests that:

> [W]e are becoming increasingly aware that we are, and always have been, intrinsically spatial beings, active participants in the social construction of our embracing spatialities. Perhaps, more than ever before, a strategic awareness of this collectively created spatiality and its social consequences has become a vital part of making both theoretical and practical sense of our contemporary life-worlds.
>
> (1996: 1)

In the field of education, it is important to note the possible social consequences of spatial construction and the use of adult-defined spaces, and to continually question: when decisions are made in the early years of school, whose constructions of space are most valued? Children are often the most silenced of participants in the educative process. While being asked to write, read, draw, group, regroup, line up, pack up and otherwise conform to institutional expectations, their perceptions of the salient features of the experience are often missing from a consideration of optimal schooling environments. Little is available to help us understand how children experience their first years of school in terms of the power of the place itself. The case studies discussed here contribute to conversations about this rich terrain, enabling children's voices to aid adult understanding of children's perspectives.

In the Convention on the Rights of the Child (United Nations 1989), children are guaranteed the right to participation in decisions that affect them. Research such as that reported here provides some children with a voice, but not necessarily in a forum that will impact on decisions affecting school structures and priorities. Therefore, finally, we stress the importance of not only creating space for children's voices, but *hearing* these voices, and, crucially, ensuring that children's perspectives are informing policy and practice, particularly in designing, creating and inhabiting the places of their learning in the early years of school.

References

Agnew, J. (2005) 'Space: place', in P. Cloke and R. Johnston (eds), *Spaces of Geographical Thought: Deconstructing Human Geography's Binaries*, London: Sage, pp. 81–96.

Bown, K. and Sumsion, J. (2007) 'Voices from the other side of the fence: Early childhood teachers' experiences with mandatory regulatory requirements', *Contemporary Issues in Early Childhood*, 8(1): 30–49.

Cannella, G. (2000) 'Critical and feminist reconstructions of early childhood education: continuing the conversations', *Contemporary Issues in Early Childhood Education*, 1(2): 215–221.

Clark, A. and Moss, P. (2001) *Listening to Young Children: The Mosaic Approach*, London: National Children's Bureau and Joseph Rowntree Foundation.

Cole, A. and Knowles, J. G. (2008) 'Arts-informed research', in J. G. Knowles and A. Cole (eds), *Handbook of the Arts in Qualitative Research*, Thousand Oaks, CA: Sage, pp. 55–70.

Cole, A., Neilsen, L., Knowles, J. G., and Luciani, T. C. (eds) (2004) *Provoked by Art: Theorizing Arts-Informed Research*, Nova Scotia: Backalong Books.

Creates, M. (1991) *Places of Presence: Newfoundland Kin 1989–1991*, St. John's, Newfoundland: Kellick Press.

Creates, M. (1992) *Marlene Creates: Land Works 1979–1991*, S. Gibson Garvey (ed.), St John's, Newfoundland: Memorial University of Newfoundland.

Creates, M. Artist's Statements. These Artist's Statements are single pages written for an installation. Some include reference to a particular exhibition. They may have been handouts or wall information; there is no pagination or publication information available. They were collected by J. Gary Knowles, OISE, Toronto.

Deleuze, G. and Guattari, F. (1987) *A Thousand Plateaus: Capitalism and Schizophrenia*, London: The Athlone Press.

Devine, D. (2003) *Children, Power and Schooling: How Childhood Is Structured in the Primary School*, Stoke on Trent: Trentham Books.

Edwards, C., Gandini, L. and Forman, G. (1998) *One Hundred Languages of Children: Advanced Reflections*, Norwood, NJ: Ablex.

Eisner, E. (2008) 'Art and knowledge', in J. G. Knowles and A. Cole (eds), *Handbook of the Arts in Qualitative Research*, Thousand Oaks, CA: Sage, pp. 3–12.

Foucault, M. (1988) 'The dangerous individual', in L. Kritzman (ed.), *Politics, Philosophy, Culture: Interviews and Other Writings of Michel Foucault, 1977–1984*, New York: Routledge, pp. 125–150.

Gahan, D. (2009) 'Memories of childhood at kindergarten: What endures? What can we learn from this?' Paper presented at the New Zealand Early Childhood Research conference. January. Wellington.

Glasman, N. S. and Crowson, R. L. (2001) 'Reexamining relations and a sense of place between schools and their constituents: Introduction', *Peabody Journal of Education*, 76(2): 1–8.

Gordon, T. and Lahelma, E. (1996) ' "School is like an ant's nest": spatiality and embodiment in schools', *Gender and Education*, 8(5): 301–310.

Greene, S. and Hogan, D. (2005) *Researching Children's Experience: Approaches and Methods*, London: Sage.

Gruenewald, D. (2003) 'The best of both worlds: A critical pedagogy of place', *Educational Researcher*, 32(4): 3–12.

Jalongo, M. R. (2007) *Learning to Listen, Listening to Learn*, Washington, DC: NAEYC.

Knowles, J. G. and Thomas, S. M. (2002) 'Artistry, inquiry, and sense of place: Secondary school students portrayed in context', in C. Bagley and M.B. Cancienne (eds), *Dancing the data*, New York: Peter Lang, pp. 121–132.

Lind, U. (2005) 'Identity and power, "meaning", gender and age: Children's creative work as signifying practice', *Contemporary Issues in Early Childhood*, 6(3): 256–268.

MacNaughton, G. (2005) *Doing Foucault in Early Childhood Studies: Applying Poststructural Ideas*, London: Routledge.

McKenzie, M. (2008) 'The places of pedagogy: or, what can we do with culture through intersubjective experiences?', *Environmental Education Research*, 14(3): 361–373.

Miles, R. (2008) 'Rural-Regional sustainability through revitalising the commons: a case study', Symposium presentation at the annual Conference of the Australian Association of Research in Education. Available at: www.aare.edu.au/08pap/mil081075.pdf. (accessed 21 May 2009).

Moss, P. and Petrie, P. (2002) *From Children's Services to Children's Spaces: Public Policy, Children and Childhood*, London: RoutledgeFalmer.

Noone, G. (2006) 'Teaching and place – a mutual relation', in *Sharing Wisdom for Our Future. Environmental Education in Action: Proceedings of the 2006 Conference of the Australian Association of Environmental Education*. Bunbury, W.A. Available at: www.bournda-e.schools.nsw.edu.au/OSPR/page45/documents /24_Noone.pdf (accessed 15 June 2008).

Olds, A. R. (2001) *Child Care Design Guide*, New York: McGraw-Hill.

Richardson, L. (1997) *Fields of Play: Constructing an Academic Life*, New Brunswick, NJ: Rutgers University Press.

Rinaldi, C. (2006) *In Dialogue with Reggio Emilia: Listening, Researching and Learning*, London: Routledge.

Soja, E. (1996) *Thirdspace: Journeys to Los Angeles and Other Real-And-Imagined Spaces*, Cambridge, MA: Blackwell.

Somerville, M. (2008) 'Waiting in the chaotic place of unknowing: Articulating postmodern emergence', *International Journal of Qualitative Studies in Education*, 21(3): 209–220.

United Nations (1989) *Convention on the Rights of the Child*. Document A/RES/44/25 with annex. Available at: http://www.wunrn.com/reference/pdf/Convention_Rights_Child.PDF (accessed 20 June 2009).

Chapter 11

In tune with the learner's perspective in music

Theoretical and analytical considerations when interviewing children

Cecilia Wallerstedt, Niklas Pramling and Ingrid Pramling Samuelsson

In this chapter, two contemporary challenges posed by sociocultural theory to research on children's learning, and one more long-standing challenge introduced by Piaget are considered in the context of interviewing children with the intent to find out their discernment of time (metre) in music. These three issues are: (1) the situated nature of knowing; (2) the need to analyse the interview as a social practice; and (3) the analytical necessity to pay attention to learning from the learner's perspective. Through analysis of empirical excerpts it is shown what these notions mean in a concrete sense when analysing children's learning and understanding.

Introduction

In educational research and related fields of inquiry, the issue of learners understanding tasks differently from what the researchers have intended has often, albeit implicitly, been a matter of concern. For example, in psychological research, the basic empirical fact that learners make sense rather than 'store' information was demonstrated in a powerful way in the pioneering work of Sir Frederic Bartlett in his seminal study on remembering in 1932. However, this basic fact has not sat comfortably in subsequent psychological investigation. Rather, in test situations (e.g., interviews), what Bartlett referred to as humans' effort after meaning has tended to be considered a nuisance, a kind of source of error threatening well-defined experimental procedures. The focus has been on a quantitative view of learning and remembering, i.e., on more or less measuring information. However, as Bruner (1990) has cogently argued, processing information and making sense are fundamentally distinct processes. Paradoxically, while a basic premise of cognitive psychology was to account for higher mental functions such as understanding and related phenomena, respondents' (e.g., children's) answers to tests tend to be valued in terms of right or wrong, and related to age, rather than as the object of inquiry as such. In another influential strand of research, children's alleged misconceptions have been extensively studied. However, an inherent problem with these studies, from our point of view, is that they consider these conceptions to be held by the children rather than as replies to communicative (and cognitive) challenges children face in the interview. When studying children's understanding, these are defined as correct or not, alternatively, as misconceptions that need to be abandoned and replaced with correct concepts. Both these lines of research can be seen in terms of what Rommetveit (1980) has referred to as the negative scholarly rationalism (Säljö 2002) of psychological research, i.e., a preoccupation with what children at various ages, levels of development, etc. *cannot* do. This means, among other things, that children's answers are not seen and analysed as rational responses to the question/test as the child has understood it (Elbers 2004; Hundeide 2003).

In child development research, Piaget ([1923]1926, [1926]1951) was, of course, a pivotal figure in introducing the child's perspective. Being critical of the tradition (of intelligence testing) focusing on the number of correct and incorrect responses by children at various ages, he argued that it would be more fruitful to analyse children's answers in terms of their grounding in children's reasoning. As Wood (1998: 29) explains, 'Unlike most child psychologists before him, Piaget did not simply set out to discover what children could *not* do in comparisons with adults, but sought to find out what they could do and what they actually did' (italics in original). By arguing and illustrating how children perceive and think differently from adults, depending on differences in experience and maturity, he put the child on the research agenda as a subject rather than an object. It lies outside the scope of the present chapter to review critiques subsequently raised against Piaget's understanding of child development. However, a few points need to be made very briefly. There is reason to claim that Piaget himself disregarded the importance of the adult in the child's development (see e.g., Piaget 1983). Closely related to this omission was a view of capability as an inherent property in the child acquired through exploring the physical world. However, it has been argued, the child grows up in relationships to and with other people (Nelson 1996). As a consequence, in more recent work, learning is conceived of as a social phenomenon and understanding as a negotiated, emergent, feature of interaction (Säljö 2000). This means that, in an analysis of sense-making, it is necessary to account for how sense is negotiated and produced in interaction between, e.g., an interviewer and a child. Another development since Piaget is the growing realisation that knowledge is contingent upon perspectives. There is no neutral knowledge. All knowledge presumes certain perspectives on phenomena.

Even in research, we have to presume, explicitly or implicitly, certain things, such as what constitutes knowing, how we gain access to it (others' understanding), the nature of communication and sense-making (Säljö 2002). The perspective we take affects what 'knowing' we produce in research and what is at stake here are the views of the capabilities of children that we generate in research (Pramling 2006). We shall consider these issues with the help of an example in which the musical-listening skills of children are analysed. This domain of study largely lacks what can be referred to as 'the learner's perspective' (Sommer, Pramling Samuelsson and Hundeide 2010). A similar idea – if not in these terms or much further developed – was put forward in two recent studies on children's musical listening.

An example: studying musical-listening skills in children

In relation to Kellett's (2000) study of young children's listening skills, Marshall and Hargreaves (2007: 35f.) write that 'She noted that research on music often used the judgements of professional adult musicians to norm reference children's responses rather than exploring those responses for their own intrinsic value.' Concluding their own empirical study of young children's style discrimination, Marshall and Hargreaves (ibid.: 44f.) make the point that 'Amongst younger participants, it was difficult to establish whether the participants who performed poorly did so because they did not understand the task, or because they were unable to discriminate between the musical excerpts.' Hence, in the terminology of the present chapter (as will be explained below), it is important to add a learner's perspective to the analyst's perspective of musical development research. In this chapter, we will attempt to take on this challenge, this gap in our knowing, within the framework of the two overarching challenges that sociocultural theory poses to research on children's understanding based on interviews.

Since the example chosen for this analysis concerns musical listening skills, a few words on this issue are necessary. Listening, as Peterson (2006: 15) points out, 'is really at the heart of all musical activities, because musical activity of any kind invariably involves attention to sound through listening (Marshall and Hargreaves 2007)' In fact, listening may be considered fundamental as both a *form of*, and as a *means of*, gaining other, *musical knowledge* (Reimer 2003). Listening entails more than simply having ears that are in order. Listening may be understood as an activity, or rather, as a set or different activities or practices. Hence, there are many ways of listening to music, for example, being exposed to a background wall of sound (DeNora 2000; Young and Gillen 2007), for mood regulation (Saarikallio and Erkkilä 2007; Sloboda and O'Neill 2001) as a tool for learning (in other domains, such as mathematics, language, social abilities) (Pound and Harrison 2003; Winner and Cooper 2000), as a strategy for enhancing musical self-esteem in children who do not consider themselves to be musical (Kellett 2000), for experience or pedagogy (Zerull 2006), or aesthetic appreciation (Hargreaves, North and Tarrant 2006). Listening to music may cover a wide range of practices. In the present case, music-listening skills are understood in terms of developing one's capability of discerning features of music in an increasingly fine way. However, music-listening should be seen as the background to the present study, which will focus instead on theoretical and analytical issues of more general relevance to studies of children's capabilities.

In this chapter, we will focus on the following theoretical notions:

1   the situated nature of knowing;
2   the necessity to analyse the interview as a social practice, and the analytical necessity to pay attention to learning from the learner's perspective.

Theoretical frame: contemporary challenges in researching children's understanding and capabilities

The theoretical point of departure consists of two challenges posed by sociocultural theory to research on children's (and adults') learning: (1) the socially situated nature of human knowing; and (2) the need to analyse interviews as social practices. First, we will present these contemporary challenges, and then we will show, through analysis of empirical data, what these notions mean in doing analytical work on children's learning and understanding.

According to sociocultural theory (Säljö 2000, 2005), children's (as well as adults') knowing is socially situated (Wells 1999). This means that what the child knows is not clear-cut in a general sense. Instead, his or her understanding will be contingent upon how a certain task is communicatively framed (Hundeide 2003), including the tools, artefacts (Schoultz, Säljö and Wyndhamn 2001) and scaffolding (Wood, Bruner and Ross [1976] 2006) present or absent in the situation. This claim has clear implications for researching children's knowledge and skills. We can no longer measure/quantify the child's knowledge and conclude what he or she understands or knows in general. Instead, we must study and show under what circumstances the child is able to do or understand something in a certain way. This makes the task for the researcher much more difficult and, arguably, more interesting.

Sociocultural theory also argues that interviews, as a common kind of data-generating method in researching children's understanding, need to be analysed as social practices, not as individual cognition in the child (Säljö 2000). This is another challenge for the researcher to consider and try to manage in doing research. It is due to the situated (i.e., communicatively contingent) nature of knowing, that analyses of children's understanding need to be analyses of what he or she considers to be relevant replies as participants in social practices rather than as individual cognition. As researchers, we cannot tap the child of his or her understanding or capability. Rather, in an interview, understanding is an interactive achievement where various – potentially discrepant – perspectives need to be coordinated and negotiated in some manner. The interviewer is not alone in defining how the question is (to be) understood.

The third theoretical notion – shared by sociocultural theory and others – considered in this chapter concerns the importance of analysing learning from the learner's perspective (Sommer *et al.* 2010). If we analyse learning from the learner's perspective, we presume that what the child answers is rational and relevant according to his or her understanding. The task for the analyst is then to clarify what this response is a response to, as distinct from the question as understood by the interviewer (teacher, researcher). Hence, the child's answer is not judged in the first instance as correct or incorrect (or as a misconception as it were) according to some pre-established criteria. In this chapter, we intend to illustrate, through empirical analysis, what such a learner's perspective means when studying children's understanding and discuss why such a perspective is essential to research (and teaching). The premise of considering the interview as a social practice implies a way of paying critical attention to the learner's perspectives as well as the interviewer's (or analyst's, we will use these latter terms interchangeably in this text) perspective when studying children's understanding and capabilities.

Empirical work: interviewing children about musical listening

Data from an ongoing research project on the development of children's musical listening skills are presented and analysed in terms of the concepts presented in the previous section. What does it mean, in a concrete sense, to focus on the learner's perspective in research informed by the contemporary challenges posed by sociocultural theory?

The first excerpt is not an interview in a strict sense. It consists of data from a classroom conversation. However, the teacher conducts what could be conceived of as a 'spontaneous interview' trying to find out what the children have understood and/or noted in the musical activity. This excerpt is then followed by briefer excerpts from actual interviews with the children. In these empirical excerpts, patterns of variation and invariance are used in order to help children discern (Marton and Tsui 2004) aspects of the music, i.e., the interviews are based on the idea that some features of the music must be varied while others are kept invariant to make it easier for the children to single out particular features and researchers to record their responses. The empirical data are derived from one (of three) lesson(s) and its follow-up interviews revolving around the issue of trying to develop children's musical listening skills. More specifically, the teacher's intention is to develop the children's (aged six–eight years old in an integrated class) capability to discern time in music (i.e., to be able to distinguish between three–four time and two–four time). In order to follow the conversations to be analysed, the musical novice may need some music-theoretical concepts. 'Time' (or time signature as indicated in a score) or 'metre' refers to the number of beats (pulse) in a bar. 'Dynamics' refers to a variation in volume. When a beat (usually the first beat in a bar) is emphasised, we say that it is accentuated, in contrast to the other beats in the bar, which are unaccentuated. The 'tempo' of the music refers to the pace of the beat (faster/slower).

Knowing/figuring out what to count

Before proceeding to listen to music and deciding what time different pieces have, the teacher and children do a movement activity. The teacher claps her hands, waves her hand like a conductor, and so on, to demonstrate different rhythms and then asks children what time she is indicating. Some of these representations are completely soundless, e.g., waving a hand, making the task a matter of visual discernment. The teacher's intention (so we were told) with the activity to be analysed below was to give the children a chance to try to decide the time of the examples only through listening to an even pulse with an accent on every other or every third beat. Some of the children also try to make movements, challenging their classmates to decide their time:

Excerpt 1
1　*Teacher*: Now I'm going to do like this, curtsy, and then you have to guess if there are two beats or three beats to a bar (if it's in two–four time or three–four time). And then you can do it too, to see if we're doing the same (bends her knees and stands up keeping time).
2　(Several children copy the teacher's movements.)
3　*Teacher*: Does Eskil know what time this is in? What can you count to? (Still continues with the movements.)
4　*Eskil*: Nine hundred.
5　*Teacher*: No, I mean if you can count to two or three, like we did before when we counted the bars.
6　*Eskil*: Three.
7　*Teacher*: Can you count to three when I do this, while I bend my knees?
8　*Eskil*: One, two, three (bending his knees at the same time as the teacher and counting the number of bends, i.e. every other beat in the two–four time that the teacher wants to illustrate).
9　*Teacher*: Watch me now! (Continues with the movements, saying one, two; *one* on the way down, *two* on the way up.) That's what I mean (continues to bend her knees and count, laying the emphasis on *one*). How many beats to a bar can that be? What do you think, Cajsa?
10　*Cajsa*: Two beats to a bar.
—
15　*Teacher*: I'm going to clap (starts clapping her hands).
16　(Several children copy her and clap their hands.)
17　*Teacher*: Listen first! (Places her hands over her ears. Claps two beats to a bar, accentuating every other beat.) Fredrik?
18　*Fredrik*: Two beats to a bar.
19　*Teacher*: (Answers by counting while she claps) one, two, one, two.

What are you supposed to count in order to find out the time of the sound (and the movement)? At first, Eskil does not understand the teacher's question (turn

4), or, rather, if conceived in terms of the learner's perspective, he answers a different question from the one the teacher intended. Nine hundred (turn 4) is as far as he can count, according to himself. This is a rational answer if seen in relation to what the teacher actually says (in turn 3) in posing her question. The teacher follows up Eskil's reply and tries to clarify what she meant (turn 5). The fact that the teacher has to meta-communicate in order to clarify her intention (turns 5 and 9) indicates that something is at stake here, a difficulty establishing intersubjectivity (i.e., coordinating different perspectives). Through her follow-up in turn 5, the teacher recontextualizes the activity in terms of a previous activity that may or may not be related in the child's understanding. Note that, in doing so, the teacher says 'when we counted the bars' (turn 5) and not, e.g., 'when we counted the beats to the bars'. Eskil continues to count bars, whole bars. He counts to three: 'one' (1, 2), 'two' (1, 2), 'three' (1, 2). In this way it is possible to keep counting, even to 900. This brief example illustrates how sensitive the management of intersubjectivity is in this kind of conversation. It is possible to understand the utterance, 'count the bars' in markedly different ways, from the teacher's or from the learner's perspective. It is important here to note that in Swedish, 'bar' is 'takt' and 'time' is 'taktart', presumably making the task of distinguishing between the two words more difficult than in English where these are more distinct.

The activity was introduced through a silent form of representation. If one imagines the sound of the soundless movement, it is possible to 'find' it in the deepest point of the curtsy (as if the body was a hand banging on a drum). Perhaps one can also imagine the movements up and down as parts of a slower pace, i.e., not 1, 2, 1, 2, but 1 and 2 and . . . The issue of coordinating and/or separating sound and movement runs through this lesson (see e.g., turns 15–17). Hence, the challenge of this learning practice is considerable for both teacher and children in several ways. Great care needs to be taken in the details of talk and non-verbal acts when promoting this learning and analysing children's understanding and capabilities.

As a meta-comment we may conclude that if we take the theoretical stance described above, the interview cannot be considered merely a way for the researcher (or the teacher) to find out what the child already knows. Rather, the interview is, in itself, an opportunity for learning and gaining new insight. Hence our ambiguous titles of 'knowing/figuring out'. It is precisely this tension between what someone knows and how we as researchers (or teachers) gain access to and contribute to this knowing that is at play in the reasoning of the present chapter.

Knowing/figuring out what to discern when several dimensions are at play

The lessons, one excerpt of which we have analysed here, were followed up through interviewing children about the time of the music listened to. Three excerpts taken from these interviews will now be analysed. In the interviews, interviewer and child listened to music and, as in the excerpt below, played on a drum:

Excerpt 2a

45 *Interviewer:* And I thought I'd play a bar, and then you have to say what it seems to be. What do you think this is, for example? (Plays two beats to a bar, alternating between the right and left hand.)

46 *Ella:* Two beats to a bar.

47 *Interviewer:* It was two beats to a bar. OK, why do you think that?

48 *Ella:* Because you have two hands.

49 *Interviewer:* Yes, OK. What about this then? (Plays three beats to a bar. One beat with one hand and two beats with the other.)

50 *Ella:* Three beats to a bar.

51 *Interviewer:* Three beats, OK. Why is that so? I still have two hands (holds up her hands). So what happened now?

52 *Ella:* You do one (beats knee with one hand) and then two (showing this with the other hand).

53 *Interviewer:* Two with this (indicating the left hand), exactly. If I do this, then? (Plays two beats to a bar, using only the right hand.)

54 *Ella:* One beat to a bar.

55 *Interviewer:* One beat to a bar. Why?

56 *Ella:* Because you are doing it with only one hand and then it sounds like one beat to a bar.

In the first two cases (turns 45–52), the interviewer plays on the drum with two hands while the time varies (between two beats to a bar and three beats to a bar). In the first and third case, the time is kept constant (two beats to a bar), while the number of hands playing varies. In all three cases, Ella's explanation relates to something visual, the number of hands playing or where the hands hit the drum. Ella seems to relate the time to the number of hands playing. According to this view, two–four time is played with two hands and one–four time (non-existent really) is played with one hand. This response is challenged when three–four time is also played with two hands. Ella is then noticing where the hands are placed:

Excerpt 2b

57 *Interviewer:* Yes, that's right. Er, we'll do this way then (three beats to a bar with one hand).

58 *Ella:* Three beats to a bar.

59 *Interviewer:* Really, why?

60 *Ella:* You beat once hard and then twice (slow?) lower (softer).

61 *Interviewer:* Yes, that's right. Yes, that's exactly what I did. And what about this then? (Plays two beats to a bar using one hand.)

62 *Ella:* Two beats to a bar.

63 *Interviewer:* OK, why?

64 *Ella:* Because you do it hard one time and loosely one time (demonstrating this on knee).

In this sequence, the number of hands is invariant (1) while the time varies, from two beats to a bar (turn 53) to three beats to a bar (turns 57–60) and back again to two beats to a bar (turns 61–64). In the latter two cases, Ella changes her replies from speaking about something visual to saying how it sounds. She speaks about hard and loose beats, which seems to refer to what in the language of musical theory would be labelled accentuated and unaccentuated beats. She now answers correctly to the 'same' question that she had previously answered incorrectly (two beats to a bar with one hand, turns 53–56). Does this mean that she has now learnt this? It is not certain. At this point, the interviewer introduces a new variable, tempo:

Excerpt 2c
65 *Interviewer*: This one then? (Plays two beats to a bar in a fast tempo, using one hand.)
66 *Ella*: Er, one beat to a bar.
67 *Interviewer*: One beat to a bar. Do I make the beats strong all the time now then?
68 *Ella*: No.
69 *Interviewer*: Is it one beat to a bar, all the same?
70 *Ella*: (Nods.)

Ella now seems to be unsure, as indicated by 'Er' (turn 66). The interviewer returns to the 'the strength of the beat' that Ella herself previously referred to (turns 60 and 64). However, at this point, she does not make this connection as decisive for deciding the time. Perhaps she is unable to discern the accent when the tempo increases or perhaps she is guessing.

In the following sequence, the number of hands (1), time (two beats to a bar) and tempo (slow) are invariant while the dynamics vary:

Excerpt 2d
71 *Interviewer*: And what about this? (Plays two beats to a bar in a slow tempo, using one hand, weak accent.)
72 *Ella*: I think it's one beat to a bar.
73 *Interviewer*: Yes, and this one? (Plays two beats to a bar in a slow tempo, using one hand, strong accent on first note.)
74 *Ella*: Two beats to a bar.

Perhaps the changing dynamics introduced here is what Ella pays attention to now. More softly becomes one beat to a bar and louder becomes two beats to a bar. Even louder would perhaps have appeared to her to be three beats to a bar?

Excerpt 2e
75 *Interviewer*: Two beats to a bar. Mm. Now I'll do like this, I'll do it behind my back (holds the drum behind her back). What do you think this is? (Plays three beats to a bar.)

76   *Ella*: Three beats to a bar.
77   *Interviewer*: This one then? (Plays three beats to a bar in a faster tempo.)
78   *Ella*: Three beats to a bar.
79   *Interviewer*: OK, why do you think so?
80   *Ella*: Because it sounds as if you do one time (hitting her knee once), two, three (marking two beats with the other hand on the same knee). One time (hitting her knee once), one, two, three (hitting her knee three times with the other hand, and doing it again).
81   *Interviewer*: Yes, OK, so it's one plus three, four.
82   *Ella*: Yes.
83   *Interviewer*: Mm. This, then (playing three beats to a bar in a quick tempo).
84   *Ella*: Two beats to a bar.
85   *Interviewer*: OK, why?
86   *Ella*: Because it sounds as if you do one time (making an accentuated beat on her knee with one hand, then an unaccentuated beat with the other hand).

In these last three cases, the number of hands is unknown since the drum is held and played behind the back of the interviewer. Ella cannot see how the sound is produced, she can only hear how it sounds. The time is invariant (three beats to a bar throughout), while the tempo varies. In the first two cases, she says that she hears the same time, in contrast to the 'same' cases previously listened to (turns 61–70) when the interviewer played in the same time (two beats to a bar) in a different tempo and the drum was visible. Is it easier for Ella to hear the time when she does not need to think of the visual aspect at the same time? In turn 80, she explains how she has experienced the time. First she reproduces a bar correctly, one accentuated and two unaccentuated beats (made with the other hand), then she adds a fourth beat. Perhaps she is confused by, and aligns with, the interviewer's follow-up (turn 81). But when the tempo is further increased, three beats to a bar seems like two beats to a bar to Ella. She explains this by making one accentuated and one unaccentuated beat on her knees.

Throughout these excerpts (2a–e), what the child is capable of discerning is continuously negotiated through the interviewer following up the child's responses by posing subsequent challenges. By presenting this evolving exploration of knowing (through empirical excerpts) and analysing this collaborative 'finding out' as a social practice where the occasional discrepancy between the interviewer's and the child's perspective is managed and negotiated in talk between the interlocutors, we demonstrate how the teacher takes 'footing' in the child's perspective (what the child has discerned) in further questioning and how the child's capacity is not static throughout but, rather, contingent or situated. When we examine the original data, the child does not seem to be simply guessing. Rather, she seems to be concerned with making sense of what is being asked of her. In our analysis, we try to follow this evolving and negotiated sense-making process.

Wrong answers and/or informative replies?

The following excerpts exemplify two different ways of responding to the challenge of discerning time. Both responses are incorrect if read from the interviewer's perspective. However, if we read them from the child's perspective, both responses are highly informative. They indicate what the children have paid attention to and discerned:

Excerpt 3
(a) Dynamics
111   *Interviewer*: OK. Well, in fact, there were different times. Two beats to a bar and three beats to a bar. Do you recognize that?
112   *Dan*: No.
113   *Interviewer*: No.
114   *Dan*: A bit.
115   *Interviewer*: A bit, we'll try it out. I'll play one and then you have to guess if you think that this can be two beats to a bar or three beats to a bar. What do you think about this one? (Plays two beats to a bar, using two hands.)
116   *Dan*: It seems like four beats to a bar.
117   *Interviewer*: Four beats to a bar? Why do you think it's four beats to a bar?
118   *Dan*: It sounds so loud.
119   *Interviewer*: Sounds so loud. Mm, this one then, what can it be? (Plays two beats to a bar in the same way but more softly.)
120   *Dan*: Two.
121   *Interviewer*: Two, mm, this one then? (Plays even more softly.)
122   *Dan*: One.
123   *Interviewer*: OK, this one then? (Plays the same way but very loudly.)
124   *Dan*: Five! (Lies down on the floor.)

Excerpt 4
(b) The number of beats
145   *Interviewer*: Now I'm going to clap, play the drum for you. And you may guess if it's two or three.
146   *Elias*: Mm.
147   *Interviewer*: What do you think this is? (Plays two beats to a bar with two hands.)
148   *Elias*: Do it again!
149   *Interviewer*: OK. (Begins again.)
150   *Elias*: One, two, three, four . . . (counting all the beats).
151   *Interviewer*: (Stops playing.)
152   *Elias*: Fifteen.
153   *Interviewer*: Goodness, how far you could count!
154   *Elias*: Fifteen.

155   *Interviewer:* Yes. You counted all the beats I played.
156   *Elias:* Yes.
157   *Interviewer:* Yes. This then? (Plays three beats to a bar.)
158   *Elias:* One, two (pause), one, two (pause) . . . No, now you'll have to do it again!
159   *Interviewer:* Yes, now I'll do it again then.
160   *Elias:* One, two . . . three, four. But! Do it again.
161   *Interviewer:* I'll do it again. (Starts again.)
162   *Elias:* One, two, three, four . . . (counts all beats). Fourteen.
163   *Interviewer:* Yes. Was it two or three beats to a bar then?
164   *Elias:* (Shrugs his shoulders.) I don't know.

These last two excerpts may appear to be clear cases of children not having understood or discerned what the teacher intended to develop in the children (and the interviewer intended to find out). However, even these two cases are ambiguous in terms of what the children are capable. In the first case (excerpt 3), Dan distinguishes between pieces on the basis of differences in dynamics. Hence, from the interviewer's perspective, Dan misunderstands or is unable to discern the time. However, if seen from the learner's perspective, it is evident that he has discerned one decisive feature of time. In fact, time is marked out through variation in the dynamics of the beats (i.e., between accentuated and unaccentuated beats). But Dan seems to over-generalise this feature, rather than noticing its variation as marking out a temporal regularity.

Elias, finally (in excerpt 4), is perhaps not able to keep up in his counting so that he can say whether it is two or three beats to a bar, even if he may be able to hear the regularity between accentuated and unaccentuated beats, which mark out the time. That is, he may have trouble coordinating his counting and the accent. As a consequence, he shifts back to counting all beats, which would be easier to do. Not even his concluding remark (in turn 164) about not knowing should be interpreted at face value as indicating an inability. People frequently say that they do not know for all sorts of reasons, to end a conversation, to say that one is not interested, etc. Hence, even when the interviewees themselves say explicitly that they do not know, we need to be careful about concluding that they do not know what we ask of them.

Discussion: implications for studying and developing children's capabilities

We will discuss what we who are interested in the development of children's capabilities (teachers as well as researchers) may learn from research guided by the principle of the learner's perspective (Elbers 2004; Hundeide 2003; Sommer *et al.* 2010). Finally, we will discuss how analysing children's interview responses from the learner's perspective, which is potentially dissonant with the interviewer's perspective, is not only an analytical necessity but also an ethical one.

That children (as well as adults) make sense of what they encounter is a basic fact of human psychological life. People do not simply receive, store, process, and transmit information. This simple reminder has important implications for researching children's understanding and capabilities. In this chapter, we have tried to outline and illustrate an approach to managing this insight when analysing and discussing children's capabilities, exemplified through the skill of discerning time in music.

From the observations made in this study, we *cannot say* that the children do not understand or are not able to discern time in music. What we *can say* in relation to these examples is that the answers show the children's understanding and knowing in relation to what they have understood is being asked of them. While it is difficult to conclude what someone does *not* understand or is *not* capable of, accepting the premises of the present study, what we (as researchers and teachers) gain access to is what sense the child has made of the encounter. This sense provides us with a basis for posing further challenges to the child to develop his or her understanding or capability. This may seem like a pessimistic stance to take, but, in fact, it tells us more than the traditional alternative of viewing children's capabilities strictly from the analyst's perspective.

The first excerpt analysed in this study was taken from a classroom conversation between a teacher and children, and if we return to the distinction of the analyst's and the child's perspective, we can see that it is also important to consider these perspectives in teaching practice, not only in researching children's understanding. Much important information can be gained from analysing children's responses in terms of the child's perspective. It clarifies for the teacher precisely what children notice and what they still need help to discern. Analysing children's responses in terms of the analyst's perspective, i.e., in terms of right or wrong according to a predefined criterion, does not help the teacher to 'get hold' of the children's understanding so that s/he can develop it further. This issue may be particularly emphasised in the case of children's listening. 'Unlike performing and composing, listening is a problematic area for research because there is no natural end product', as Marshall and Hargreaves (2007: 43) remind us. Leaving 'communicative space' and providing scaffolding for the child in order to try to clarify what and how he or she has heard, rather than asking her or him to discriminate between pre-established alternatives, may provide a first step in the right direction towards researching children's listening skills.

In the excerpts that we have analysed, children give several incorrect replies, if analysed from the analyst's perspective. If we analyse the excerpts from the child's perspective, instead, these responses could each be understood as a correct answer to the question as the child has understood it. Taking this analytical stance, it becomes evident that we need to analyse children's replies as contributions to a negotiation of meaning, i.e., the interview as a social practice rather than as a way of 'tapping' children of their conceptualisation, intellectual stage, etc. This kind of analysis also illustrates how sensitive children are in their replies to the interviewer's phrasing of the question (see e.g., above, excerpt 1, the examples of 'takt'

[bar] instead of 'taktart' [time] and 900). Allowing children to come to their right (rather than being seen as 'inadequate') as capable of giving relevant replies to questions as they have understood them is not only of analytical importance. It also illustrates how the interview is not only a social practice but also an ethical one. As analysts, we need to pay due attention to how the children understand our questions. Interpreting answers like the ones exemplified in this analysis as incorrect (i.e., from the analyst's perspective) makes us 'rationally blind' (Shotter 1993) – or, if you will, 'rationally deaf' – to ourselves as analysts and to the nature of the things we do when we conduct, and make analyses of, interviews. Analytical sensitivity (perspective awareness) and ethical consideration go hand in hand when we analyse interviews as social practices and take the learner's perspective as advocated in this study.

Acknowledgement

The research reported here has been financed by The Swedish Research Council.

References

Bartlett, F. C., Sir ([1932] 1995) *Remembering: A Study in Experimental and Social Psychology*, Cambridge: Cambridge University Press.

Bruner, J. S. (1990) *Acts of Meaning*, Cambridge, MA: Harvard University Press.

DeNora, T. (2000) *Music in Everyday Life*, Cambridge: Cambridge University Press.

Elbers, E. (2004) 'Conversational asymmetry and the child's perspective in development and educational research', *International Journal of Disability, Development and Education*, 51(2): 201–215.

Hargreaves, D. J., North, A. C. and Tarrant, M. (2006) 'Musical preference and taste in childhood and adolescence', in G. McPherson (ed.), *The Child as Musician: A Handbook of Music Development*, New York: Oxford University Press, pp. 135–154.

Hundeide, K. (2003) *Barns livsverden: Sosiokulturelle rammer for barns utvikling* [Children's lifeworld: Sociocultural frames for children's development], Oslo: Cappelen.

Kellett, M. (2000) 'Raising musical esteem in the primary classroom: An exploratory study of young children's listening skills', *British Journal of Music Education*, 17(2): 157–181.

Marshall, N. A., and Hargreaves, D. J. (2007) 'Musical style discrimination in the early years', *Journal of Early Childhood Research*, 5(1): 32–46.

Marton, F. and Tsui, A. B. M. (eds) (2004) *Classroom Discourse and the Space of Learning*, Mahwah, NJ: Lawrence Erlbaum.

Nelson, K. (1996) *Language in Cognitive Development: The Emergence of the Mediated Mind*, New York: Cambridge University Press.

Peterson, E. M. (2006) 'Creativity in music listening', *Arts Education Policy Review*, 107(3): 15–21.

Piaget, J. ([1923] 1926) *The Language and Thought of the Child*, trans. M. Warden, New York: Harcourt, Brace.

Piaget, J. ([1926] 1951) *The Child's Conception of the World*, trans. J. Tomlinson and A. Tomlinson, Savage, MD: Littlefield Adams.

Piaget, J. (1983). 'Piaget's theory', in P. H. Mussen (ed.), *Carmichael's Manual of Child Psychology*, vol. I, New York: John Wiley and Sons, pp. 703–732.

Pound, L. and Harrison, C. (2003) *Supporting Musical Development in the Early Years*, Buckingham: Open University Press.

Pramling, N. (2006) '"The clouds are alive because they fly in the air as if they were birds": A re-analysis of what children say and mean in clinical interviews in the work of Jean Piaget', *European Journal of Psychology of Education*, 21(4): 453–466.

Reimer, B. (2003) *A Philosophy of Music Education: Advancing the Vision*, 3rd edn, Upper Saddle River, NJ: Prentice-Hall.

Rommetveit, R. (1980) 'On meanings of acts and what is meant and made known by what is said in a pluralistic social world', in M. Brenner (ed.), *The Structure of Action*, Oxford: Blackwell, pp. 108–149.

Saarikallio, S. and Erkkilä, J. (2007) 'The role of music in adolescents' mood regulation', *Psychology of Music*, 35(1): 88–109.

Säljö, R. (2000) *Lärande i praktiken. Ett sociokulturellt perspektiv* [Learning in practice: A sociocultural perspective], Stockholm: Prisma.

Säljö, R. (2002) 'My brain's running slow today: The preference for "things ontologies" in research and everyday discourse on human thinking', *Studies in Philosophy and Education*, 21(4–5): 389–405.

Säljö, R. (2005) *Lärande och kulturella redskap: Om lärprocesser och det kollektiva minnet* [Learning and cultural tools: On processes of learning and collective memory], Stockholm: Norstedts Akademiska.

Schoultz, J., Säljö, R. and Wyndhamn, J. (2001) 'Heavenly talk: Discourse, artifacts, and children's understanding of elementary astronomy', *Human Development*, 44: 103–118.

Shotter, J. (1993) *Conversational Realities: Constructing Life through Language*, London: Sage.

Sloboda, J. A., and O'Neill, S. A. (2001) 'Emotions in everyday listening to music', in P. N. Juslin and J. A. Sloboda (eds), *Music and Emotion: Theory and Research*, Oxford: Oxford University Press, pp. 415–430.

Sommer, D., Pramling Samuelsson, I. and Hundeide, K. (2010) *Child Perspectives and Children's Perspectives in Theory and Practice*, New York: Springer.

Wells, G. (1999) *Dialogic Inquiry: Towards a Sociocultural Practice and Theory of Education*, New York: Cambridge University Press.

Winner, E. and Cooper, M. (2000) 'Mute those claims. No evidence (yet) for a causal link between arts study and academic achievement', *Journal of Aesthetic Education*, 34(3–4): 11–75.

Wood, D. (1998) *How Children Think and Learn: The Social Contexts of Cognitive Development*, 2nd edn, Oxford: Blackwell.

Wood, D., Bruner, J. S. and Ross, G. ([1976] 2006) 'The role of tutoring in problem solving', in *In Search of Pedagogy*, vol.1 *The Selected Works of Jerome S. Bruner*, London: Routledge, pp. 198–208.

Young, S. and Gillen, J. (2007) 'Toward a revised understanding of young children's musical activities: Reflections from the "Day in the Life" project', *Current Musicology*, 84: 79–99.

Zerull, D. S. (2006) 'Developing musical listening in performance ensemble classes', *Arts Education Policy Review*, 107(3): 41–46.

Chapter 12

Producing and using video data with young children

A case study of ethical questions and practical consequences

Sue Robson

This case study focuses on ethical questions and practical challenges occurring as part of the production of video data in research with young children, especially as a way of eliciting their thoughts about themselves and what they do. It considers a number of questions, particularly in the context of the production of video data: 'Who decides on participants?'; 'How can you try to ensure children's consent?'; 'How can you try to ensure anonymity and protect confidentiality?'; 'How can researchers try to be aware of their impact on participants?'; and 'How can researchers provide young children with feedback about their involvement?' It is suggested that video can be a valuable means of listening to children's perspectives. It provides a context for interaction between researchers, children and video episodes for the purposes of research, as well as contexts for interaction between practitioners, children and video episodes for pedagogical purposes.

Introduction

This chapter looks at our experiences of researching the perspectives of children about their thinking, as part of the Froebel Research Fellowship Project *The Voice of the Child: Ownership and Autonomy in Early Learning*. The project began in 2003 with an initial focus on practitioners' perspectives on supporting young children's thinking (Fumoto and Robson 2006; Robson 2006; Robson and Hargreaves 2005). From 2005 onwards, the focus was widened to consider the views of the children and their families.

Any research project which aims to work directly with young children as participants poses questions and challenges of ethical, methodological and practical kinds. In recent years, many of these have been sensitively addressed (for example, Alderson 2005; Christensen and James 2008). My concern is not to go over this ground again, but to focus on ethical questions and practical challenges arising out of the production of video data with young children, especially as a way of eliciting their thoughts about themselves and what they do in early childhood settings. The use of video recorders as tools in research is not new, and, after its beginnings in the fields of social and visual anthropology and ethnography, is now widespread across the social sciences, and increasingly popular in research which focuses on participatory approaches. However, methodological discussion of video remains underdeveloped (Knoblauch *et al.* 2009), and, where it has been used in relation to young children, it has often been for the purposes of practitioner reflection on the data (for example, Moyles *et al.* 2002). In addition, more emphasis has often been placed upon analysis of the video data itself, by researchers using tools such as Transana (www.transana.org), with less emphasis on the children's own responses, interpretations and analyses. Notable exceptions have been the work of authors such as Forman (1999) and Morgan (2007). The use of video data may be particularly helpful in research with children, given their interest in image-making, including mark-making and photography. The 'image-saturated everyday lives' (Thomson 2008: 11) of many children means that they are, from a young age, practised consumers of images, with experience of interpreting and making meaning from the television and video images they view.

Two things, in particular, are emphasized here as central in the use of video data. First, that such data is produced or 'constructed' (Dahlberg *et al.* 2007) in what is (and should be) a collaborative, mutually influencing process involving all participants (Banks 2001), and second, that there is a reciprocal relationship between ethics and practice. Morrow and Richards (1996: 90) outline this relationship in their definition of ethics as 'a set of moral principles and rules of conduct', with the clear implication that ethical considerations are relevant throughout the entire research process, rather than a 'hurdle to be got out of the way at the beginning' (Hill 2005: 65).

Setting the context

The research focused on here forms part of the project *The Voice of the Child: Ownership and Autonomy in Early Learning* (2003–) and addresses the research question 'How do social relationships in early childhood settings support and influence children's creative thinking?'. The research seeks to elicit the views of practitioners, parents and carers, and children, with this sub-question asked with particular regard to the children: what are the children's perspectives on their activities in early childhood settings, and how do they reflect upon these? The children who participated were drawn from three early childhood settings in London, England: a Children's Centre, a Foundation Stage Unit in a Primary School and a Workplace Nursery, and ranged in age from 3.10 to 4.10, with a mean age of four years three months.

The project is underpinned by a theoretical framework which draws on post-Vygotskian sociocultural theory and self-determination theory (Deci and Ryan 2002; Vygotsky 1978). Vygotsky's (1986) emphasis on language as a tool for self-regulation suggests the value of talk, particularly dialogue, as a key way for children to both express and develop their thoughts. Pramling (1988) demonstrates how explicit talk about learning and thinking may help to make young children more consciously aware of their thinking, and contribute to their metacognitive under-standing. However, Morgan (2007), in an analysis of lesson observations of children aged three–seven years, concludes that the children had few opportunities to talk about how they learnt, or reflect on their thinking. She suggests that 'in general young children's perspectives on their own learning process are not being acknowledged, valued or documented' (ibid.: 221), a view supported by Woodhead and Faulkner (2008).

In order that our research question be addressed, we were conscious of the central importance of contexts for talk which had meaning for the children, acknowledged them as experts in their own lives, and were capable of being shared between the different participants. As a result, the team decided to use, as starting points for discussion, excerpts of researcher-recorded video data of children's self-initiated activities or 'Reflective Dialogues' (RDs) about activity and thinking between child and practitioner, generally each child's key person (defined in the English *Statutory Framework for the Early Years Foundation Stage* as 'a member of staff assigned to an individual child to support their development and act as the key point of contact with that child's parents' [DfES 2007: 52]). As such, the video data and RDs both function as semiotic tools (Vygotsky 1978) in support of young children's thinking.

Playing back video data can help both adults and children recall context, and is multimodal, carrying evidence of action, body language, facial expression and verbal interaction (Dockett and Perry 2005), in a linear narrative form. The possibility the medium affords for replaying such data over and over again, to different participants, supports richer and more diverse interpretations, the potential for intersubjectivity, and provides a site for discussion and collaborative reflection (Dahlberg and Perry 2007), as in this extract from the RD between Tom and James, his key person, as they watch a video episode together:

> *James*: What are you asking Katie?
> *Tom*: *Push* me up.
> *James*: To *push* you up there, ah . . .
> *Tom*: It's . . . and I done that.
> *James*: You're asking her to push you. Well, that was a good idea, wasn't it? Because the trolley's very heavy, isn't it? So if you get [someone to . . .]
> *Tom*: Well, no, when I *checked* it, it's not very heavy for me.
> *James*: Oh, right. What when there's no-one in the back it's not very heavy? Oh, I see. But when there's someone in the back . . .
> *Tom*: Yeah.

Thomson (2008, citing Freedman 2003) highlights how images elicit emotional and aesthetic responses as much as intellectual ones, and thus have the potential for drawing out different responses to research which is primarily language-based. Anderson (cited in Bickham *et al.* 2001) has demonstrated that children pay closest attention to, and have strongest recall of, television images which they best comprehend. It seems reasonable to infer that they would comprehend images of themselves and their actions, and, as a result, might be likely to recall the circumstances under which they were recorded. This was strongly borne out in practice, with children consistently displaying excellent recall, knowledge and expertise in their discussions with their key person about the video. This included comments about themselves and their appearance in the video, for example Daniel observing: 'Hey I'm not wearing them shoes today, I'm wearing shoelaces', and appraisals of their own actions and those of others. For example, Rachel's observations of other participants in the activity she and her key person were watching:

> *Rachel*: (looking at screen, children playing with large construction materials, outdoors) Rebecca's spoiling it. That's Jasmin, that's Harry. Jakie's ruining it as well. I'm not. I asked Harry if we needed string, yeah, but Harry said no. I had a good idea. Move them along, yeah, then they can play fine whatever they wanna do with it, and they can break it.

Forman (1999) suggests that one of the benefits of using video data is that it can act as a 'tool of the mind', allowing children to 'download' details of their actions as part of replaying the video, freeing their minds to think about what those actions mean. He also suggests a phenomenon of particular benefit in the context of a project which looks at young children's thinking:

> Children would see me approach with my camera. Their knowledge that I was recording gave the children a reason to consider what in the classroom or in their own play was interesting. It turns out that thinking about what is interesting requires rather high-level thinking.
>
> (ibid.: 5)

At the same time, as Mondada (2009) suggests, participants also observe and seek to interpret the actions and focus of the camera operator, inferring possible topics of interest on the operator's part, making this process highly interpretative and subjective.

Our starting point was that young children can be competent research participants, with rights to be treated as such (Christensen and James 2008). Children's rights to express their views are enshrined in Article 12 of the UNCRC (United Nations 1989):

> Parties shall assure to the child who is capable of forming his or her own views the right to express those views freely in all matters affecting the child, the views of the child being given due weight in accordance with the age and maturity of the child.
>
> (ibid.)

In research *with* children, attention to Article 13 is also important:

> The child shall have the right to freedom of expression; this right shall include freedom to seek, receive and impart information and ideas of all kinds, regardless of frontiers, either orally, in writing or in print, in the form of art, or through any other media of the child's choice.
>
> (ibid.)

This right to freedom of expression, particularly for young children, is emphasized in the more recent United Nations General Comment No. 7 (OHCHR 2005), including with regard to research and in the development of policies and services.

Methods

Who decided on the participants?

While the starting point of the project team was that children should be active participants (Alderson 2005), decisions about which children would be involved rested initially with gatekeepers in the form of head teachers, managers, practitioners, parents and carers. Before approaching anyone connected with the settings we needed permission from the head teacher or manager, who negotiated with individual practitioners over which of them would opt in to the project, and thus which children might potentially be involved. A letter outlining the project, and a questionnaire, was then sent to all parents of children in the practitioners' key groups. Parents' participation was solicited, along with consent for their children's involvement, including video recording. As with practitioners, emphasis was on parents and carers positively opting in to, rather than out of, the project. This raises an initial question: 'Were there children who would have wanted to be involved but could not, because their parents did not opt in, through lack of confidence or time?' Conversely, it is not possible to know whether any parents gave consent out of a sense of obligation, fearing that relationships with the settings could be compromised if they did not, however much we attempted to reassure them that there would be no negative impact if they did not participate.

More generally, we were conscious that some parents may have consented to their children's participation while the children themselves might be more reluctant. Compliance, or adult direction framed as 'request', are often features of children's lives in schools and nurseries, and it may be challenging for children to distinguish occasions when they truly have freedom of choice from those when compliance is required. The 'power dynamics of age' (Mauthner 1997: 19) impacts on relationships between children and adults generally, and, along with relationships between researcher and 'researched', may mean that young children are doubly disadvantaged (Christensen 2004). Drawing on Foucault, Dahlberg *et al.* identify 'local settings' (2007: 35), such as early childhood institutions, as sites for the exercise of such disciplinary power, and further research which examines how these constructed power relationships impact on research with young children would be beneficial.

On return of the questionnaires, we worked with practitioners to select children for inclusion, within our target age range of three–five years. Thus, it was only after a number of processes that children's opportunities to participate were realized. These processes impact on the outcomes of the research itself, by including some children, and excluding others (Flewitt 2005). They also mean that, unlike the adults, children were only able to effectively signal their views by opting out, rather than positively opting in, at the start of the project.

How did we try to ensure children's consent?

The idea that all those involved in research should give their permission to participate has general acceptance globally. How this permission is established and expressed varies across countries, partly as a result of beliefs about children's development, with some suggestions that children under the age of 14 may not be competent to give consent (Bray 2007), but also as a function of the legal status of participants' views. Under English law, competent minors can give consent, with competence being defined as having sufficient understanding and intelligence to understand the proposed project (Alderson and Morrow 2004). By contrast, in Singapore and Australia, the legal ages of consent are 21 and 18 respectively (Conroy and Harcourt 2009). As a result, Conroy and Harcourt argue for use of the term 'assent' rather than 'consent'. In practice, and in the literature, assent and consent are often used interchangeably (Bray 2007), and, as Gibson and Twycross (2007) point out, in a UK context at least, the legal difference remains unclear. Here, I use the term consent explicitly, partly because this research was conducted in England, but also as a way of affirming young children's competence to engage in 'the invisible act of evaluating information and making a decision, and the visible act of signifying the decision' (Alderson and Morrow 2004: 96).

The UNCRC (United Nations 1989) asserts children's rights to express their views on all matters that affect them, and to seek, receive and impart information and ideas. Central to this must, however, be the extent to which children are able to make sense of that information, and to understand what is being proposed, in order to ensure that their consent is 'informed'. The British Educational Research Association (BERA) Revised Ethical Guidelines emphasize that 'children should . . . be facilitated to give fully informed consent before research begins' (BERA 2004: 7). Some imaginative and thoughtful ways have been developed to try to support such facilitation, including tape-recorded explanations (Hill 2005), opportunities for children to think about the research and consult with others (Dockett and Perry 2007), illustrated information leaflets shared between researcher and children (Alderson 2004), an 'activity board' (Bray 2007) and, in the context of video data, showing potential participants video already produced as a way of supporting their understanding (Banks 2001). However, the construction and appearance of such material are not neutral, and carry messages about the positioning of children and the purposes of research which children may read in very particular ways (David *et al*. 2001). In addition, decisions need to be made about what is enough information, and what might be too much, and potentially confusing for young children (Dockett and Perry 2007).

For this project, the children in each setting were made aware that I, as researcher and camcorder operator, would be coming in and spending time there. I began by playing alongside the children, before focusing on potential participants, explaining that I was coming in to find out more about what they did, what they themselves thought about this, and asking their permission to observe and record them, and their consent to participate. I then gave the children a camcorder to experiment with, and play back, looking at their recordings. All the children wanted to use the camcorder, which I felt was vitally important if they were to give their informed consent, and see themselves as 'active participants' (Alderson 2005) with a sense of ownership of the project. However, a tension that is, in some ways, unique to video recording, remains: as stated above, BERA Ethical Guidelines (2004) emphasize the importance of facilitating children's informed consent before beginning research. In the case of video data, it is arguable that part of that facilitation should include opportunities for children to see themselves on video, and reflect on how that feels for them, before giving their consent. Logically, therefore, we needed the children's consent to record them before they could really have that opportunity to provide such fully informed consent.

As the use of digital video cameras, and visual research methods in general, becomes more embedded in early childhood settings, this tension may become less marked. In the meantime, and where this is not the case, we felt it was valuable to ensure that children had opportunities for periods of extended play and exploration with the camcorder before the project, and data collection, began. As Alderson (2008) suggests, children act as researchers in their everyday activities in settings, for example, collecting data about favourite foods and researching their surroundings, and the use of camcorders in such contexts may be helpful in giving them opportunities to consider their feelings about appearing in recordings.

Flewitt (2005) suggests that the idea of 'informed' consent should be replaced with one of 'provisional' consent, which continues to be negotiated and revisited, with children's consent positively, and frequently, reaffirmed. In this respect, camcorders as research tools are little different to other means, except that they may be physically more intrusive than, say, a notepad and pencil. With this in mind, we emphasized that camcorders would not be taken into areas regarded as private, for example, where children's personal care was being attended to, or concealed play areas. This does, though, leave a lot of open ground to be continually negotiated. Trying to remain sensitive to children expressing their consent or dissent implicitly, through body language and gesture as well as talk, is not always easy if you have one eye on a camcorder screen. There is also a tension between trying to remain unobtrusive in order not to disrupt the everyday life of the setting, and the children always being aware that they were being filmed, and thus able to give their consent knowingly. In the majority of instances, children were keen to participate, wanting what they were doing to be recorded, and wanting to see it played back, as in Rachel's suggestion one afternoon when I was recording inside: 'if you want to carry on videoing you'll have to come outside with me now', a clear example of a statement which affirmed her desire to continue to 'opt in'. Her comment was also characteristic of a phenomenon common to all three settings: where children were playing alone, they would more frequently seek to involve me while recording than when they were in a group. This could be by look or gesture, but was often through talk, and as part of the narrative of the play, for example, Rosie's comment to me as I filmed her: 'Look, I've built a wall!' Children also clearly signified when their interest waned, both during recording and in the RDs. Harun effectively curtailed a discussion with his key person, and clearly exercised his right to opt out, by saying 'Can we finish it? It's making my head go dizzy.'

How did we try to ensure anonymity and protect confidentiality?

Conventional methods of data collection such as questionnaires and observations make it relatively easy to protect participants' anonymity and confidentiality, by altering names and identifying features. Visual material of any kind, particularly video data, makes this more problematic. 'Raw' recordings may leave settings recognizable: children in two of the settings in this project wore distinctive school clothing, featuring logos. Participants themselves were recognizable, and often identified one another by name in their conversations. In addition, participant children and adults talk and play with children who are not part of the project but are in the setting. Trying to 'screen' these children out is challenging, and necessitated either seeking further permission, or editing. The use of video, then, demands particular actions on the part of researchers, and 'puts children at particular risk and renders parents and practitioners vulnerable to criticism, anxiety and self-doubt' (Flewitt 2005: 558).

   We sought participants' permission to use the data only for the purposes of the project and in research presentations, and gave undertakings that no images would be placed on internet sites. The nature of the research design meant that all participants viewed and actively commented on the videos, and were able to request that material be altered or deleted. However, we saw it as our respon-sibility, as researchers, to ensure that both children and adults were regularly reminded of their rights of choice and veto. Flewitt suggests that, in making use of visual images for presentations 'the researcher should reflect on the degree of visual detail that is relevant to the research claim' (ibid.: 559), and consider reducing pixel counts, rendering faces and distinctive clothing 'fuzzy', or making drawings of images. The nature of the project, which sought to take advantage of the medium for recording aspects such as facial expression and direction of gaze to infer aspects of metacognitive activity, meant that valuable data could potentially be lost, should we have to alter images. In addition, Banks (2001) suggests that such devices may invoke ideas of criminality in viewers. In the event, all participants gave their consent for the data to be used without alteration.

One aspect which remains a concern was that of the potential for participants' attitudes to change over time. As they age, the children may be less happy for recordings of their younger selves to be used. On completion of any research project, data is stored for a period of time, and then may be destroyed (guidelines in the United Kingdom vary on this across institutions and research bodies). Decisions about data storage, its potential re-use, and possible disposal, raise the question 'who owns the video?' (Morgan 2007: 223). Ownership, copyright and access to data are recognized in the UK as potentially 'hazy areas' (Polydoratou 2009: 306) for academic and research staff, in need of further exploration. Ownership may most often be seen as attributing to researchers, funders, institutions, either singly or in combination (ibid.). Less often is it seen as a right of those being researched. During the course of this project, our belief in the moral rights of all participants to share ownership of the data assumed increasing importance for us as a team, and copies of the video material were kept by children and families as records of their participation, as well as by researchers. This does, however, raise issues with regard to our undertaking as researchers not to place material on websites: once parents and carers have copies of their own, it is no longer possible for us to guarantee that such material will not find its way into wider public domains. Traditionally, ethics policies have focused on the ownership of institutions and researchers: more consideration now needs to be given to the more complex questions of shared ownership, the rights associated with ownership and access, and how to ensure that all participants' rights and wishes are respected. For example, participant consent forms may need to make more explicit the responsibilities of participants, and solicit their agreement, with regard to such shared ownership of data.

How did we try to be aware of our impact as researchers on the participants?

Researchers will always have an impact, just by intervening in participants' lives. In the context of this project, this impact has three distinct, but overlapping, aspects: first, my position as an adult coming into the children's domain; second, my role in producing video data, which, like any data, is never neutral; and third, the effect of my choices of what data was shared with the children. In the case of the first aspect, as an adult introduced to the children by teachers and nursery officers I came with a set of expectations, and the children may have seen me as another 'teacher', or at least someone with some kind of power. O'Kane (2008) identifies disparities of power and status as the biggest challenge for researchers working with children. Although, as Dahlberg *et al.* (2007) point out, it is not a simple dualism of adult and child: children themselves exercise power, and, in this context, had an impact on my behaviour towards them, and the choices I made about how to position myself. Mandell (1991) advocates the adoption of a 'least-adult role' with the children, with the researcher 'operating physically and meta-phorically on the children's level in their social worlds' (Mayall 2008: 110). Christensen, however, points to what she regards as the danger of this looking like a 'dubious attempt to be a child' (Christensen 2004: 174), which could easily be seen by the children as patronizing. It seemed to me inescapable that the children would see me as *an* adult, and thus that Christensen's idea of presenting as 'an unusual type of adult'(ibid.: 174), continually trying to balance being recognized as *an* adult while avoiding preconceived ideas children may have about 'adult-hood', particularly teachers and parents, might be most likely to be successful. This included sitting with them, rather than alongside other adults, during whole-group times, and avoiding making 'controlling' or 'managing' comments during play.

Looking at the second aspect, the production of video data, it is important to acknowledge that the camera was inevitably part of my identity for the children, and continued to impact on our relationships with one another (Pink 2007). While watching an extract, Anju asked her keyperson 'Where's Sue?' He replied that I had gone back to my work. Her firm response 'In *there*', pointing at the video, expressed the identity I had for her, as part of the video process. Time spent collecting as much data as possible may be one way of attempting to minimize the impact of the researcher. This may reduce the potential 'observer effect' of children playing 'role(s)' (Valkanova *et al.* 2004), and help to minimize any unconscious biases I may also have had, for example, towards recording particular types of activities. It is, however, hugely time-consuming, and it was neither practical nor desirable to use the camcorder constantly. In addition, tracking individual children was often challenging, and participant children were sometimes absent on days I visited. However, this did mean I had more time to develop richer relationships with children, conducive to enhanced intersubjectivity and reflexivity (Lahman 2008). It was also the reason why, in one setting, a practitioner became involved in making recordings, which added another voice to the process of production.

It is perhaps the idea of selection which is the most important challenge with respect to the impact of the observer. Images are never neutral, they are literally and socially constructed (Thomson 2008). As operator of the camcorder, I saw 'with' the camera, rather than 'through' it (Mondada 2009), and it was my deci-sion what to record, and, importantly, what to leave out. This included decisions I made about the temporal elements of an activity, particularly with regard to when an activity chosen for replaying began and ended. These decisions have aesthetic and ethical dimensions at the very least (Bourdieu 1990), and represent a level of analysis taking place during recording which is not readily apparent on later viewing (Plowman and Stephen 2008). This effectively conditioned what extracts were selected for discussion by participants. In addition, the physical act of using the camcorder, while seemingly unconscious, including decisions I made 'on the move' about framing shots, and about positioning myself, had an impact on what was recorded, and on how it was then interpreted by viewers. What impact did decisions I made about zooming in on an activity have on how children and parents subsequently 'read' the importance of what was happening? Data presented to them was inevitably from my point of view, and from frontal angles. While this may act to engage the viewer (Rose 2001), it may also have had the effect of positioning me as controller of both space and time (ibid.), thus reinforcing my position of power in the children's eyes.

Bourdieu's analysis that understanding a photograph 'means not only recovering the meanings which it *proclaims* . . . it also means deciphering the surplus of meanings which it *betrays*' (emphasis in original) (1990: 7) holds true for video data as well. Children are practised interpreters of the semiotics of television, and may have inferred particular meaning in my decisions. They will also 'bring their own social and cultural understandings as well as their unique life trajectories to the act of interpretation' (Thomson 2008: 10). It is not possible to know the extent to which this may have influenced their talk in the RDs, but it is important to be aware of this as a possible factor, and to continue to bear in mind the impact of the processes of the researcher's selection, processing and editing of recorded images on participants (ibid.).

My physical proximity to children when I was recording varied. On some occasions, this was pragmatic: I spotted something happening and started recording. At other times, by being further away, I hoped to minimize the potential impact of my presence. There is, of course, a trade-off here with quality, particularly sound quality. After piloting our approach, we had decided that asking the children to wear microphones could prove intrusive and impractical, so I was reliant upon the quality of the camcorder microphone. Whilst in most instances this worked well, in some circumstances what children said was not always clear. Interestingly, in playing such material back to the children, they would often spontaneously recount what they remembered they had been saying, showing good recall, and providing us with valuable evidence of their competence, in particular, their ability to recall past events and think abstractly. This included occasions where, for reasons such as illness, there was sometimes a gap of weeks between the recording of the activity and the RD. At these times children's recall still proved strong, assisted by the replaying of the video, as suggested by Forman (1999). In one RD while watching the video, Harry playfully asked James, his key person, 'Guess what I'm doing!' More generally, the discussions afforded children opportunities to display their knowledge and expertise, often in ways which might otherwise have remained invisible to the adults. This is borne out by the data, which, overall, showed much higher levels of evidence of metacognitive knowledge in the RDs than was apparent in the activities themselves. Importantly, this supports the idea of video reflection as a pedagogical as well as research tool.

How can researchers provide young children with feedback about their involvement?

Provision of personal feedback to any research participants can be problematic for many reasons, including lack of time and money (Hill 2005). The project design meant that participants had ongoing feedback and opportunities to look at the data. Alderson (2008) asserts that children may be particularly interested in those aspects of research which have the potential to impact positively on their everyday lives. MacNaughton *et al.* (2007: 461) link such early opportunities for young children's involvement in decisions which affect them with their later 'abilities, identities and well-being'. This suggests it may be particularly important to find really effective ways of ensuring that longer-term outcomes are shared with the children, along with their involvement in dissemination and implementation of findings. This is a challenge, particularly given that many of the children have moved on to other settings.

Conclusion

This chapter has considered some of the ethical and practical considerations in the production and use of video data with young children and suggests that such data should be seen as constructed collaboratively by all participants. Video can be a highly motivating research tool, and a valuable means of eliciting children's perspectives, different in scope to other methods, and possibly of particular benefit in research which focuses on children's thinking. However, it poses challenges for adults seeking to ensure that children are active participants, and able to give informed consent.

The construction of video research data is not an 'innocent act' (Dahlberg *et al.* 2007: 154), and is influenced by the experiences and perceptions of those making the recordings, and of those being recorded. While the collection of large amounts of data may help to ameliorate the observer effect, this also poses practical challenges. In addition, young children are practised consumers and interpreters of the semiotics of television. Their responses to video data will be influenced by their reading of the actions of the researcher in selecting and framing images, and in the use of devices such as zooming and panning. Awareness of this influence will be vital in readings of the data, albeit that it will be impossible to know, with any certainty, of its impact.

Video data, as a semiotic tool (Vygotsky 1978), provides a context for inter-action between the researcher, the child and the video episode, with the potential for producing rich data for the purposes of research. However, it also has similar potential for providing contexts for interaction between practitioners, children and video episode, for pedagogical purposes, serving to remind children and adults of context (Forman 1999), and acting as a valuable support and stimulus for the development of young children's thinking and learning. In addition, the use of video data for the purposes of both research and practice has the potential to influence all participants' views about what happens in settings, and to impact upon change.

References

Alderson, P. (2004) 'Ethics', in A. Fraser, V. Lewis, S. Ding, M. Kellett and C. Robinson (eds), *Doing Research with Children and Young People*, London: Sage Publications, pp. 97–111.

Alderson, P. (2005) 'Designing ethical research with children', in A. Farrell (ed.), *Ethical Research with Children*, Maidenhead: Open University Press, pp. 27–36.

Alderson, P. (2008) 'Children as researchers: participation rights and research methods', in P. Christensen and A. James (eds), *Research with Children: Perspectives and Practices*, 2nd edn, London: Routledge, pp. 276–290.

Alderson P. and Morrow V. (2004) *Ethics, Social Research and Consulting with Children and Young People*, Ilford: Barnardos.

Banks, M. (2001) *Visual Methods in Social Research*, London: Sage.

Bickham, D., Wright, J. C. and Huston, A. C. (2001) 'Attention, comprehension and the educational influences of television', in D. G. Singer and J. L. Singer, (eds), *Handbook of Children and the Media*, Thousand Oaks, CA: Sage Publications, pp. 101–119.

Bourdieu, P. (1990) *Photography: A Middle-brow Art*, Cambridge: Polity Press.

Bray, L. (2007) 'Developing an activity to aid informed assent when interviewing children and young people', *Journal of Research in Nursing*, 12: 447–457.

British Educational Research Association (BERA) (2004) *Revised Ethical Guidelines for Educational Research*. Available at: http://www.bera.ac.uk/publications/pdfs/ETHICA1.PDF (accessed 29 January 2008).

Christensen, P. H. (2004) 'Children's participation in ethnographic research: issues of power and representation', *Children and Society*, 18: 165–176.

Christensen, P. and James, A. (eds) (2008) *Research with Children: Perspectives and Practices*, 2nd edn, London: Routledge.

Conroy, H. and Harcourt, D. (2009) 'Informed agreement to participate: beginning the partnership with children in research', *Early Child Development and Care*, 179(2): 157–165.

Dahlberg, G., Moss, P. and Pence, A. (2007) *Beyond Quality in Early Childhood Education and Care*, London: Routledge.

David, M., Edwards, R. and Alldred, P. (2001) 'Children and school-based research: "informed consent" or "educated consent"?', *British Educational Research Journal*, 27(3): 347–365.

Deci, E. L. and Ryan, R. M. (eds) (2002) *Handbook of Self-Determination Research*, New York: University of Rochester.

Department for Education and Skills (DfES) (2007) *Statutory Framework for the Early Years Foundation Stage*, Nottingham: DfES.

Dockett, S. and Perry, B. (2005) 'Researching with children: insights from the Starting School Research Project', *Early Child Development and Care*, 175(6): 507–521.

Dockett, S. and Perry, B. (2007) 'Trusting children's accounts in research', *Journal of Early Childhood Research*, 5(1): 47–63.

Flewitt, R. (2005) 'Conducting research with young children: some ethical considerations', *Early Child Development and Care*, 175(6): 553–565.

Forman, G. (1999) 'Instant video revisiting: the video camera as a "tool of the mind" for young children', *Early Childhood Research and Practice*, 1(2). Available at: http://ecrp.uiuc.edu/v1n2/forman.html (accessed 20 June 2005).

Fumoto, H. and Robson, S. (2006) 'Early childhood professionals' experience of time to facilitate children's thinking', *European Early Childhood Education Research Journal*, 14(2): 97–111.

Gibson, F. and Twycross, A. (2007) 'Children's participation in research: A position statement on behalf of the Royal College of Nursing's Research in Child Health (RiCH) Group and Children's and Young People's Rights and Ethics Group', *Paediatric Nursing*, 19(4): 14–17.

Hill, M. (2005) 'Ethical considerations in researching children's experiences', in S. Green and D. Hogan (eds), *Researching Children's Experience: Methods and Approaches*, London: Sage, pp. 61–86.

Knoblauch, H., Schnettler, B., Raab, J. and Soeffner, H-G. (eds) (2009) *Video Analysis: Methodology and Methods*, 2nd edn, Oxford: Peter Lang.

Lahman, M. (2008) 'Always othered: ethical research with children', *Journal of Early Childhood Research*, 6(3): 281–300.

MacNaughton, G., Hughes, P. and Smith, K. (2007) 'Young children's rights and public policy: practices and possibilities for citizenship in the early years', *Children and Society*, 21: 458–469.

Mandell, N. (1991) 'The least adult role in studying children, in F. Waksler (ed.), *Studying the Social Worlds of Children*, London: Falmer Press.

Mauthner, M. (1997) 'Methodological aspects of collecting data from children: lessons from three research projects', *Children and Society*, 11: 16–28.

Mayall, B. (2008) 'Conversations with children: working with generational issues', in P. Christensen and A. James (eds), *Research with Children: Perspectives and Practices*, 2nd edn, London: Routledge, pp. 109–124.

Mondada, L. (2009) 'Video recording as the reflexive preservation and configuration of phenomenal features for analysis', in H. Knoblauch, B. Schnettler, J. Raab and H-G. Soeffner (eds), *Video Analysis: Methodology and Methods*, 2nd edn, Oxford: Peter Lang.

Morgan, A. (2007) 'Using video-stimulated recall to understand young children's perceptions of learning in classroom settings', *European Early Childhood Education Research Journal*, 15(2): 213–226.

Morrow, V. and Richards, M. (1996) 'The ethics of social research with children: An overview', *Children and Society*, 10: 90–105.

Moyles, J., Adams, S. and Musgrove, A. (2002) *SPEEL Study of Pedagogical Effectiveness in Early Learning*, London: DfES.

OHCHR (2005) *General Comment No. 7 (2005: 01/11/2005. Implementing Child Rights in Early Childhood*. Available at: http://www2.ohchr.org/english/bodies/crc/comments. htm (accessed 13 July 2009).

O'Kane, C. (2008) 'The development of participatory techniques', in P. Christensen and A. James (eds), *Research with Children: Perspectives and Practices*, 2nd edn, London: Routledge, pp. 125–155.

Pink, S. (2007) *Doing Visual Ethnography*, 2nd edn, London: Sage.

Plowman, L. and Stephen, C. (2008) 'The big picture? Video and the representation of interaction', *British Educational Research Journal*, 34(4): 541–565.

Polydoratou, P. (2009) 'Experimenting with the trial of a research data audit: some preliminary findings about data types, access to data and factors for long term preservation', in *ELPUB 2009: 13th International Conference on Electronic Publishing:*

Rethinking Electronic Publishing: Innovation in Communication (Conference Proceedings), Italy: Nuova Cultura, pp. 291–307.

Pramling, I. (1988) 'Developing children's thinking about their own thinking', *British Journal of Educational Psychology*, 58: 266–278.

Robson, S. (2006) 'Supporting children's thinking in the Foundation Stage: Practitioners' views on the role of initial training and continuing professional development', *Journal of In-Service Education*, 32(3): 341–358.

Robson, S. and Hargreaves, D. J. (2005) 'What do early childhood practitioners think about young children's thinking?', *European Early Childhood Education Research Journal*, 13(1): 81–96.

Rose, G. (2001) *Visual Methodologies*, London: Sage.

Thomson, P. (2008) *Doing Visual Research with Children and Young People*, London: Routledge.

United Nations (1989) *Convention on the Rights of the Child*. Available at: http://www.unhchr.ch/html/menu3/b/k2crc.htm (accessed 22 January 2008).

Valkanova, Y., Watts, M. and Jackson, A. (2004) 'Enhancing self-reflection in children: The use of digital video in the primary science classroom', *JeLit Journal of eLiteracy*, 1(1): 42–55. Available at: http://www.jelit.org/9/ (accessed 12 November 2008).

Vygotsky, L. S. (1978) *Mind in Society*, Cambridge, MA: Harvard University Press.

Vygotsky, L. S. (1986) *Thought and Language*, Cambridge, MA: MIT Press.

Woodhead, M. and Faulkner, D. (2008) 'Subjects, objects or participants? Dilemmas of psychological research with children', in P. Christensen and A. James (eds), *Research with Children: Perspectives and Practices*, 2nd edn, London: Routledge, pp. 10–39.

Index